THROUGH A BRICK WALL

The real story
of The South African Breweries'
global triumph

By Ally Hewitt

ISBN: 978-0-6397-2810-0 (print)
ISBN: 978-0-6397-2811-7 (e-book)

Publisher: Ally Hewitt
Editor: Neville Barber
Copy Editor: Reina Luck
Cover design: Berge, Farrell Designs
Typesetting: Megan Barber Designs

Printed in South Africa

Dedication

As this book moved closer to completion, Meyer Kahn, the former chairman and managing director of South African Breweries, passed away. It was a devastating loss of our cheerleader, muse, mentor, colleague and friend.

For me personally, not only was he an inspiration for writing this book, but I had been hoping to present the first copy to him, as he had endorsed the project to record SAB's emergence from South Africa.

When I had sought the opportunity to meet to review some of the stories he remembered so well and in so much detail, he had suggested in his humorous way that we hire a room at his favourite hotel, The Beverly Hills, fill the bath with ice and Castle Lagers, and sit on the balcony reflecting on this wonderful company.

Meyer observed the pandemic lockdown fastidiously and eventually I managed to set up a two-hour phone call to capture the invaluable insights that I was delighted to add to our story.

Towards the end of our conversation, Meyer understandably admitted to feeling fatigued and invited me to call at any time for more anecdotes. Sadly I didn't. He ended the call with one of his famous quips: '*Fluit fluit, my storie is uit.*' (Whistle, whistle, my story is finished).

'I don't envy you writing this story but good luck, I can't wait to read it,' he said. Regrettably, I can't present the book to him and he will never see it.

I will be forever glad that Meyer Kahn's stories are woven into our tale, whether personally narrated, from his friends and colleagues or from me. His rich legacy will live on.

Contents

Prologue

The greatest company to emerge from post-apartheid South Africa is arguably The South African Breweries Limited (SAB): a beer giant in the context of South Africa, born on the dusty streets of Johannesburg in the late nineteenth century, which became a household name across our nation over the decades.

In the era of global isolation, the maxim of *'n Boer maak 'n plan* guided SAB's diversification and growth at home through companies like OK Bazaars, PG Glass, Southern Sun, Amalgamated Beverage Industries, and Appletiser.

Of course, the crown jewel was SAB, the brewing company. At the same time, the company grew the industries that supported it – suppliers, farmers, retailers and liquor store owners – and it was the inspiration for the legalisation of township shebeens in South Africa where prohibition had been in force for decades.

As another example shows, SAB found a way of growing hops at the southern tip of the continent, where hours of daylight in winter are less than ideal for cultivating the Humulus Lupulus plant. We erected spotlights in the fields to extend daylight hours, which is a requirement to grow hops successfully. We had a talent for always finding a way to make things happen.

I joined SAB in February 1985, in an era when the company had just emerged from the 'beer wars' waged between Dr Louis Luyt, founder of Luyt Breweries, and SAB, which at that time chairman Meyer Kahn dubbed a 'temporary sole supplier' as voted by our consumers.

In the years that followed, change was palpable as preparations began for South Africa's new democracy, bringing with it opportunities for South Africans to compete on the global stage. When the doors eventually opened, SAB was in the front row to seize the moment and run at the chance to brew beer beyond our borders.

When those doors closed in October 2016, we had spread the business across six continents and 84 countries and were the second-largest brewer in the world after the US brewing giant ABInBev (formed by Anheuser-Busch and InBev), who eventually bought us.

I began my career as a sales analyst hunched over a keyboard at a small desk with a mainframe computer taking up almost all of my tiny office. I tapped away to extract sales numbers for our Northern Region's sales teams, printing reams of computer data on blue and white lined paper and packing the reports into cardboard boxes for weekly dispatch to our sales managers across the region.

The grounding I received was profound. It gave me an insightful perspective of how the business operated and allowed me to travel the region from time to time to present the analyses to the sales teams by brand, pack, and customer segment.

The data was powerful, and I was welcomed by the sales fraternity. The relationships I built became an important theme throughout my career. Our story was about 'Making Beer, Making Friends'. It was a catchphrase that was at the heart of SAB in the '90s and was synonymous with the company, what we did, and how we behaved.

SAB was a company that, combined with my passion for South Africa, the country of my birth, became an integral part of my life. I ended up spending 32 years with SAB and a further two years with ABInBev, who had taken us over. Our SAB chapter finally closed after 121 years, ending a sensational journey that, like our flagship brand Castle Lager, truly stood the test of time.

What stood out for me throughout the journey was the incredible passion and dedication of all the people of SAB, across the value chain and around the world. It was this that led me to pen the title 'Through a Brick Wall' which speaks volumes for what drove the amazing people of our company to do extraordinary things that defied the odds.

When I left the company, I knew that if SAB in its previous guise had survived, I would have worked for the company until the last hour of the 63rd year of my life and hope that the retirement age could be delayed, allowing me to stay longer. This would have given me 40 years of service, a true indication of my great affection for this distinguished company.

Somebody once said that if a surgeon were to cut off my arm, I would bleed Castle Lager, such was the passion and dedication that I felt for SAB and the band of friends that I made during my 34 years in it.

Were I to have written a life script, I could not have created a tale of a more fulfilling, pleasing, journey. It took me around the world and had me working on more than 50 beer brands throughout my career. It was a dream company. Every role was meaningful; every day was a learning day. The characters I met along the way were on another level.

One of my favourite quotes is: 'If you can't have fun in the marketing department of a beer company, you have a problem.' This is true, although one certainly did need to stay mindful of the need for a balance between work, home life, and the love of beer itself.

Writing this book has not only been pleasurable but has also brought memories of many emotional moments flooding back and, at the same time, highlighted many stories and accomplishments hitherto unheralded. So ingrained in my mind are these recollections that I remember the finest details without having to delve too deeply into my memory bank.

I believe that a company with this pedigree and its extraordinary journey deserves to have its story told and to be remembered as an icon in the commercial landscape of South Africa. Hopefully, the story will engender a wider appreciation of what made this company great and of learnings that might inform and inspire others to try new ways of making things happen. At the very centre of the story are the people who believed that the impossible was possible and that no brick wall could stand in their way.

I have never written a book but have a love for storytelling. Storytelling is not just part of who we are as a nation, but the bedrock of much of the communication that we built into our brands, particularly my favourite, Castle Lager. Brand stories often reflected what was happening in our country and drove emotional connections with all our stakeholders.

I also had no idea where to begin and end this story. My friend Maurice Egan suggested I just start writing and something might come of it. It was never the intention to pen a definitive history of the company. So this book is not that.

During the Covid-19 pandemic lockdown, I spent time in the South African bushveld writing more than 30 short stories. Then I decided I should interview some 30 executives – and several of SAB's many 'characters' – who had played a key role in creating this rich narrative of SAB's odyssey and to discover the key themes and nuggets that made SAB great.

I felt I needed to ask someone's permission to write this story. It belongs, after all, to South Africa and to the great people of SAB who dedicated their lives to creating a global phenomenon. I had lunch with Meyer Kahn. He cautioned me that several employees had tried and failed. However, he thought I should give it a go and that I was well placed to write the story. I thank Meyer for supporting me in tackling this book.

01 Inspiration
out of the Dark

The room was dark and foreboding. As it began to fill, its occupants became increasingly restless and began whispering amongst themselves. It had already been unsettling when they were shepherded through a South African Police Force security check before entering the Sun City Superbowl.

Most thought it was a hoax to have that level of security at a conference. Others were genuinely disconcerted. What the ... was going on?

A spotlight swung to the entrance door at the right of the stage. At first, most of the audience doubted what they saw. Some rubbed their eyes. Then the light picked out a figure with a familiar walk – a saunter back to freedom – as he made his way through the audience on the left to reach the podium.

Nelson Rolihlahla Mandela.

This unexpected, mind-boggling appearance of one of the greatest statesmen of our time and the first democratically elected president of South Africa on the opening Thursday afternoon of the Marketing, Sales and Distribution Conference (MS&D) was especially appropriate as the conference theme for that year was 'Heroes'.

The fatherly figure of the man the nation knew as Madiba shook hands with each delegate in the front row and the three behind it. Those beyond clambered over seats to reach him. The applause was thunderous. It took 40 minutes for him to reach the podium.

Tears rolled down cheeks as the folks of the SAB marketing, sales and distribution operations treasured these moments of adulation which they would never forget.

From the stage, Madiba spoke of his time in prison on Robben Island, and how he admired SAB as a company that had embraced democracy long before anyone knew what that was, and how proud he was of the work we had done in communities across the country – in education; in sport, to unite the country; and in business, to give benefits back to the economy. It was a celebrated address. We hung on to every word.

At the end of his speech, Madiba proceeded to leave the Superbowl in the same way he had arrived. Another 30 minutes of applause ensued. It was the most emotional hundred minutes back-to-back that I'd ever experienced.

The annual SAB MS&D conference was a star-studded event; an inspiring 48-hour extravaganza that drove the business forward and motivated our people to extraordinary accomplishments.

It was a highlight in the lives of every SAB staffer who was fortunate enough to attend. It gave the business a real sense of purpose, a reflection of where we had come from and a way forward for the year ahead. It was a celebration of accomplishment and – more important than reward – a recognition of extraordinary achievement, and encouragement to all.

The real heroes, of course, were the winning delegates. At the gala banquet on the last night, accolades were bestowed on them amid joyous celebrations, and heartfelt commiserations were afforded to those who didn't quite make it.

This was the X-Factor at work – that special something that made SAB the best company to emerge out of Africa in the 20th century. It was in a different league. It was an organisation for which its people were willing to run through a brick wall.

SAB's Journey:
The Early Days

My journey with SAB began on 11 February 1985. I had the option to join Johnson & Johnson for the same salary – R750 a month – but the SAB offer included 56 dozen beers a year and my fellow residents in the commune I lived in persuaded me that the choice was a no-brainer.

My interview was with the Northern Region's Human Resources guy, Graham-Louden Carter. He began by asking me who I was. Evidently I resembled a friend of his and he suspected he might be the victim of a prank.

'How many toes does your friend have?' I asked him.

'Ten ... '

I removed my right shoe and revealed the result of an encounter with a lawnmower some years earlier, a missing small toe.

He thought it was hilarious, and, satisfied that I was who I said I was, he took me straight through to the General Manager, John Eastwood, without any further questions. The rest is history.

My induction was in the Northern Region's head office, the Poynton's building in Church Street, Pretoria. This is where an explosion in May 1983 killed 19 people and injured more than 200 after a car with 40 kg of explosives on board was detonated outside the South African Air Force headquarters.

I was paging through several files – induction in those days was less than rigorous – when a dear new colleague, Carla van der Boegaard, introduced herself and offered to take me to the pub for a beer after work.

I diligently paged through file after file and became so engrossed that when she arrived to fetch me at 5 p.m. I was taken by surprise.

We went to the bar on the floor below. She ordered me a cold Castle Draught. I immediately offered to pick up the bill. Everyone around us burst into laughter.

I realised then that every SAB venue had a staff bar where employees were free to enjoy the amber nectar between 5 p.m. and 7 p.m., Monday to Friday, as part of the conditions of employment.

I figured that this was probably a company unlike any other. What surprised me over time was the quality of the conversation and the resultant productivity garnered around bar counters throughout the company, which gave birth to some of the great innovations.

Given the calibre of people and the intellectual capital present in every business meeting, there was also no lack of confrontation in the workplace, yet there were never any hard feelings between people, be they right or wrong. Disagreements were resolved over a drink after work. It was a 'work hard, play hard' culture that was ingrained in the company's DNA.

Of course, by 1985 SAB already boasted a glittering history, as a brewer and as a successful business conglomerate. It was only a decade from celebrating its centenary and its status as a cornerstone of South Africa's economic development.

Beer is perhaps man's oldest friend. The ancient Babylonians produced the first written records of the beverage. The Egyptians buried beer with their pharaohs. Julius Caesar called it a 'high and mighty liquid'.

In South Africa, beer is as old as the country itself, arriving with Jan van Riebeeck in 1652 and establishing a pedigree older than wine's. The sparkling streams of the Cape watered a fledgling brewing industry that was to follow the course of South African history.

Beer accompanied the fortune hunters to the diamond diggings of Kimberley, soothed the throats of pioneer miners on the Witwatersrand goldfields, and offered solace to troops in the Anglo-Boer war. Breweries that are today captured in sepia photographs sprang up across the country.

The colourful story of beer and brewing's development in South Africa is, of course, well recorded, but SAB's story emanates essentially from three pioneers: Anders Ohlsson, Frederick Mead, and Charles Glass.

Ohlsson, a burly, thick-set man with an abundant moustache, came ashore in Cape Town in 1860, intending to start a business selling Swedish tools and other hardware. Over the years, his business interests developed and prospered. By then brewing in the Cape was relatively well established.

Between 1840 and 1884, four breweries were built in the Cape in the Papenboom area of Cape Town (now Newlands), taking advantage of the water that bubbled down the slopes of Table Mountain before becoming the famous Newlands Spring, considered the finest quality water for the finest quality of beer in the Cape.

First, in 1840, Jacob Letterstedt established the Mariendahl Brewery. Sixteen years later, Daniel Cloete set up the Newlands Brewery (also known as Cloete's Brewery) opposite the Foresters Arms, an established inn still popular today. In 1874, Dr Jonas M. Hiddingh started Cannon Breweries and bought several public houses and canteens to handle the sale of his brews.

Ohlsson was by then beginning to see a prosperous future in brewing. After Letterstedt's passing in 1862, he leased Mariendahl Brewery and Josephine's Mill (with options to purchase) and gained the rights to access water from the Newlands Spring.

He also bought Newlands Brewery from Daniel Cloete's family as he had passed away, and the Foresters Arms from David Mausen.

In 1883, he built the Annaberg Brewery, converted from the Annaberg Mill. Six years later, he obtained the leases of all canteens and public houses from Jonas Hiddingh, who had decided to shut down Cannon Breweries.

The major event in his career, however, came in November 1889, when his interests were consolidated and registered as Ohlsson's Cape Breweries. With investment capital of £350,000, it was then the largest industrial enterprise in South Africa outside of mining.

Meanwhile, around the mid-1880s, a red-faced, red-haired Englishman by the name of Charles Glass, who had been brewing beer at a troop station in India, arrived in KwaZuluNatal. After the discovery of the Witwatersrand's goldfields, Glass believed there might be an opening for a successful brewery in the expanding mining camp of Johannesburg.

He approached a transport coach operator named Jim Welsh, and his partner, a Johannesburg pioneer named H.B. (Henry) Marshall, and they started the Castle Brewery in Marshall's Township (now Marshalltown) in Johannesburg.

Charles ran it with his wife, Lisa, and a few labourers, and, despite the couple's short tempers and frequent quarrels, the brewery was successful, and expanded.

Around 1890, Marshall bought the Castle Brewery for £18,000 in toto but kept the trademark logo of the three castles. A newspaper reported: 'The old established business of Glass & Co. has been taken over by a new English company which is going to erect extensive machinery and supply us with a really good draught beer. If they do this at a reasonable price, we dust-breathing Johannesburgers will be grateful, and the shareholders of the new company will deserve to be rewarded by large dividends.'

After selling out, Glass had returned to England but came back to South Africa after the Anglo-Boer War and revived the once well-known Stag Brewery on the Witwatersrand. In 1899, as a 19-year-old sailor, Frederick Mead left his ship in Durban to work in the canteen of a local army garrison in Fort Napier.

As it had been in the old country, the favourite drink of the Tommy (British) soldiers was beer, and Mead watched barrel after barrel drain down their thirsty throats. In the summer, demand grew such that the tiny local brewery was unable to meet it. Shipments from overseas were still the British forces' mainstay.

One day Mead told a friend, George Raw, about the growing demand for beer. Raw pricked up his ears at the opportunity of taking over and expanding the little brewery.

'No,' said Fred. 'Let's put up an entirely new, up-to-date plant. We can, if necessary, get money from overseas.'

After Frederick bought a site and returned to England to buy machinery and raise capital, his company was registered in 1890 as the Natal Brewery Syndicate (South East Africa) and brewed its first beer in July 1891.

As gold mining developed and fortune seekers' thirsts grew, it became inevitable that Frederick would move to the Witwatersrand. It is on record that in 1892 the mining town of Johannesburg had more than 300 bars. Mead made the acquaintance of Charles Glass, won support from Marshall, and in the same year closed a deal to acquire the Castle Brewery.

The Natal Syndicate went into liquidation and an entirely new concern, the South African United Breweries, appeared, with investment capital of £100,000.

To Mead and Raw, Glass's buildings were unsuited for adaptation to handle a larger trade, whereas the Castle Brewery was an ideal site for a new brewery to be built in the middle of town.

By 1894 South African United Breweries put up the complex of buildings adjoining Fox Street, Johannesburg, where today's Carlton Centre stands.

It was not much later that the brewing industry on the Witwatersand was revolutionised. The celebrated Barney Barnato, mining entrepreneur and rival of Cecil John Rhodes, decided there were vast opportunities in the trade – his father had been a publican in the East End of London – and he put together the sponsorship for what was to become The South African Breweries Limited.

The Natal syndicate's chairman, W.H. Hackblock, Mead and others of the older board, membership were joined by Sammy Marks, who with his partner Isaac Lewis, fathered many of South Africa's important industries.

SAB's story is really about its beers and its people. But it's useful, I think, to offer a context to the narrative with a thumbnail chronicle of its development.

Two years after SAB was listed on the London Stock Exchange (LSE) in 1895, it became the first industrial company to be listed on the Johannesburg Stock Exchange (JSE), assuring it access to additional investor capital.

When war broke out between British colonial forces and the Dutch and Huguenot settlers known as the Boers, many residents fled Johannesburg. The Castle Brewery was closed for almost a year but sustained little damage during hostilities.

British authorities regarded the plant as an essential industry and encouraged the company to resume production in August 1900. Disrupted supply lines caused shortages of yeast and other raw materials but within a year production had returned to full capacity.

Although the war ended in 1902 and was followed by severe economic depression, the brewing industry was not as adversely affected as others, and SAB was able to expand across southern Africa.

The company acquired the Durban Breweries and the Distillers Company and established a new plant in Bloemfontein.

It bought Morgan's Brewery in Port Elizabeth in 1906. Five years later it acquired another brewery in Salisbury, Rhodesia (now Harare, Zimbabwe) and established a second one in Ndola, Northern Rhodesia (now Zambia).

The chairman, Sydney Chambers, who succeeded William H. Hackblock after his death in 1907, spearheaded an arrangement to cultivate hops at a farm near George, between Port Elizabeth and Cape Town. A subsidiary, Union Hop Growers, spent several years developing new hybrids, which delayed the first commercial use of South African-grown hops until 1920.

After Frederick Mead died in August 1915, John Stroyan, who had succeeded Sydney Chambers a few months earlier, became the most important figure in SAB management.

When hostilities during World War I interrupted the supply of bottles to South Africa, SAB set up its own bottle making plants in 1917 and began actual production in 1919, the year after the war ended.

Another economic depression followed World War I but steady growth in the demand for beer reduced many of its detrimental effects, and SAB was financially strong enough in 1921 to buy the Grand Hotel in Cape Town, an important addition to the company's lodging business.

It gained a foothold in the mineral water business in 1925, by buying an interest in the Schweppes Company.

Like earlier blights, the Great Depression of the early 1930s had little effect on the South African brewing industry; SAB continued to expand its operations and improve its facilities. Its biggest problems were shortages of labour and capital.

Castle Beer accompanied South African soldiers to the East African and Mediterranean theatres of World War II; however, apart from its involvement in Europe and North Africa, South Africa was relatively unaffected by the war. When hostilities ended in 1945, SAB turned its attention to further modernisation and expansion.

Under the leadership of John Stroyan, it concentrated on establishing a South African barley industry. In the midst of a large corporate modernisation programme in 1950, it moved its head office from London to Johannesburg.

After its inception, SAB produced nothing but beer for more than 60 years, until an increase in taxes on beer prompted a fall in beer consumption for the first time on record and showed every indication of further decline.

Senior management of SAB, Ohlsson's Cape Breweries, and United Breweries met in London and Johannesburg on several occasions to discuss the viability of competing in a declining market.

In 1956 they agreed that the three companies should merge. SAB acquired all the shares of Ohlsson's and United Breweries, thus retaining The South African Breweries name.

Arrival of
a 'Proper' Company

It was at this time that, in the words of Meyer Kahn, SA Breweries became a 'proper company'.

Although the new company controlled 90 percent of the SA beer market, antiquated production facilities narrowed profit margins. In response, company activities were centralised in the Transvaal and the Western Province. In addition, the old Castle Brewery in Johannesburg was closed in 1958.

With its further diversification into wines, SAB acquired the Stellenbosch Farmers' Winery (SFW) in 1960, and later added Monis Wineries in Paarl in the Western Cape.

The company ran into another financial crisis in 1966 when Whitbread and Heineken entered the South African beer market. Worse, successive increases in excise duties made beer the most heavily taxed alcoholic beverage in the country. Consumers began to abandon beer for wine and sorghum beer, but the company was able to reduce the effects through increased sales from SFW.

Further diversification came when CEO Ted Sceales was instrumental in creating a new subsidiary, Barsab Investment Trust (Pty) Ltd, jointly held by SAB and Thomas Barlow & Sons Ltd (later Barlow Rand), the rapidly expanding mining services group. It enabled SAB and Barlow Rand to invest in one another and pool their managerial and administrative resources. It also provided SAB with the resources needed to adapt to changing market conditions.

Sceales died after a car accident in 1967, but the success of Barsab continued under the new chief executive, Dick Goss.

SAB's bid in 1950 to move its legal domicile from Britain to South Africa was stymied by tax obligations to the British government and, as it derived about a third of its income from investments in Rhodesia and Zambia, it was bound to observe a British trade embargo against Rhodesia in 1967.

Parliamentary motions to permit the reincorporation of SAB in South Africa were initiated in 1968 but gained approval only in 1970 and, after 75 years as a British company, SAB became a *de jure* South African company.

During the late '60s SAB began brewing several new beers – some under licence from foreign brewers, including Guinness, Amstel, Carling Black Label and Rogue – and acquired the Old Dutch, Stag and Whitbread brands.

While sales of wine and spirits continued to rise, SAB sold a number of its liquor-oriented hotels, and reorganised those that remained under a new subsidiary, the Southern Sun Hotel Corporation.

Southern Sun, which operated 50 hotels in South Africa, was formed by the merger in 1969 of the existing SAB hotel interests with those of the Sol Kerzner family.

When the government barred SAB from further investment in the liquor industry and limited its ability to invest overseas, SAB and Barlow Rand decided in 1972 to dissolve Barsab. Two former Barsab holdings, Shoe Corporation and Afcol, South Africa's largest furniture manufacturer, came under SAB control. The following year, SAB acquired OK Bazaars, but disposed of other investments including ventures in banking and food products.

Various German interests set up breweries in Botswana and Swaziland in attempts to challenge SAB's dominant position in the South African market but failed to gain a foothold.

South African entrepreneur, Louis Luyt, also failed, and sold his breweries to the Rembrandt Group in 1973. Luyt Breweries, the core of Rembrandt's alcoholic beverage group, was later incorporated as the Intercontinental Breweries.

Determined to succeed, Rembrandt's chairman, Dr Anton Rupert, acquired a 49 percent share of Gilbey's, the third largest liquor group in South Africa, so gaining 100 new retail outlets and access to 450 stores.

SAB responded by acquiring Union Wine, an independent liquor retailer with 24 hotels and more than 50 retail outlets.

Again, market conditions were not conducive to competition. The government proposed a rationalisation programme in which SAB would take over Rembrandt's brewing interests and turn over its wine and spirits operations to an independent subsidiary, Cape Wine and Distillers.

By the early '80s, the South African government's apartheid regime and deteriorating social conditions for Black people had become international issues. Many business leaders openly called for change. The government resisted it and prevented companies from transferring capital out of South Africa into foreign investments.

Many foreign-owned companies with fewer restrictions on divestment sold their South African subsidiaries and closed their offices in South Africa.

Most South African companies had little choice but to reinvest their surplus money in South African ventures, making the resolution of social and human rights problems within South Africa even more crucial.

SAB took over control of the Amalgamated Beverage Industries (ABI) soft drink concern from Coca-Cola, and later added several clothing retailers, including Scotts Stores and the Edgars chain.

A government order in 1979 for SAB to sell its Solly Kramer retail liquor stores was completed in 1986, five years before its deadline.

In 1987, Meyer Kahn, continued to diversify through acquisition, adding the Lion Match Company, the leading manufacturer of safety matches in Africa, in 1987; the Da Gama Textiles Company, a leading South African textile manufacturer, in 1989; and PG Glass, a manufacturer of glass and board products, in 1992.

When democracy finally came to South Africa in 1994, things changed again. SAB sold most of its non-beer assets and looked to expanding its brewing enterprise to the global stage.

Meyer reminded me about a speech he gave at one of our conferences in 2001.

MEYER KAHN

Our beer business in South Africa became a national asset. It was owned mostly by South Africans, was managed by South Africans, and was designed and structured to service all South African consumers.

From this start we grew into being the fifth largest brewer in the world and spread ourselves over more than 20 countries, embracing many languages and cultures.

In all this, our South African beer division was a jewel; South Africa's unassailable brewmaster for more than a century. We were unquestionably a mighty marketing machine and took the message of our brands, quality, packaging, value system, low pricing, and commitment to the community and to every consumer in our land.

We never ran away from anything or anybody. We always stood our ground. We walked tall. As a company, we never abandoned the communities we served and we helped to build the country to the benefit of all its inhabitants.

We concentrated our efforts on making high quality beers for every segment in our target market, brewing them at the lowest possible cost and making them available at the right time and the right price.

In doing so, we halved the price of beer in real terms. We consistently kept our price increases below the rate of inflation and brewed the lowest priced beer in the world.

We won many international awards for the quality and taste of our beers, culminating in Castle Lager winning the Grand Champion Bottled Lager Award at the Brewing Industry International Awards at Burton-upon-Trent, England, in 1999.

Our people transferred their skills, expertise and commitment to the far-flung corners of the world. We became a giant in our field. We touched the lives of hundreds of millions of consumers in Africa, Central and Eastern Europe, Russia, India and China.

However, South Africa remained our home base. It was an integral part of our name, our heritage and our roots. We are still a country of contrasts. And we most certainly have problems. But none of these is insurmountable or unmanageable.

The difference between mediocrity and excellence was nothing other than passion, and a strong belief in our abilities, colleagues, brands and products, and we had that.

There was no place in SAB for prima donnas. The company was built by honest players. Integrity of purpose, ability, dedication, perseverance and a hunger to succeed were the main ingredients of personal success and self-empowerment in our company. Nobody ever got to the top in SAB by accident.

SAB was never a place for sissies. It was tough by any standards but, at the same time, it was fair. The golden thread that ran through its cultural behaviour was one of caring. It cared for the country, for its communities, for its assets, for its brands, and above all, for its reputation. Our business was urgent and immediate. There was no *mañana*.

At the end of every day, we could count the money in the tills. We could learn who had voted for us that day. When we had a good day, there was reason to rejoice. Every time we could string together seven good days, we had a good week. When we had four good weeks it had been a good month. When there had been two times six good months, it was a good year.

Urgency and immediacy were the name of the game when it came to fast moving consumer goods (FMCGs) like SAB's.

To me it was far more important to do the right thing, as opposed to doing things right.

GRAHAM MACKAY

Graham Mackay, who became managing director in 1997, added to the overview in a speech in 2013:

In the early '90s we saw some compelling opportunities to run beer assets better in the breweries, and out in the marketplace among retailers, and so create a better image among consumers. Perhaps unlike many US or European brewers, we focused on the potential of the markets as we sought beer growth, rather than being put off by our assets, which were often of extremely poor quality at the time.

We may have underestimated the extent to which beer would alter the mix of consumers' alcohol consumption and raise its share of total alcohol. But as we have reported for many years since then, beer's share of alcohol has risen in many markets as a result of our work to upgrade the category. Over time, beer has displaced local spirits and other subsistence alcohol on more and more occasions.

As we looked at building our original operations in South Africa, we saw opportunities in other countries to apply the capabilities we developed at home.

The Architects'
Story

Probably what contributed most meaningfully to SAB's success was that Meyer Kahn and Graham Mackay had contrasting personalities. Meyer explained the difference. He said: 'On business trips, when Graham and I arrived at hotels around the world, Graham would ask where the gym was. I asked for directions to the bar.'

Cerebral and articulate, Graham was widely regarded as a measured, forward-thinking company leader and one of the most inspirational and successful ones in international business.

A man of vision and loyalty, he held a number of senior positions in the group, including executive chairman, and oversaw a period of growth and expansion in the US, Eastern Europe, China and South America.

He graduated from the University of the Witwatersrand with a BSc in Engineering in 1972, and obtained a BCom from the University of South Africa (UNISA) in 1977. A year later he joined SAB to help the company sort out its computer systems.

He was managing director of SAB Beer Division in the late '80s before becoming CEO and leading the company's expansion outside South Africa by listing it in London in 1999. He then went on to tap into the US market by buying Miller Brewing in 2002.

He had the foresight to see what the future held for the beer industry and had the courage to join what his colleagues called 'the dance of the elephants'.

Meyer, on the other hand, who once described himself as 'just a boykie from Brits', was combative and unpretentious, an accomplished orator and inspirational speaker with a quick wit and amusingly memorable turn of phrase.

He studied law, joined SAB in 1966, became a director in 1981, MD in 1983, executive chairman in 1990 and non-executive chairman of SAB plc in 1999 when it moved its primary listing to London.

Meyer and Graham led the team that devised the company's hugely successful international strategy, which enabled it to acquire 200 brands in more than 80 countries across six continents. Under Meyer's leadership, both as group managing director and chairman, SAB grew from its South African roots to become one of the world's largest and most respected brewers.

Articulate as ever, Graham reflected in upbeat tones at an investor conference in Boca Raton in Florida, US, in 2013, on how we got there as a company, and put the current and future view of the business into a broader context.

(Note: Graham's presentation in February 2013 was his last before his untimely passing in December that year. His comments were made in the present tense. In later years, of course, some of them were overtaken by events such as the war in South Sudan and the less successful than expected Australian venture.)

Consolidation has structurally changed the global beer industry over the last 10 to 15 years. The beers we buy now are developed with a more sophisticated approach and are made to much higher quality standards than in the past.

We can choose from a range of flavours and strengths and a broad array of brand imageries. Bottles and labels are cleaner and more attractive, and the perception of beer in this period, particularly in emerging markets, has been transformed.

Before industry consolidation began, beer's value proposition in emerging markets was unclear, perhaps even paradoxical. On the one hand, beer was priced at a higher premium, certainly per unit of alcohol and in absolute terms, than most forms of local alcohol, such as vodka in Eastern Europe, sorghum beer and home brews in Africa, cane spirits in Latin America, and country liquor in India.

Beer was, and still is, intrinsically a higher-cost form of alcohol than other liquor types, both to produce and to deliver, with higher capital and operating expenses which impact on capital expenditure and margins.

On the other hand, the image of beer was scruffy and unsuited to commanding a premium. Old returnable bottles, uninspiring packaging, and rather simplistic marketing campaigns tended to have only one target in mind among consumers: the working man.

We saw that we could raise the quality of our beers, create an aspirational image for them, and for the first time engage consumers in more sophisticated brand communications. So the price that consumers pay for beer remains typically much higher than that of local subsistence alcohol. But now its quality and image are seen to warrant such a premium.

We didn't have all the answers while we were operating in South Africa. We learnt a lot from the building of new businesses, starting in Africa. What we found helped us to build enduring strategic priorities, which reflected the direction we set and which we followed over the following decade. We continue to review these strategic directions, and they have served us well.

International progress started with the fall of the Berlin Wall in 1989 and the beginning of negotiations to end apartheid in South Africa in the early '90s. We took first mover advantage, initially across Africa and then into Eastern Europe, China and India; then we took on turnaround challenges in the US and elsewhere in Western Europe; and finally, we went on to our big step into Latin America and most recently into Turkey in Central Asia via the Anadolu Efes group, and into Australia with another turnaround opportunity.

The result, where we stand now, is a footprint weighted in favour of growth markets and advantaged over our peer group. This has been driven deliberately and enabled by our skills both as turnaround practitioners and in measuring and managing risk. It informs both our due diligence and our operating management processes, equipping us, we think, better than many others to assess targets and deliver the right acquisitions.

Our strategic relationships are important, too. We are now, through our partnership with China Resources Enterprise (CRE), the largest brewer in China. We brew, ourselves and through our strategic partnership with Castel, about 60 percent of the beer consumed on the African continent. Our Central and Eastern European and Central Asian positions were also enhanced through our strategic stake in and partnership with the Efes group last year.

We do have standard analysis templates and techniques, but our approach is essentially bottom up and decentralised, with a tight grip on local operations. It is a model different from most of our FMCG and beverage peers. It's an approach that starts by assessing what local heterogeneous people really want, what their social fabric is, and where their distinct markets may be heading. It builds on what we find there, rather than force fitting the standard approach from a global headquarters.

This means renovating businesses and products with a strong focus on cost efficiency, developing full portfolios that win by covering the consumer landscape in each local market, and continual improvement by cross-pollinating best practices over 75 countries.

This all goes on across and within regions at a pace determined by local circumstances.

Of course, serial mergers and acquisitions can be built only on successful execution of what you've already done. Perhaps the significant factor enabling our start and our progress was the quality and the depth of management within our South African base.

SAB was at the time the envy of South African industry, and we have tried to build on it since then. I must point out that I take no personal credit for this. I inherited the leadership. I didn't invent it.

The key to this was a set of human resource management practices, well ahead of their time, for hiring and training the best people. The foundation for this was laid in the '60s and '70s, and what it produced was a cadre of resourceful, self-reliant, committed managers; always dissatisfied and keen to benchmark themselves against the rest of the world, and crucially, when it came to it, willing to be posted to almost anywhere in the world with their – sometimes kicking and screaming – wives and families in tow.

Back in South Africa that benchmarking was important because of the inducement to idleness posed by our very high market share. We did fight two bruising 'beer wars' as they were called, against bigger and wealthier competitors at the time, but we emerged victorious both times.

For most of our time in South Africa we enjoyed more than a 90 percent market share of beer, which we referred to as a 'good start'. Nevertheless, despite that, we managed to bring down costs in excruciating detail and to pass on real price reductions to consumers. The tangible result was the real decrease in the price of beer for over 40 years.

We halved the real price of beer and increased our share of alcohol from around 11 percent to almost 60 percent now. This had the dual effects of discouraging competitive challengers, growing the category, and, of course, creating a big industry.

We combined this with a passion for perfecting operations and pioneering and using modern techniques such as six sigma, world class manufacturing, and best operating practices.

Our initial success was based on taking that culture and the operational skills we had established in South Africa and applying them across a range of markets, and across continents, where assets were scruffy at best and where commerce in beer and across consumer goods was very underdeveloped.

We learnt from each new situation and developed bespoke solutions rather than applying a formula.

We deployed a corps of generalist beer management who didn't come to market with predefined answers. They looked for growth and profit in the local context, based on analysis of long-term potential.

I hope that we've been humble enough to learn from some of the mistakes we made, and from the occasional sub-par performances – fortunately in low-cost and low-consequence markets – and then swiftly applying our learnings on site and across to other local markets.

Local beer markets remain highly distinct in their consumer drinking occasions, brand preferences, purchase channels, routes to market, regulation, and so on.

We adapted as quickly as we could to this patchwork of diverse and challenging markets, and we began to see patterns and devise ways of dealing with them. In time, these ways became known as the series of 'SABMiller Ways' which codified and spread our best practices.

Cost productivity appropriate to market scale and structure, zero-based budgeting, and continual improvement have always been part of our 'business as usual'. We have been ahead of our peers in markets where we compete.

As our businesses grow, we are bringing to bear systems that will use our above-market scale, driving cost reduction and better line of sight from the centre across markets to cross-pollinate best practices quickly.

Beer remains different from other FMCG categories. Alcohol is a mood-enhancing product and beer, in particular, has a history as old as civilisation, omnipresent across many societies.

All over our plants, beer is seen as local, and expected to be local, with consumers' brand loyalty driven by local associations and heritage. This emotional reality is reinforced by the economics of producing and distributing what is a bulky perishable product.

Our approach to local consumer insights drives us to segmentations and projections for profit pool segments in each country, to understand the financial landscape of that industry, and to ensure that our portfolios are well targeted,

In Poland, for example, we saw that the mainstream and local premium segments would dwarf the profit contributions of the other segments. So we focused on those.

In Central and Eastern Europe, we took local regional brands and developed them as national icons, tapping into a sense of pride in and belonging to the country based on deep local insights. Local pride of origin has become one of the core themes among our national brands globally.

We also developed local premium as a further sweet spot of national profit pools with premium cues, affording opportunities for consumers to trade up, to differentiate, or to show off with local prominence. These brands have a 10 to 40 percent price premium over mainstream, with significantly higher margins, and are far larger than international premium brands in those markets.

In Latin America the situation is similar, with well-known local brands that lacked clear positioning and differentiation from one another. Based on needs and occasions analysis, we have been able to create daylight between them, letting them stand on their own with distinct relevance to different target groups.

We now have sharper brands and better differentiated portfolios which are expanding in both product and package range and are successfully taking significant share of alcohol from local spirits.

In Africa, the story is similar; building from a much lower base, of course, but accelerating in recent years.

In Moçambique, the portfolio has been completely renovated and now consists of a full brand range with an extensive price ladder, which is important in a country where price points are key.

We've also opened new geographical areas previously isolated by poor infrastructure. In the past few years, we have opened new breweries in the more rural parts of Africa, such as Nampula in northern Moçambique and Mbeya in southeast Tanzania.

Despite the difficult conditions, returns on these new investments have generally been high. The most extreme example of that was South Sudan, the newest country in the world. At the invitation of the government of the new nation, we made the first real manufacturing investment of any industry in this market, in frontier conditions where employment was scarce and tarred roads few and far between.

Despite the risky nature of this investment, in fewer than 18 months we filled the capacity of the brewery. We then doubled its capacity, and filled it again. We are now in the process of doubling it yet again. And we have yet to see the limits of the market.

Our brand strategy for CR Snow in China has been remarkably similar to that in Eastern Europe. We took a regional brand from Manchuria, Shenyang City, Liaoning province, and through relentless focus created the number one national brand, which now exceeds 21 percent market share, more than double the volume of the next biggest brand. Snow is now the largest beer brand in the world. The volume and value of the Snow franchise is being rapidly expanded with premium variants targeting different cohorts with distinct positioning.

We are seeing a continual steady drift towards premium in almost all mature markets and in many emerging markets.

That drift is not exactly in the way that many thought it would play out a decade or even less ago. Trade up in beer is now being led by the rapid emergence of craft, local premium and speciality beers, all premium priced. This challenges, and in some cases reverses, the rise of international premium brands and emphatically re-establishes the need for localism in beer.

Even as our industry, like others, faces top-end fragmentation and the relative decline of old mainstream segments, the leading edge of growth remains resolutely local. Which is notable in the US in the craft segment, and there are variations of this across most of the world.

Of course, none of this is static. Our consumers' tastes are evolving and so are our portfolios.

To appeal to changing taste profiles, perceptions of 'cool', and desires to experiment across a wide range of flavours and styles, our innovations in product and packaging have increased across all our businesses.

Whereas innovation in spirits tends towards mixology, in which the original flavour of drinks such as vodka is disguised later in the bottle, or even at the last step in the bar, innovation in beer is now fundamentally a part of the process even in the brewhouse. These are new products *ab initio*.

In addition to using a very wide range of ingredients in craft beer recipes, we've developed shandies, radlers (essentially the Eastern European variation of a shandy), and beers with fruit, with specific hops, or even using wine or champagne yeasts.

Contrary to some perceptions that existed strongly a while ago, the scope for innovation and flavour variety in beer is very wide. However, doing this all at once is not easy. We've long understood the difficulty of trying to run business models which simultaneously cater to high volume mainstream brands i.e. our local flagships, and low volume, high touch, high growth premium portfolios, all within the same local business.

In some cases, we tried running these together; in many other places, apart. Our current model in the US is one construct that has been successful so far.

In Europe, we launched numerous premium priced innovations across our markets, aimed particularly at younger adults. These include sweeter tasting products, such as low alcohol radlers and speciality premium beers, such as Sha Jenstsha in Poland, which is available in wheat, red and dark variants, and St Stephanos in Belgium.

Our innovation rate will continue to increase. It's not limited to the developed markets. The success of Club Colombia's variants and Redd's variants in Africa demonstrates consumers' appetite for variety in the developing world. There, too, they are expanding the premium beer segment.

In Africa, non-commercial alcohol is around four times the volume of the commercial market, and it varies from home brewed traditional beer to spirits, occasionally adulterated with battery acid or other chemicals.

In this context we are also innovating lower down the alcohol price ladder. We have pioneered the creation of an affordable beer category, which began with Eagle Lager made principally from sorghum, and more recently with Impala, made principally from cassava. We're expanding our distribution and packaging of Chibuku, a traditional African beer made using sorghum or maize, across nine countries and rising.

We sell a carton of Chibuku, a commercialised version of home brewed sorghum beer, at about two days old when the alcohol is still around 1-2 percent by volume. It continues to ferment in the package by 'breathing' through a spout at the top. It lasts about five days, by which time it has typically reached about 4.0 percent alcohol by volume. Being an unfiltered, unpasteurised product, its shelf life is a few days, which tends to relegate it to an informal, relatively unsophisticated, off premise occasion.

Chibuku packaged in PET bottles, a technical innovation, is taking off like wildfire. It's much longer shelf life makes it easier for retailers to stock and store.

Cassava is a subsistence crop which is very difficult to commercialise, but we created a lot of interest from farmers and government when we engaged with stakeholders in its development as a commercial crop – at this stage in Moçambique.

In 2009, we began producing Impala, a light lager version of traditional African sorghum beer using cassava root. Cassava root is widely available throughout Africa and is a cheaper alternative to maize and millet. We replaced the maize in the beer with cassava root to produce a reduced-price beer to appeal to consumers drinking traditional brews. The beer produced was a clear lager type beer, as opposed to the opaque versions of traditional brews.

Improving beer's retail presence and creating more appealing drinking environments have been other core components of our strategy. In the US, the world's most developed market, I perhaps need to highlight the opportunity and the challenge in the developing world, where many retail markets are just beginning the journey towards creating a comfortable drinking environment and broad product choice.

Our efforts to help upgrade points of sale in emerging markets are truly transformative. They create shining examples of sustainable small businesses, enhance the consumer experience, and allow us to show the positioning of our products' merchandising in the outlet.

We have been ahead of the FMCG pack in this retail engagement in many emerging markets and we're often among the largest suppliers of the outlets.

In Africa, for example, for the last two years, we have tripled the number of outlets that are now able to serve cold beer in markets such as Tanzania and Uganda. This is accompanied by a range of basic retailer support, oriented towards our own brands, from wall paint to furniture and lighting. That would be illegal in the US but in Africa it is very welcome.

In Colombia, we have structured, tiered and tailored direct store delivery service packages to more than 420,000 outlets.

At the same time, the influence of modern trade and discounting strategies in developed markets requires brewers to use a more sophisticated partnership model.

This is one area where the beer industry is, quite frankly, still catching up with other categories as an average around the world. Revenue management tools are, however, becoming more advanced, as more complex assortments of products evolve to suit a range of tastes and to help drive revenue and profit growth from premiumisation.

There is plenty of evidence of our progress here. In the US our new category management systems are increasingly accepted by retail chains to grow the overall category while helping to make sense of SKU proliferation. It is increasing category captaincies, creating better positioning for our brands, and ensuring an appropriate balance between segments.

There are examples in Europe where our partnerships with Spar in the Czech Republic and Alma in Poland have led to impactful secondary placements, thereby influencing decisions at the point of purchase.

It's the same direction we're heading in Australia, where the turnaround of Carlton United Breweries depends on new relationships with the two big retailers there, Woolworths and Coles. The relationships are oriented towards joint business planning and win-win solutions to bring beer back to growth.

Overall complexity is a natural consequence of our global footprint and the price we pay for having locally relevant portfolios. We are making good strides in developing best practices and organising ourselves to take better advantage of our scale.

One principle is the use of market archetypes to cluster and simplify approaches to brand portfolios, to channels, and to routes to market by direct vs indirect distribution etc. We are centralising our back office to reduce costs by optimising procurement, enabling local businesses to focus more on the purely commercial with less back-office distraction, and globalising IT to drive cross-border sharing within defined market archetypes.

Over the years we have evolved our growth model by codifying and sharing management techniques across our businesses for a wide range of business functions in brands, category, and revenue management, and in operations.

For our commercial functions, our guide, the SAB Marketing Way, continues to be refreshed and evolved. It is currently on its fifth iteration and pre-eminent among our series of SABMiller Ways.

Creating the culture and the structures to systematically cross-pollinate between business functions is complex, but we believe it's worth it. I have already highlighted the benefits of our decentralised model.

I believe there is no alternative if we are to capture the growth opportunities for which our decentralised model is designed, while still managing a business that is not unmanageably complex.

The Carlton United Breweries acquisition should be seen in this light. There were obvious areas for improvement at every turn, in brands, portfolio, sales, procurement and operations. It is gratifying to see how efficiently we could bring our skills, processes and culture to bear. It supports our belief that we can transform that business and drive a renaissance for beer in Australia.

In summary, we have created an advantaged position, in our footprint and in our commercial strategy, to enable best-in-class growth by transforming the business of brewing and selling beer. There is room for per capita consumption to grow far beyond current levels within our emerging markets as consumers enter the commercial alcohol space.

Consumer tastes are staying resolutely local, and in some cases becoming even more so as living standards rise. Our local portfolios and intensified innovation into new products are well suited to this context.

Our commercial capabilities are continually being enhanced beyond brand management into revenue and category management, dealing with modernising channels and moving into the digital age.

Our systems, processes and organisational design are evolving to allow us even greater leverage from our scale, with continual improvement to raise the bar internally and maintain our competitive lead in the sector.

The essence of our successful strategy and opportunity in global beer remains the same: local portfolios and businesses with global skills and efficiency, meeting evolving consumer needs and increasing beer's presence across all drinking occasions.

MEYER KAHN

Of course, there were some seriously bad times for SAB as well. Here are my top five.

The first was in 1989 when we changed the label of Castle Lager, but not the beer in the bottle. What a catastrophe that was. People in those days used to argue that a brand's worth equaled its worth in sales. Castle Lager, which had 60 percent share of the alcoholic beverages market, plunged to 30 percent in six months. It made the 'Real Coke' saga look like tea with Mother Theresa. How did we survive that, in the full glare of the public eye? It wasn't as if it happened quietly, and nobody knew about it. Everybody was talking about it. We very nearly destroyed the brand.

In any other company, Graham Mackay and Peter Savory (who was Marketing Director at the time) would have been fired, and maybe even I, as a non-operating head of beer at this stage, would have been shown the door. In Japan, Graham would have fallen on his sword. Savory would have jumped from a 20-storey building. But we carried on, and we survived.

That was a bad time, and it lasted a long time. Imagine if we had had a formidable competitor at that stage. They could have broken us into pieces.

The second mistake was the Heineken Amstel debacle. Heineken invoked a contract clause that ended our right to brew and distribute Amstel Lager. It cost us nine percent of our sales and 20 percent of our profits. It all came down to the fact that they cuckolded us. We brought it upon ourselves by not using decent lawyers for the reappraisal of the agreement.

Our in-house lawyers, the kind who were good at drawing up decent leases and suing people for debt, took it upon themselves to finalise this agreement, which precluded SAB from doing anything that would damage the Amstel brand anywhere. We needed to have added Africa or South Africa. We left out one word, the 'South' in South Africa. In court, two out of three judges ruled against us. The loss was self-inflicted.

The third bad time was when we revamped Lion Lager, which was selling about a million hectolitres a year at the time; it was drunk, amongst others, by the tough okes in the pubs of Vereeniging on Saturday nights while they were playing snooker. We put it in an effeminate bottle, changed the red and gold label to blue, and reduced the alcohol content, but still called it Lion and expected people to want it. That's like taking Stalin and putting him in a dressing gown and calling him a priest.

Number four is not widely known but was dangerous beyond belief. A man named Franklin Sonn was vice chancellor of the University of Cape Town at the time and a good friend of SAB. He then became a lecturer in the US and the US brewing giant, Anheuser-Busch, pressured him to persuade SAB to distribute AB's beers. They didn't want to brew their beer in the US – they didn't want to invest; they just wanted to export it to South Africa for us to distribute on their behalf.

AB convinced Sonn to speak to Alec Irwin, then Minister of Trade and Industry, and he did. He sold Irwin on this lock, stock, and barrel. They sent out several American consultants to advise Irwin. They all went back and reported that political pressure and open markets determined that SAB should be distributing anybody's beer, not just their own. They claimed that to have an exclusive beer distributor such as SAB flew in the face of fair competition.

It started while I was still chairman; then Cyril Ramaphosa became acting chairman while I spent some time heading the South African Police Services, and Graham became acting managing director. Graham phoned me one evening in a panic to say that the government had decided they would regulate distribution, but it applied only to SAB. They would never make Proctor and Gamble distribute for Lever Brothers, but beer was now open season.

Graham arranged a meeting at the Industrial Development Corporation. I came in from my work at the cops, Cyril was there, and Alec with some of his handlangers looking very pious and proud that they were now opening the market and the Americans would applaud them. And people would be able to drink Anheuser-Busch beers.

In reality, we would have been spending our share of the revenue generated to introduce a competitor's beer.

Alex explained the whole strategy sweetly, detailing how they were effectively going to destroy us.

Eventually I turned to Alec – I knew him quite well and called him by his first name – and said: 'Alec, you must know that this will happen only over my dead body. If you do this, I must tell you in all fairness, what we will do.

'In the first place, we will close down all ten of our distributors, all black owned, and explain to South Africa why we are doing this.

'Secondly, we will extend the warehouse space at our breweries and instead of delivering to our customers from our distribution centres, we will deliver from our breweries.

'That will cost us a lot more. We will have to put up the price of beer and we will do so while explaining to South Africa why we were being forced into this.

'So, understand the repercussions. I am not threatening you. I am telling you on my life that is what we will do.'

He went pale. The meeting broke up, and not on a friendly note. Over time that plan just dissipated until eventually they sought a compromise. By then I was back at SAB, and they came back asking would we, then, with no animosity and just through our normal distribution channels, distribute one or two AB products in Africa?

I asked that if we did that, would they take one or two of our brands and distribute them in North America? If they were prepared to do that, then we would be prepared to consider doing the same here. Then they went away altogether.

The last black day was when we listed on the London Stock Exchange (LSE) in '99. We were number 80 on the FTSE 100 ('footsie') – very comfortably placed. Our whole business was Africa at that stage. And then the rand collapsed. Our earnings in rands, converted into sterling and US dollars, plummeted. We dropped from 80 on the FTSE 100 to about number 94. Our listing stabilised at 95 because of so many guys pitching up to get into the FTSE 100. If you stabilise at 95, you lose your place on the FTSE.

You can imagine the fallout, especially after all the *snot en trane* that we were being disloyal to our country and disinvesting from South Africa; and now we were getting a *snotklap* for being eliminated from the FTSE.

Every reporter and every analyst in the world was waiting to say they told us so. That lasted for about a year, the longest year of my life that I can remember.

Then the rand recovered a little, we began trading better, we began to climb, and over time we peaked at number nine.

Positive game changers? There were many. In South Africa, international sanctions in the latter years of apartheid had a huge negative impact on the economy. They bled South Africa dry. In a positive sense, they hardened our managers enormously. With sanctions, we also had inflation and interest rates at 25 percent, labour troubles, and war in the townships. For us to have survived that time was almost a miracle. Yet we not only survived – we blossomed.

Another landmark was our purchase of Amalgamated Beverage Industries, ABI. It wasn't a normal purchase because we paid R1 per share at the time when Coca-Cola disinvested from South Africa and moved their plant to Swaziland so that they weren't in violation of sanctions. We sold the business eventually for R94 a share. What a pisspot full of money we made there. It was one of the highlights of that period.

The 'beer wars' with Louis Luyt, and later Anton Rupert, were another significant event. Luyt was a business tycoon who had made his fortune selling fertiliser to the country's farmers. His birth name was Oswald Louis Petrus Poley, but he took the surname of his stepfather, Charles Luyt, when his mother remarried.

A rugby player as a young man, he was a burly heavyweight who set out in 1972 to contest our dominance of the South African beer market, expecting, in particular, support from the farming community.

Into a market dominated by Castle Lager, Lion Lager and Carling Black Label came Luyt Lager, brewed in a new brewery in Chamdor on the West Rand, ostensibly offering a crisp, clean taste to compete with Castle. Luyt's company also marketed and sold Becks and Madison.

These brands attracted a small following, largely of beer drinkers who felt a kinship with the local underdog and some who were willing to try a new taste. The new operation, however, grossly underestimated not only the fervency of SAB's sales force to protect its market, but also its unshakeable relationship with retailers, particularly in the urban black communities.

Even before prohibition of township sales was lifted, more than four out of five beers drunk by South Africans was poured down Black drinkers' throats. Our reps knew exactly how township shebeens operated and the difficulties their owners faced.

Storage space was limited. Shebeen owners knew their customers' brand preferences. They could not afford to stock slow selling brands. And often they faced police interference. So they saw minimal value in trying to sell untested brands, and especially not brands offered by a 'super-Afrikaner' who fraternised with the political bigwigs of the day, among them head of the Bureau of State Security, General Hendrik van den Bergh, and Prime Minister John Vorster. Luyt had difficulty both distributing and selling his brands, to say the least.

The 'Treaty of Versailles' we signed afterwards was for us to take over all the beer interests, and they would take over wine and spirits – though we maintained a 30 percent share – while they had no share in beer. It rattled the industry and put SAB on its feet.

To make matters even more dramatic there was the case of Colt 45 and Stallion 54. It is still a case study at Harvard University, more than 40 years after the event. It was one of the highest profile game changers you've ever seen.

In the early '70s, Intercontinental Breweries (ICB) were brewing Kronenbrau 1308, Heidelberg Lager, and Sportsman Lager.

We heard that it was ready to launch an American beer called Colt 45. Its alcohol content at 5.4 percent by volume was higher than any other lager in South Africa at the time. To demonstrate the 'extra kick', the label depicted a kicking colt.

We never knew when Rupert was going to launch it. Then somebody at the Sunday Times tipped us off that ICB had bought two or three pages of advertising for an upcoming weekend. For us that was the clincher that the launch would be that weekend.

Our marketing director at the time, Peter Savory, was lying in his bath when he had the idea of 'muddying the waters' in the market with a competitive brand.

Inside a week, SAB developed a new brand, signed off its name and the design of its packaging, and offered it to beer drinkers as Stallion 54. The label showed a rearing horse; it had the same packaging colours as Colt 45; and the name had a similar meaning.

The two brands reached retailers within days of one another, arousing not just confusion among them, but also frustration and anger. Inevitably, they rejected both and re-ordered the more familiar SAB brands.

What followed was a battery of court cases, death threats, accusations of the Hoggenheimers dominating the little guys, and a shower of shit like you won't believe.

The court ruled that there could be no confusion between a stallion and a colt. A stallion represented vigour and virility while a colt represented youth. A month later we withdrew Stallion 54 from the market. There was consternation in the market second to none.

SAB was unique among companies. From 1956 when SAB became a 'proper company', in the next 60 years we had only four managing directors (MDs). That's unheard of. Each MD was in office for 15 years on average.

Ted Sceales died in a car accident. He was in office for seven or eight years. He was the SAB lawyer who put together the deal to establish SAB, because the brewers couldn't decide who should be the boss. They saw him as neutral. He knew nothing about business.

Then came Dick Goss, who did 12 years. Then I came, and between MD and chairman, I probably did more than 30 years. Graham Mackay did 10.

It meant continuity was assured. When we needed to appoint a new chairman, it flew in the face of corporate governance because the worst thing you could do was take the ex-managing director and make him chairman. There was pandemonium. It was the worst scenario of governance you could imagine.

Our advisors in the UK kept telling us that we'd better look for a replacement for the chairman, because there was no way that the institutions or the analysts would agree at that stage to an MD becoming chairman. That had happened to me, and we were trying to make it happen to Graham.

I promised Graham that I would get it through. I spent two days in London seeing every one of the institutions there and spent a day on the phone here in South Africa, and eventually the shareholders voted in favour of Graham becoming chairman. He was chairman for 18 months before he took ill, and his passing in 2013 put a stop to the continuity.

I challenge anyone to find a company that is not family owned that, over that many years, had only four different MDs. Continuity worked for us. It was the most important theme in our lives.

Making Beer,
Making Friends

My own career began as a computer analyst and ended as director of global brands across Africa, working with ABInBev. I worked in 19 roles in the company over 34 years, travelled to more than 50 countries to do business, and worked on more than 50 beer brands in my marketing journey. It was a lifetime of experience, and it just happened to be my lifetime.

I awoke each morning around five – irrespective of the time I'd gone to bed, which was sometimes very late after social commitments – hit the shower, prepared for the day, had a coffee, and made sure I was at my desk before 6.30 a.m. ensuring I was organised for every meeting scheduled and ready for anything that might come my way ... well, just about.

A rough calculation suggests that I probably consumed 31 pallets of beer in my career, equating to 25,316 beers – about one and a half fully-loaded beer trucks. Strangely this was not reflected in my medical check-up records.

We sold sociability. My career was mostly on the front line, marketing and selling our brands, working with consumers, customers, stakeholders, sportsmen and women, government, investors, suppliers and many others.

The SAB catchphrase 'Making Beer, Making Friends' was interwoven with the company's story. We were popular people wherever we went and our generosity in the way we treated everyone, especially in a social setting, was unrivalled.

Such were our people practices that if one was willing to seize the moment, the opportunities were endless.

My first role was as a computer analyst. It was really just a toe (one of my nine) in the water. I saw myself as a passionate marketer. I went on to become a consultant training retailers in core business practice.

It was not only rewarding for me but built great trust and credibility for SAB. We were offering something never seen before in the market.

In October 1986, I was plying my trade teaching new taverners and shebeeners in Tzaneen to run their businesses through our 'Partners for Profit' training models, focusing mainly on financial management and stock procedures.

My role as retail consultant was particularly rewarding. I was helping liquor businessmen to become astute and to make money. But it was a lonely lifestyle. I was teaching during the day and alone away from home most evenings.

It had been a long, sweltering day as I drove from the township back to the comfort of my hotel, the Coach House Hotel in Tzaneen, Limpopo, a landmark in the area, which had a spa, luxurious facilities, stunning views and food to match. After a shower, I adjourned to the bar for a customary cold Castle Lager before dinner.

The barman recognised me and reached into the undercounter fridge for a cold pint of Castle Lager and a frozen glass. I poured the beer at an angle and then straightened the glass to ensure a tidy head of foam that made up around 20 percent of the liquid, as I had been taught. It ensured proper carbonation and appetite appeal.

I took a long rejuvenating swallow as I looked across the bar, which was filling up. I did a double-take when I spotted a young, familiar-looking fellow waiting for service on the opposite end of the bar. I walked over to enquire where we had met and to offer to buy him a bitterly cold. 'Howzit.' I held out my hand in greeting. 'I know you from somewhere – you look so familiar.'

To which he replied: 'My name is Paul. Paul Simon.'

At that time, Simon & Garfunkel were among the most popular musicians in the world. Their songs were topping the charts from London to New York to Johannesburg. It dawned on me that this was the real Paul Simon.

We set about discussing how he had come to be at the Coach House, given that we were living under apartheid and no musicians of global stature were prepared to play music in our country. It turned out that he was there to appear in a Tracy Chapman concert in Salisbury (now Harare), Zimbabwe, and the Anglo-American Corporation had secretly flown him into Tzaneen that evening in a private jet for a surprise dinner in an aircraft hangar. He was to return afterwards under cover of darkness.

We became so engrossed in conversation that his driver had to interrupt us to remind him it was time to leave for the function. He wished out loud that he could enjoy another Castle Lager with me but knew he had to meet his social obligations.

He got up and embraced me. 'Remind me what your name was again,' he said.

I quipped: 'You can call me Al.'

I moved to the warehouse in Waltloo, Pretoria, the largest depot in the country, managing some 80 people with around 90 truckloads of beer moving through the premises daily.

In distribution my colleagues Mark de Wille and Zybrand Fourie were the gurus of operations and took our standards to new levels, developing innovative programmes to enhance the business.

For instance, by introducing forklifts into big liquor retailers like Makro, we improved our truck turnaround times by hours, thus increasing our truckloads per day.

The SAB operation across South Africa, and eventually globally, was slick and efficient. We could access geographic areas beyond the reach of anyone else. We were an integral part of the communities in which we operated. For instance, in the fight to prevent the spread of HIV/AIDS, we distributed condoms in rural areas. While anti-apartheid activists regularly torched trucks going into Soweto, SAB vehicles remained untouched.

When a fire broke out or floodwaters ravaged a community, SAB was first on the scene, rescuing people, providing food, shelter and warmth, and rebuilding.

A philosophy of caring and generosity helped us to build trust, loyalty and love for our brands among all South Africans.

Several times in the '90s and later, SAB won awards as the 'Best Company to Work for'. People practices and ways of working, measures, and performance management were maintained at the highest levels.

Corporate South Africa drew on the success of SAB. Many leaders who left the company adopted similar practices and standards that remain in other businesses to this day.

Development of people was a pillar of the business model. I had ongoing training both in the classroom and in my various roles, and I was privileged to attend some of the best global programmes at the top tertiary institutions in the world.

The Battle for Shelf and Mind Space programme at INSEAD University outside Paris; the Value Chain Alignment Programme at Kellogg's in Chicago; and the Executive Development Programme at the Gordon Institute of Business Science in Malaysia, Singapore, and in South Africa. I went through them all.

The company valued its people and invested heavily in their advancement. In return, it had smart people working smartly to deliver excellence in everything they did.

Through the performance management process, we took an honest and frank approach to the way we worked, set and reached goals, and used key performance indicators (KPIs) to measure 'what good looks like'. Performance management was linked to promotability and reward and became ingrained in the leadership. It was very fair. You always knew exactly where you stood.

Inspiration was everywhere. Leadership was empowering. Accountability was clear and personal. The quality and level of questioning was what stood out for me as one of the greatest strengths of the company. Just when you thought you had all the bases covered, someone would pose a different question and you were left to go away and think about it, perhaps even to consult the experts, before returning with your answer.

Recognition almost eclipsed reward. The pride of standing in front of 1,700 peers at the MS&D conference made for some of the most memorable moments in some people's careers. Be it for team or individual, the inspiration received was profound.

(Initially, share options seemed underwhelming as a retention opportunity but, as the company grew exponentially, those who held onto their shares received handsome pay-outs, particularly around October 2016 when ABInBev purchased SABMiller.)

Every year we looked forward to MS&D, which was a combination of reflection and strategic thinking, and whose agenda included motivational speakers, leadership presentations, and outside-in thinking that was both inspiring and thought provoking.

I worked in Pretoria as the marketing services manager under a legendary character named Willie Odendaal. Our team became best-in-class and won all the sales awards annually – a golden team of passionate people. Several of them went on to become senior managers in SAB and outside the company. The grounding was exceptional, and the learnings were immense.

I headed up sponsorships, events and draught beer, managed 25 promotions hostesses, and made friends with all of Pretoria. That was what we were about. The SAB 'wolf pack' was revered wherever we went, and consumers were drawn to us. The township of Mamelodi was my favourite stamping ground and became a second home to me. We worked hard, played hard, and enjoyed the friendships we made both inside and outside the business.

Staying in shape in SAB became important. Most SAB people were trim and lean. I decided to take on ultra-marathon running and ran five successive Comrades Marathons. It taught me a lot personally about what was possible and how you could take on anything if you put your mind to it.

After about five years at the rock face in numerous roles, I crossed the Moreleta Spruit from Pretoria to the City of Gold to take up a role in brand marketing.

I had staged a Lion Lager roadshow with 10,000 attendees and was proud of its success. Robin Goetzsche told me that it was the best they had seen and suggested I move to SAB Central Office to join his team.

Working initially on both Hansa Pilsener and Castle Milk Stout, I found them to be an odd combination, but they became giant brands over time and the grounding could not have been better for me.

Hansa Pilsener was a crisp, refreshing beer which appealed to youthful consumers, playing on the difference between lagers and pilsners. It became a popular choice for consumers after the Castle Lager label change, and the franchise became famous as we moved into the '90s. It was also very profitable. As a brand with an alcohol content lower than the mainstream (4.5 percent alcohol by volume), it attracted a lesser excise and boosted our bottom line.

(Over time, excise became almost one third of the total price of beer. At its peak, SAB contributed more to the government in taxes than the entire South African gold mining industry.)

Castle Milk Stout had a strong franchise in the Transkei. Consumers believed there was a baby in every bottle. They thought that Castle Milk Stout made you strong. An underrated brand, it was extremely profitable. I enjoyed it and often mixed it with a lager to make a 'black and tan', as it was known.

In 1990, my dream came true. I was offered custodianship of SAB's flagship brand, Castle Lager – our founding brand, the brand that rallied our company, our people and our country. The brand was woven into the story of South Africa, and it was a passion for me and an integral part of my life.

My sense is that Castle Lager played a central role in influencing the political landscape of South Africa. The stories told by the brand were visionary and created hope for the future. When there was despair, Castle Lager portrayed optimism and unity.

In a mixed-race TV commercial in the mid - '80s, the hero was seen taking his pet Collie for a run but making a detour to a bar to share a cold Castle Lager with his mates for the duration of what would have been a decent jog. As he left, they sprayed him with water so that he looked the part when he arrived home.

The ad portrayed the future democracy of South Africa and that the country needed multiracial sociability. Only much later did that come about.

I always told our creative gurus that we should dream of the future before it happened and reflect that in a brand that united, celebrated and welcomed all.

In the '90s, Castle Lager was bonding the nation both through its stories and through the inaugural sponsorships of Bafana Bafana, the Proteas, and the Springboks.

To jolt beer lovers into action – the brand had been in decline since the label change in 1989 – we launched the 'Homecoming' advert that showed 'Mike' bidding a long-term farewell to his mates in Sachmo's Bar. Five years later he returns to the bar to an emotional and stirring homecoming.

The underlying story talked to former Castle Lager consumers returning to what they knew to be the best and the most trusted. It so happened at the time that a number of exiles were also returning to South Africa and the interpretation just prior to democracy's arrival was that we should all come home to Castle Lager.

The sequels to our story saw the lads put Diego Maradona's boots up for sale for a friend to win a ticket to London to try out for a top English team around the time that our first footballers were heading for the UK to play in the premiership.

The second of them depicted the welcoming of an American to South Africa and teaching him to order a round of Castles in the vernacular. *Inqaba!* became the rallying call for a round of Castles and lives on to this day.

These emotional communications enabled Castle Lager to gain a full percentage market share each month for just on 30 months, lifting the brand back to close on 60 percent market share. Consumers forgave us for changing the label. Castle Lager was king once more.

Meanwhile, Africa was waiting. I had the privilege of two great stints on the African continent to work across our business units in Southern Africa, East Africa and West Africa. At the same time, my international role at the turn of the century took me on visits to the UK and India, to due diligence visits in Argentina and India, and to the US launch of Castle Lager before our acquisition of the Miller Brewing Company.

In the US we conducted research in Washington to understand resonance and differentiation and created meaningful positionings for Castle Lager. After good progress, we were about to launch the brand when Graham Mackay told me that he was announcing the SAB purchase of Miller Brewing.

We had learnt a lot in our two years of research. It kept the due diligence team interested in the Miller deal and brought us a greater understanding of the US beer market and the brands.

In the UK, we were a small player with Castle Lager. Our main sales were in areas where ex-South Africans lived and longed for home, clutching on to their Castle Lager, Mrs Ball's Chutney, biltong, and Ouma Rusks.

Custodianship of Castle Lager in the UK was exciting and challenging in probably the most prolific and competitive beer market in the world. I worked with our distributor, UBEVCO, out of Dorking in Surrey, and visited for a week once a quarter to review our status and the steps we needed to move up a notch.

Using my own office keys, I was in office two hours before anyone arrived, worked through lunch when everyone left to go to the local, and remained in the office after everyone went home.

It was evidence, I think, that South Africans have a unique work ethic that is part of the X-Factor that enabled SAB to take on the world and win.

We worked hard to gain listings in Tesco and Sainsbury's, and the Rugby World Cup in '99 provided an ideal platform for us to link our brand proposition to other rugby nations' beers such as Stein Lager and Castlemaine XXXX (pronounced 'four X'). We rocked the event and our impact in stadia in the major cities of Edinburgh, London and Cardiff made them look like Castle strongholds. Indeed, many thought that Castle, not Guinness, was the beer sponsor.

The year 1999 saw an epic moment for South African Breweries when we listed on the London Stock Exchange (LSE).

I was with a colleague, Jane Gilroy, visiting Tesco in Birmingham, when my cell phone rang. In those times it was the size of a brick.

'Ally Hewitt here, how can I help?' I answered.

'Hi Ally, it's Graham here, how are you doing?'

Graham was our trade marketing fellow in UBEVCO, so I proceeded to tell him how unhappy I was with the minimal shelf runs we had for Castle Lager in Tesco.

Then it dawned on me that this sounded like a different Graham. It was Graham Mackay, then CEO.

'Ally, Meyer and I are in London, and we'd like you to join us for the listing of SAB on the London Stock Exchange tomorrow morning.' I was over the moon and battled to keep an even tone in my response.

'I'd love nothing more than the privilege of witnessing this historic event. Thank you, see you at 7.30 a.m.' I said.

I turned to Jane: 'I need to ask you a favour. Please can you get me back to my B&B in Dorking? I've been summoned to an urgent meeting in the morning.'

I was shaking with excitement as I packed my suitcase and grabbed a cab to head for the station and the train down to London.

I checked in at the Bloomsbury Crest Hotel, dropped my luggage, and headed for Jermyn Street to buy a new suit, tie, and shoes, and a shirt that I pressed myself that evening. I turned in for an early night, eagerly anticipating the day ahead.

I awoke bright and early and headed for a coffee shop near Paternoster Square to meet Graham and Meyer Kahn.

They were the architects of SAB's global expansion after isolation and were revered in South Africa. In London in 1999, however, they were the unknown leadership of an unknown company. Things were about to change.

Meyer had entertained nine analysts at Langan's Brasserie, a landmark London restaurant, the day before. He was delighted to tell Graham and me about the experience.

He had jokingly asked the waitress in Langan's if the establishment served Castle Lager. The analysts smirked and humoured the comment until the young lady said: 'Of course sir, how many would you like?'

Meyer himself was surprised and asked what other beers they served. She replied that the only beer they served was Castle Lager. Meyer stood up and invited the nine analysts to step up to the bar to see if this was true. The undercounter fridges were stacked edge-to-edge with cold Castles.

It turned out that Langan's was owned by the English movie star, Michael Caine, who was a good mate of Dennis Miller, the CEO of our UBEVCO distributor.

On the big day, we entered the London Stock Exchange auditorium. Graham and Meyer sat at the front table while more than 200 analysts gathered and took their seats, arranged cinema-style. I sat in the middle of the auditorium and watched the formalities unfold.

The poncy fellow who headed the exchange welcomed everyone to the proceedings and gave a brief overview of formalities and a short description of the company: SAB, a beverage company from the southern tip of Africa that had its origins in the apartheid regime and had started to expand into Third World territories with the knowledge and capability of what they thought was essentially a Third World brewer.

A silver plaque was handed to Graham and the bell was rung to signify the primary listing of The South African Breweries Limited on the London Stock Exchange.

Graham graciously accepted the silver plaque and Meyer stood up to make a few comments, which by my understanding was not the 'done thing'. He was holding something fairly large in both hands, wrapped in the South African newspaper, the Sunday Times. He spoke boldly and with conviction.

'You may not be aware that SAB, The South African Breweries, was listed on the London Stock Exchange many years ago. We were forced to withdraw during the horrific apartheid era but are now really proud to return.

'You will come to know us over time but one thing I can tell you: we South Africans are friendly and generous by nature and are ready to take on the global beverage industry.'

With that, he handed the unwieldly parcel to the head of the LSE, who opened it to find a hippo carved out of wood that Meyer had purchased from a street vendor in Braamfontein, Johannesburg, on his way to the airport a few days before.

I heard an analyst near me remark: 'That was an interesting listing ... never in my time have I seen a CEO or chairman of a newly listed company hand over a gift to the LSE. We are obviously looking at a very different approach and leadership style here.'

Oh man, was he right.

I returned to South Africa in 2003 to head our trade marketing team, truly one of the greatest groups of characters with whom I worked throughout my career.

I worked across our key account groups with Riaan McGillicuddy and Antonio Rossetti, visiting the group headquarters and meeting with the great business minds that ran our top groups in the off-trade and on-trade environments. Our customer relationships were superb and the professionalism of our leadership and teams was outstanding.

Under Allison Collier's and Andrew Mundell's leadership, we used Nielsen data, customer service surveys, and other pieces of research that gave us an in-depth insight to the market and our competitors and put together analytics and measures for in-trade effectiveness, enabling us to change direction when needed to make sure we were ahead of the game from every angle.

The knowledge and information we had at our fingertips was abundant. I often thought that we perhaps paralysed ourselves with too much information. We took time to make decisions and were sometimes late in going to market. My own gut feeling was often right. Some information just cannot tell you what your gut can. Be that as it may, we were rigorous, detailed and mostly spot on.

We ran the promotions department with a strong team under Nic Scheijde's leadership, and with a merchandising team under Geraldine Scott, both of whom were a fundamental part of our in-trade 'look of success'.

I also enjoyed leading the annual awards with Tony van Kralingen, Robin Goetzsche, and 'Big Mac' Wayne M\(^c\)Cauley, when we reviewed the performance of the best teams in the country for our awards ceremony at the MS&D conference, which I organised with the likes of Simon Harvey and Francois Malan.

Around February 2008, I was summoned to Wayne's office. I was met by him and Steve Bluen, our HR director at the time. It's not always a good thing to find yourself in the company of your leader and the HR director.

My mind began to run wild as I reflected on what I might have done recently that would call for a meeting with these two giants … one in size, and both in business stature.

I was asked to sit, served a cup of tea, and offered the option to move to human resources. I would lead a strategic initiative to create a specialised team tasked with sourcing the best possible outside talent for positions in middle and upper management at SAB, amongst other things saving the company the considerable expense of commissioning headhunters to do the job.

It was an interesting proposition but not what I was after, as I was grappling with the impacts of my brother's serious illness. After much deliberation, however, I accepted the challenge.

A new high-flyer from McKinsey Consultants was about to take my place to head our trade marketing division. I handed over the baton to him in a 45-minute meeting: it turned out that I had to endure 45 minutes of being peppered with McKinsey jargon – and no handover. He had no interest in the journey we had travelled or the team we had built.

Not surprisingly, this prodigy, who was sent to take over trade marketing in one fell swoop, was moved out of the position within three months. He was replaced on a consulting basis by my friend Trevor Hughes, who was in the position for almost two years.

This episode confirmed that brains do not eclipse the importance of a balance between the 'what' and the 'how'. The X-Factor in SAB was about striking the right balance.

So there I was, facing the task of running recruitment after some 24 years in sales and marketing. I decided to give it my all and built a team of recruitment gurus whose psyches were very different from those we sought in other disciplines. Our crazy team became known as 'Ally's Angels' as we set about building a conversion recruitment funnel for each job across both SAB and ABI.

We focused mainly on finding great engineers and artisans, who were in short supply at the time, and began to achieve good traction and land some valuable talent. My own experience in understanding what it took to work in the company began to play a role in sourcing good fits for the business and across all disciplines. At the same time, my understanding of the business model, through exposure to the board and senior management in taking briefs for various roles, began to grow. Never waste a day to learn something new.

Our key performance indicators and use of performance management again came to play in the way that we set our targets and actively chased key indicators to show success from the beginning. The SAB board was pleased with our achievements and savings. My aim was to 'wash our faces' on pay and recruitment costs in year one, and to begin to show significant savings for the company in year two.

Personally, I was dealing with the sadness of watching my very competent and passionate brother, a general surgeon diagnosed with aggressive cancer that began in the prostate, as he withered away. In his final year of life, I travelled to Tasmania five times to visit him and reflect with him on our lives together and the beyond-brotherhood bond that we had.

Steve Bluen, Human Resources (HR) Director, was generous and compassionate as he helped me through these times, granting me special leave on three occasions to visit my brother. It appears the HR role came along for a reason and gave me an opportunity to breathe in the middle of a frenetic career in marketing and sales.

It took me around three months to set up the talent team and we began to operate rather well. The brilliant 'Angels' went about their work and achieved the recruitment goals we had set ourselves. My days were filled with meeting final candidates, taking briefs from management, and sometimes going to the spa around the corner from my office, which had been set up as a staff facility, for a little light relief.

As an early-morning person, I would clock in around 6.30 a.m. and go home much earlier than I did previously. It made for a longish day, but not at the frenetic pace of my previous position when I worked more like 12 hours a day and then had to attend social engagements in the evening.

When I took on the role, former managing director Norman Adami called me from SABMiller in Milwaukee to ask if the board and management team had seriously lost the plot by taking me into an HR role. Soon after, he returned to South Africa – having retired to be closer to his son and daughter – and helped me a great deal through this time.

I was in an HR review workshop one afternoon at the SAB Training Institute in Kyalami when I received a call from Norman. I excused myself from the workshop and went to Sandton to meet him for a beer at the Baron pub. He seemed excited and informed me he was returning to SAB in six weeks' time to lead the business again. I was to sit tight, he said, as he would move me as quickly as possible out of HR and back into a frontline role in marketing.

True to his word, not long into his new role he called me in to tell me that I was high on his agenda, and he would keep me informed. Around three weeks later, he summoned me to his office to tell me that he was moving me back to marketing to work with Ian Penhale once more and to lead the 2010 Soccer World Cup campaign for Castle Lager.

This was right up my 'Ally'!

The FIFA 2010 Soccer World Cup was an exhilarating time for all South Africa. It was as though the day-to-day affairs of the country were put on hold for six weeks as we welcomed the world. Castle Lager did some engaging work and mobilised South Africans to get behind our national team, Bafana Bafana, and to welcome the world with our unique hospitality. More of this later.

We developed a 'Superfan' property where our fans became the heroes of our stories as they got behind our three national teams: Bafana Bafana, the Springbok rugby team, and the Proteas cricket team. The Superfans, unmistakeable in their wacky brand regalia, followed their teams around the world to India and Australia and with their noisy, enthusiastic and colourful support, greatly inspired our players.

Proteas skipper A.B. de Villiers used to show our cricket commercial to the team in the changeroom before every game to inspire the players and to show what their fans would do to support them.

It was a special era. Through our sporting properties, we told emotional stories that resonated with consumers and instilled in them the pride that translated into brand loyalty. Castle Lager emerged once more as a giant in the beer landscape of South Africa.

This was the second time in two decades that I had led a turnaround of the flagship brand back from the brink. It puzzled me how leadership often allowed brand custodians employed from outside of the company to mess with the crown jewels to support their own egos. The same had happened with Lion Lager, of course.

The Superfans story was shared around the world as best practice, and other countries used a similar approach to amplify the fans as heroes and link them to their lead country brands.

The case study eventually won the coveted Mercatus Award for best campaign. (Mercatus was a hotly contested in-house award that recognised excellence in marketing across the SAB Group around the world and was an amazing way of sharing best practice with other marketers to understand what good looked like.)

Later, in 2016, Superfans won the Grand Prix Award for Marketing Excellence across SABMiller countries around the globe. This was an award bestowed at the end of our marketing journey just prior to the ABInBev takeover. The award was given to the top winner throughout the 10 years of the Mercatus Awards.

In 2014, Ian Penhale, marketing director Africa, asked me to join him on the African marketing team to drive and entrench our regional brands across our African businesses. I had been there before and was excited to go back to work with capable people across Africa.

These two years were special and happy years as I travelled the continent with Wayne McCauley and his sales experts, and with Ian and his branding specialists. We implemented rigorous creative processes that elevated our local and regional brands across Africa and uplifted our skills base.

Castle Lager, Castle Lite and Carling Black Label began to gain traction beyond South Africa. We proved that with perseverance, we could begin to build a continental franchise. To this day, I believe that Castle Lager could have been a global brand. It should have been a lead focus in our global story over time.

I was enjoying my African role when the announcement came that SABMiller was to be purchased by ABInbev.

Because of the knowledge base and corporate memory I had gained in years of working in SAB, I was asked to work with the ABInBev team to begin the commercial integration structure and to look at a new organisational design that was aligned to the ABInBev way of thinking.

After some six months of working with the global management consulting firm, Bain, on 10 October 2016, the ABInBev executive walked into 65 Park Lane, Sandton, our South African headquarters.

It was sad in so many ways, but I saw the opportunity to stay on and head the global brands of ABInBev. It's never too late to learn something new. More of this later in the story.

All beer people are good people. Some are better than others.

Forty-eight hour
Extravaganzas

Although there were moments in the calendar that were more hectic than others, like times for budgets, profit forecasts, brand planning, excise tax, pricing announcements and the like, as a business SAB had a subtle but powerful rhythm ingrained in the psyche of its people.

For me, one of the most stressful but rewarding times was the MS&D conference such as the one that welcomed Nelson Mandela (Madiba) in 1995.

Each April, the financial year complete, the entire marketing, sales and distribution fraternity would converge on Sun City or the International Convention Centre in Cape Town, the only two venues in the country able to accommodate a 48-hour gathering of up to 1,700 delegates.

The venues, although in sumptuous locations, were less important than an event that could be described as an extravaganza that inspired and motivated every employee and defined the company's level of commitment to communicating, motivating and aligning employees with the business roadmap.

Later, similar conferences were instituted for our other value chain colleagues in technical, manufacturing, human resources and finance.

SAB leadership from the CEO level, was passionately committed to our conference and used the platform to inspire, motivate and set new challenges to grow beyond our dreams.

We looked forward to the conference each year: to what was in store and what surprises we could expect, who the motivational speaker would be, what the leadership would share, who would win the best-in-class awards, what entertainment would be lined up, and what key messaging we would take back to inspire those who could not attend.

This entire institution of reward and recognition served to imprint that culture firmly into the business.

Of course, it's understandable for the marketing, sales and distribution forces of a beer company to enjoy every aspect of an annual conference to the utmost with a few impromptu parties, but these social occasions were much more than just boozy bun fights.

Each of the conferences was a great get-together and a lot of fun, but more importantly an opportunity to align the business and focus on what was critical. Everybody heard it from the horse's mouth. Every presenter had a clear message, and the message was always on strategy. It focused on the bold actions that we wanted to achieve.

As someone heavily engaged in the organisation of conferences, I always admired the level of detail, planning and rehearsing that the executive demanded. Days before the conference, we had to run our speeches past our leadership team to ensure that all the content resonated, the theme was central, and the messaging was right. It was choreographed to the nth degree.

Steve Bluen, HR director, saw every conference as a microcosm of the excellence of SAB and what made it great. It honoured people and acknowledged excellence in performance with the awards at the gala dinners, applauding the winners as they stood bursting with pride on the podium in front of all their peers.

Conferences changed the way we mobilised our people and engendered spirit and pride. They reinforced what we had achieved and portrayed it in a dramatic way that declared: 'Yes, we're all competitive and we celebrate our winners and our heroes; but above all, it's about the organisation.'

We used recognition and celebration to motivate and instil pride. Many young people in SAB told me that these conferences were one of the best things that had ever happened in their lives. Pottie Potgieter, a finance guy, told Grant Harries: 'I have never seen a business like this. I never want to leave.'

At the end of each conference, people would say it had been world class. And then the next year always made the previous year look amateurish. That's what defined the company: what was good enough for the 1989 conference was below par for the 1990 one, and we had to raise the bar. We never rested on our laurels.

Some felt that it was a bit pretentious for SAB people to hold black tie functions. But it wasn't about the black ties. It was about showing that we were going to a lot of trouble not only to recognise the people who had been the most successful, but to recognise them in style. At the heart of the whole undertaking was the intention of making people proud to show their peers what they had achieved.

Several people told me: 'The team spirit, the response to having won an award, and that level of recognition... guys with their white scarves and tuxedos, standing there hugging each other emotionally and not knowing how to cope with the euphoria of having been recognised at the highest level possible, was unforgettable.' The conferences were something quite extraordinary.

Wayne McCauley commented that competition was key to building the operating model, and we just got better and better. Competition was tough. When one region or district fell just short of winning against another, their teams had tears in their eyes.

Like any competition, there were times when it became a bit too competitive or lost a bit of its meaning, but these were the exception rather than the rule.

It started with the sales awards. Then the company introduced marketing awards and then manufacturing awards. World class manufacturing arrived. There were HR awards. Other functions said they wanted to compete. The people who came into the business were naturally competitive. Whether you were in HR or in manufacturing, you wanted to be the best of the best. Awards underpinned that.

There was a wonderful purpose in Making Beer, Making Friends. There was the desire for excellence; for transforming society in a positive way; for bringing in the best young, diverse and hardworking talent you could find; for learning and growing; for the idea of discovery; and for respecting its long-serving employees (of which there were many).

I had the privilege of working on some 20 conference organising committees with some wonderful agencies; VWV under Mark Steinhobel, and Omage under Graham Edmonds, were true characters and creative geniuses who understood our business intimately and knew what was required to drive the pursuit of excellence.

Madiba's epic address in 1999 was followed by an inspiring talk from young Victor Vermeulen, a talented cricketer who was rendered quadriplegic after breaking his neck diving into a near empty swimming pool.

The third speaker was an RAF pilot who had been downed in Afghanistan and held captive for more than a year.

It was an afternoon to remember: we were connecting with true heroes, in real life.

Almost equally momentous was the year that the theme was *Yadibasab* (Fanagalo for 'fantastic experience'), a gathering of delegates that began, once again, in a bland demarcated area of the Superbowl, again with black curtains and poor lighting. I heard several attendees complain about the poor setup and a welcome that was mediocre at best. Simon Harvey and I, who were running the show, were heard as muffled voices over the microphone saying that we thought the delegates had been guided to the wrong venue.

Then the lights went down, there was a loud crash, and the curtain opened to reveal the Black Eyed Peas hammering out their global hit 'Let's get it started ...'

I have no knowledge of any corporate, globally, who had the likes of the Black Eyed Peas opening their conference at one-thirty on a Thursday afternoon. The cellular networks lit up and that afternoon we trended on every major social media platform.

The balance of that conference had many more twists and turns including our own 'Fear Factor', and even the appearance of global movie star Danny Glover. (Sadly, his talk was as exciting as watching paint dry. He sat next to me at the gala banquet and fell asleep over his salad.)

A superstar speech for me will always be that of Benjamin Zander. Benjamin was the English conductor and musical director of the Boston Philharmonic Orchestra. I had contacted him personally on a tip-off that he was 'simply the best speaker ever'. He had indicated that he would be prepared to come to South Africa ... with a few conditions.

He needed exactly two hours to perform his speech, and his fee was one million rand.

This was challenging on both counts. We never allowed a speaker longer than forty-five minutes, and a million rand was a steep fee. A deal was agreed, however, and he arrived and turned out to be a wonderful human being.

We told delegates, to their horror, that they needed to be an hour earlier than scheduled for the Friday morning session because we had a big surprise in store.

We took roll call to ensure that all delegates, many of them seriously hung over, were seated by 7.50 a.m. With Benjamin's arrival spot-on at 8.00 a.m., silence descended.

His speech, 'The Art of Possibility', was also the title of his autobiography. You could hear a pin drop. He captivated every person for every minute of the two hours allotted to him. At one stage, he persuaded the audience to sing happy birthday to one of the delegates. They did so with such passion and zest that the birthday boy almost broke down in front of his colleagues.

Great South African sportsmen, too – the likes of Neil Tovey, Phil Masinga, Lucas Radebe, Graeme Smith, John Smit, Jacques Kallis, Mark Boucher and Schalk Burger – attended our conferences with alacrity and spoke with passion about their game and the brewer that had stood by the country and its sportsmen for decades.

GRAHAM EDMONDS

Big brains, big balls, and big bucks, describe what I saw. The people invited to speak at the conferences were the intellectual illuminati of business and brand strategy in South Africa and abroad.

Despite the money spent, it was not squandered. We always felt we had done a big body of work for a relative return. There was a consistent fairness in dealing with the guys on all sides.

Few people appreciated what went into a conference that started at lunchtime on a Thursday and ended on a Friday night (or often in the wee hours of Saturday morning). To be able to stage something like that required about six to eight months of work.

By the time of the event, the organisers would have been running on two or three hours of sleep a night for probably the last month before the conference. Sometimes we were not sleeping at all.

We were involved in set design and lighting design and managing comedians who drove the linkages between speeches, and celebrity MCs who led proceedings from the informal opening evening of easy, popular entertainment, to the black tie gala awards at the close.

In between, we were dealing with making entertaining brand videos, serious videos, and presenting the leading-edge strategies of the business. It was a multi-disciplinary effort and everybody at every level was required to deliver beyond expectations.

Ally

It was also entrepreneurial. Initially the price for the Black Eyed Peas was way over budget but we amortised that against them playing two concerts and appearing for the Nelson Mandela Children's Fund. We persuaded Virgin Air to sponsor some of the flights, and Sun International to fund a concert.

I saw three concerts in four days. I think that after three days I became a bit blasé about Fergie and will.I.am. After their visit they sent me a Pringle shirt and a letter to express their absolute joy around what for them was one of the most spectacular visits on any global tour. That was probably the most memorable conference, not just because we had the Black Eyed Peas but also because we decided to name the theme in the vernacular, *Yadibasab*.

At the end of something like that, you had 1,700 people with clear direction who left that conference inspired. They raced back to the business. Even if they hadn't won an award, they were raring to go to win it next year and do it for the business again.

Everybody had clear direction and initiative. There were people – some probably from finance – who questioned the amount of money spent, but the motivational outcome of doing things on that level and on that scale was real value for money.

The attendance of Nelson Mandela in 1995 confirmed how special the organisation was, that we were able to line up speakers of such calibre in society and in business. It wasn't just a jolly. It was a real mixture of business sessions and exposure to things ranging from those that might make you feel uncomfortable, to enjoying a great social evening, to the formal dinner on the last night when the awards were presented. It was a great way of exposing every element of the business to all 1,700 people.

One memorable anecdote is when we received a call from Alan Henning from SAB Newlands to say that the bus bringing the Cape Town team had broken down about 20 km from Sun City. I said we'd see what we could do. We phoned back and said there was a flatbed cattle truck that could bring them in. Alan was not too keen. Was some form of indemnity needed?

When we told him that there was a truly spectacular opening and he wouldn't want to miss it, he agreed, and the truck brought them in.

He was later to discover that there was a photographer on board the flatbed and that he and his team had been duped into featuring in a video which was aired at the conference the next day and invoked much hilarity.

So special experiences create special memories. (He never forgave me, but I am sure he will never forget his arrival at Sun City on a flatbed truck.)

At a four-way stop some 50 kilometres from Sun City, people from the local village are often out in force to collect funds for their cricket team. For the Yadibasab conference, we arranged for Protea cricketers Makhaya Ntini and Mark Boucher to collect funds at the intersection. Our own people were astonished to be ambushed by these sporting heroes and gave generously, as did many motorists who had no idea of what it was all about.

We raised more than R15,000 for the village team. It had been a prank but demonstrated our willingness as a business to make a meaningful contribution to the communities in which we operated.

Understandably and appropriately, colleague and friend Stuart Scott suggested that: 'By midnight on Friday evening each year, people are ready to run through a brick wall for SAB.'

The What
and the How

The X-Factor of arguably the best company to come out of Africa is to be found in the people who were selected through a rigorous battery of psychometric tests and interview processes carried out by line managers who covered all the bases. They tested not just for cleverness, but for the emotional intelligence needed to work in the SAB environment.

The performance management culture was established in the late '80s when ambassadors such as Barry Smith, Roy Bagattini and Robin Goetzsche underwent 'train the trainer' programmes abroad to bring the frameworks home and forge a culture of instilling discipline and process throughout the company.

The performance management process set rigorous goals that articulated precisely what 'excellent looks like' and defined the quality requirements to bring the outputs to life and establish a set of key performance indicators (KPIs) to measure the results and evaluate success.

Performance management defined job descriptions for every role. In the Hay Job Evaluation System (a method used by corporates and organisations to map out job roles within the context of the organisational structure), points were assigned to each job description to determine the complexity and grading of that job.

SAB conducted two performance reviews a year and required weekly one-on-one interactions between manager and subordinate to ensure short-term feedback brought corrections and learnings. Remuneration was structured around the performance rating: high achievers received a greater slice of the pie.

Accountability was clear and personal. There could be no finger-pointing about who had the responsibility to deliver.

While the 'what' was clearly defined, the 'how' showed the way the goals and key outputs were to be achieved.

I seldom came across a below-average recruit in SAB, but I did meet several employees who failed miserably on the 'how'. The psychometrics were not right every time. In the main, however, the system sorted out the wrong 'how' and eventually these square pegs exited the business after open and honest feedback.

I had huge conviction about the value of the performance management approach. I lived by the fairness of the process and the backing it gave me to fight for above average increases for star performers and to back the 'less good' performances fairly.

My colleague and friend Steve Bluen was at the forefront of understanding the psychology of the business; the psychometric test battery, talent selection, and career paths that were created for people, among many other facets of the company's human resources. He found that the X-Factor in the people at SAB was something exceptional.

STEVE BLUEN

It's hard to wrap your head around that X-Factor, but I knew we had it and I could tell you today if someone has it or not. It's an intangible that has nothing to do with language, religion, size, function or intelligence, nor with humour, intellect, physical prowess, sporting or drinking ability. It's to do with everything. It's simply that something extra.

You can't describe it. You know who has it and who hasn't. It's just something that tells you this person is going to make it. You can feel it. I could feel it.

There was, for example, a list of guys who were potential general managers. Every time a position came up, one would get it and 15 wouldn't. Fifteen people would be at my door asking why. I would say to them, 'Trust me, you have what it takes. But it's horses for courses. We can only select one guy.' All the guys on the list had the X-Factor.

ANDRÉ PARKER

SAB and its successes were all about its people. One group were the bright, cerebral people like Graham Mackay, Pete Lloyd, Norman Adami and Gert Goedhals, who turned out to be our leaders. We had a lot of brainpower, which helped a hell of a lot with defining strategy and vision. At the stage when we went global, you needed some serious vision.

The second bunch was okes like you and me, not too doff, who liked challenges, enjoyed being part of successful teams, worked hard, and played hard. They enabled us to go out into the world.

The expats we relied on in those early days were the solid, hardworking, experienced blokes, trustworthy and loyal, with a lot to offer especially when they were out on their own. They were the backbone of SAB in its glory years.

When Pete Lloyd was CEO at SAB in the middle '80s, we also took on the affirmative action challenge. We moved early in bringing black talent into the business. We produced some excellent businessmen: Monwa Fandeso, who ran some of the country operations; Lon Mtongana, who ran Botswana; and Hloni Motsela in Lesotho, to mention just three. There were many more. SAB had the best Black talent in South Africa.

The culture was to work together as a team. It was quite competitive. Nobody sat back complacently. But there was always a sense of sociability, which came from the sector we were in. Beer calls for friendship, fellowship, and a bit of fun.

Steve

One of the most effective instruments we used was the Minnesota Multiphasic Personality Inventory (MMPI). It was designed to assess an individual's state of mental health and to evaluate several different issues to identify, with accuracy, struggles with substance abuse, depression, anxiety and personality disorders.

It posed a few hundred questions that seemed bizarre. Most psychological tests used in selection would, if they were checking for depression, ask something like: 'Do you feel tired?' or 'Do you feel there is no point in life?'

The MMPI is different. It's an empirically based test. Its creators went to mental institutions and gave questionnaires to hundreds of mental patients diagnosed as schizophrenics, or suffering from depression, bipolar mood disorder, anxiety disorder, or whatever.

They would phrase the questions as: 'If you go to the theatre, would you prefer to watch a drama or a ballet?' They found, for example, that people suffering from depression preferred drama.

It was completely empirically derived. You never knew what the right answer was. It was one of the most powerful instruments we used. What it did for us was that it weeded out the people with 'bad wiring'.

I remember a woman at SAB who became head of treasury, an important job in which she would deal with billions of rands, who reported to Gary Whitlie.

She said she had found the perfect candidate for a job. He worked with one of the big five consulting companies, they had recommended him, and his knowledge, CV and qualifications were a good fit. She had interviewed him and was certain he was right for the job.

'But', she told me, 'Gary says I have to have you and your psychologists test him.'

We did so and I went back to her and said sorry, no go.

Here's why: If you divide a population into three groups, one would be people who were a perfect fit for a job; another third is people who are okay, but you never know. If their CV is good and they've interviewed well, go for it. The third group were those you shouldn't touch with a barge pole.

'Your candidate is in the third category,' I reported. 'He doesn't want a job. He wants a mother, and you will be her.' She said she would appoint him anyway.

I advised Gary that she had looked long and hard to find this guy and had interviewed him accordingly. But he was 'badly wired'. We couldn't have him in the company. Gary took me at my word and blocked it.

She wouldn't speak to me for weeks. A month later, however, she came into my office and said: 'I owe you an apology.' The candidate had gone back to his company where they asked what had happened. He had left them with their blessing and thought that the new job was assured.

He said: 'The effing shrink at SAB blocked me.'

Their response was: 'Can you give us his name?'

At SAB, because of MMPI, there were very few people who were badly wired. They were normal.

Transactional analysis says every person has three states: parent, adult, and child.

The parent has two parts: one is the nurturing period (would you like to do this?); the other is dictatorial (you must do this).

The adult state is about talking adult to adult.

The child state has the free child (let's go and have another beer), the withdrawn child (hiding in the corner), and the rebellious child (I won't do as you ask).

The message here is that you do business only when you are in your adult state. That's what SAB was all about. We did business as adults, but we would go to the pub as free children, drink, and have a good time.

In many companies you find all kinds of games being played. Given the number of people in SAB, the playing of political games was minimal. People spoke honestly to each other.

The first thing for SAB was weeding out the bad eggs. In other companies you run into weird people. We employed normal people as a baseline. The calibre of the people we employed was high and psychometrics played a huge role.

When I came out of Witwatersrand University as a researcher and professor, one of the first things I did was conduct a validity study of the SAB psychometric battery of tests. I obtained the psychometrics of the top 500 people in the business and their performance management data. Then I went to each member of the board and asked: 'Of all the execs across the business, tell me who are your stars and who are the 'dogs' (under-performers).'

I created two groups. If more than two directors identified a person as a 'dog', they were in the 'dog' group. If more than two people were called a star, they were in the star group. I took those sub-categories, about 100 in each, and compared all the psychometric tests across them, and compared these to their grades and salaries. I also did many triangulated studies and out of that refined the whole battery.

Based on that study, I created a targeted SAB battery that would differentiate between those who would succeed and those who wouldn't.

When Graham Mackay left SAB's Beer Division to go to SAB Group in London, we had a party for him, and he made a speech. One of the things he said really resonated. He said there were many things that made SAB a great company, and he listed many of them, 'but', he said, 'one characteristic that makes SAB unique is the calibre of its people.'

I left SAB in 2010 and have worked in many blue-chip companies afterwards, but I never met the calibre of people that we had at Breweries anywhere else. The quality of the people we employed was phenomenal.

Ally

Team dynamics were important. I had the privilege of working with some magnificent teams; 'golden' teams that seemed to gel collectively to hone their skills and recognise their shortcomings. Often, I kept the wider business politics away from my teams, enabling them to focus on the task at hand and deliver excellence.

The teams that really stood out in my career were our international marketing team, who took on the world at the turn of the century, particularly Africa; the trade marketing team of 2004; the Castle brand team who ran the 2010 World Cup; and the global brand team who launched Budweiser, Stella Artois and Corona in South Africa.

The common themes across them all were an understanding of strengths and weaknesses, trust as a key dimension of leadership, empowerment of all members, and a work hard, play hard ethic that built camaraderie and spirit.

Working with agency partners who felt like they belonged to the team also made a great difference. Our creative, media and research partners were an extension of our teams, never part of a supplier-client relationship. The operation was inclusive. Everyone on the team understood their role and the collective vision. We believed 'People make the world go round; people made SAB go round the world'.

JOHN COCHRAN

My goodness, what SAB meant to me in my life: 30 years, a family, a tightly knit band of absolute rebels, a gang of wonderful people.

In five years' time, if you put out the word that there would be a reunion, you would get 100 to 200 people who would gladly pay their way just to get together. I think that's the mark of the organisation that we worked for.

We individually and collectively put our shoulders to the wheel, with joy and happiness and sometimes with a dreadful hangover, but what a wonderful organisation of magnificent people. I don't know if it was the recruitment process or just the culture that we all became part of. I felt honoured and blessed that there wasn't a day in those 30 years that wasn't an absolute pleasure working at SAB.

It was a truly South African icon that went out into the world and became a global giant in many respects. We had balls beyond the size of the animal. We went out initially into Africa with those balls, and into neglected old businesses that had been nationalised, run into the ground, and stolen blind. We made them into profitable, well-run organisations, put in some basic processes, and began to build a bit of culture. I look back with pride.

Some of those markets were tough places. We turned them around and they delivered. The people grew and changed and began to live the values of the SAB Way.

When I was offered the marketing director position in Tanzania, I took it gladly. I was tired of travelling around Africa, of 130 days a year of changing underpants and toiletries over a weekend. It was nice to settle down. Plus, I had just got married.

I took my wife and off we went to Tanzania. In those days it was still pretty rough. When the local Checkers got chickens in, all the mommies did a run for the supermarket; it was quite fun.

But working with the people and developing them was the most rewarding aspect. We took local brands that were pretty hammered, put a crown on the bottle (which was in itself quite legendary), added a label and a neck label and then, for goodness' sake, we actually added a back label and a story about the brand … it was ground-breaking stuff. Then we did posters and TV commercials. Developing all that was just wonderful. It was an absolute honour.

André

When we sent expat families into Africa – and at the height of our expat tally we had more than 100 families in Africa – there was fear and trepidation, especially amongst the women, about moving to the dark continent, but we experienced not one single incident of anti-South African sentiment in any of those territories.

It was remarkable that the local folk knew we came from South Africa, which had a bad reputation, but nobody ever raised it or took anybody on about it. Nobody ever accused us about our apartheid background and journey or suggested we had screwed up in our country. They would judge you as a person and by your actions.

We never specifically picked people we thought would be good in this situation. The normal SAB person knew what was right and what was wrong and was sensitive to all situations. I think that's why they found us so acceptable. We were genuinely there to make a difference, to train people, and we didn't espouse any of what was generally thought to be 'a white South African attitude'. The locals accepted us, and everybody had good relationships. It sounds almost too good to be true.

Wives were incredibly important in every sense. The men worked 10 to 12 hours a day. The women sat at home, unable to phone folks back in South Africa, and worried about the kids at school. Often the accommodation wasn't that flash. It was fantastic what those families did.

We did, of course, try to make it comfortable for expats. It wasn't all bad. They also received an offshore package that helped them in their later years.

Danie Niemandt set the example when we got to Tanzania. He said the first thing he spent money on was the facilities for the workers. We started our revamps with ablution facilities. Then we got the canteen right. The workers then saw what was happening.

Legend had it that bribery and corruption was the way to survive in Africa. Expats were happy when we told them they did not have that option.

Danie was faced with that issue early on. He phoned me and said: 'We have a container stuck at the dock and I must get it out, but I agree I can't bribe the guy.' He went to see government officials and became personally involved in moving the container out. It was a good early example for our expats to see that there were legal ways of doing things. These might have been difficult, and they may have needed to eat a bit of humble pie, but it could be done.

TONY VAN KRALINGEN

Resilience is a theme that will come through among SAB people, no matter whom you talk to. We expected our people to be tough, to stand up against hardship, and to keep going.

It was like a broad-based family rather than a business. In SAB, your work life, social life, and entertainment life were all part of the same mix. It was aided and abetted by what we produced.

You quickly come to learn, whether you work at SAB, Heineken or any beer company, that everybody is interested in the product. It was so easy to integrate with many groups because the product was just a natural talking point.

The sports and sponsorships we were associated with were also big talking points. Everybody was interested in what lay behind some of the issues. It was really rewarding in more than just the business.

A couple of things drove that.

One was our care with recruitment. We recruited a certain type of person. It was a broad spectrum of a type – but it was a type.

Peter Savory summarised it well when he talked about the criteria he sought in marketing. He said he wanted someone with a high IQ, who played or followed a team sport, and who could present themselves well. In the business we were in, some of those things made a lot of sense. In marketing you were always presenting things to persuade someone of something. If you couldn't hold your own, you were probably going to fail.

If you weren't smart, you probably wouldn't see the agendas of other people and what your opportunities were, and sport was just an integral part of sociability. We looked for intelligence and an ability to lead through people and through sport.

As I understand it, the first company in South Africa to introduce psychometric testing was SAB in the 1960s. We hired a professor of psychology named Simon Biesheuwel. He introduced psychometric testing to SAB at the time. During the years we went through a variety of experiments the hire the best people.

When I joined, a man named Ronnie Gluckman was a consulting psychologist to SAB and I was fortunate to spend many hours with him, one-on-one and in workshops, where he was managing team interfaces and issues that would arise from them. He was the guy who interpreted 100 percent of the thematic apperception tests (a widely used test designed to reveal an individual's perception of interpersonal relationships) which we ran at the time.

This practice of undergoing a battery of psychometric assessment when you joined SAB in the '60s, to when we sold in 2016, never changed. The reliance, emphasis, demand, and rigour of going through three to five hours of psychometric assessments before you were either recruited or promoted into managerial ranks, was non-negotiable. Through that we learnt a lot about which type of people were successful in SAB and which were not. As a result, we erred on the side of people who were more likely to stay with us than to leave us.

One of the things that struck me when I joined SAB was how many people had long service and how few people left. Probably the biggest turnover at that time was in the sales force.

I went to Cape Town and John Seton interviewed me. We talked about personalities, culture and leadership, and there were two interesting bits.

He asked me: 'What kind of leader are you? How do you manage?'

I said: 'I think I'm more about painting the picture and encouraging people where to go.'

He said: 'If Norman (Adami) is here (he gestured), where are you?'

I said: 'I'm probably that side.'

He walked right to other side of the boardroom and said: 'You mean here?'

What he was really saying to me was that you can be successful both ways. You can be very successful being a command-type leader and just as successful by being more thoughtful and asking: 'how do I get someone to see the answer, rather than how do I give them the answer?' It's the what and the how. I'll tell you the 'what', but it's better if you learn the 'how'.

He then told me that I had the job. 'Here's your package. Open it.' I opened it and he said: 'How do you feel?'

I said: 'I thought you would offer me more. I'm going from one of the smallest regions to one of the biggest.'

He said: 'Tony, have you ever built a house? Do you pay the builder for the whole house before he's built it, or do you pay him as he builds? That's how I'm treating you. Start building the house and I'll pay you as you go.' I think that's a great lesson.

People who were successful at SAB hardly ever had to apply for a job. That was his view: that if you spent your time looking for a job, you were spending too much of your time worrying about yourself, and not enough time worrying about what you needed to do in the business. It meant that if you had your head down and you did well, you would perform ahead of others. People would notice you and they would want you. It was simple logic.

John was one of those guys who spent 40 years at SAB and that was how he grew up. He grew up saying: 'If I keep my head down, worry about how well I do, how well the business I run is doing, about the people I manage and how I look after them, life will look after me.'

Steve

The winning aspect of our recruitment was that we had a mandate to recruit for potential, rather than simply for a job. We were given the authority that if we came across someone who had the right fit for SAB, we could bring them in. Its origins lay with the company's expansion.

I remember Graham Mackay coming into the HR team and saying: 'This is what's going to happen now. We're going to go from a local hero company into a global operation with a base initially in Africa and Eastern Europe. As we do that, we will be making acquisitions. By their nature, they will be strictly confidential. You will be given very little warning to put together a team that will be expatriated to whichever country. Because we will be investing big bucks, we don't want B-team players. We want A-team players.

'There is a statistic that says expatriation costs are four to five times the cost of locals. If you're a marketing director in South Africa and your cost to company is half a million (all things included), your expat cost will be two-and-a-half million. So we need to expatriate people who know what they were doing.

'But for the first decade SAB Beer Division will still be the cash cow for the group. So we need an A-team in South Africa as well. We need to make two A-teams out of one A-team.'

Our mission was to find people who had the essence of what SAB was all about. They had to have the qualifications and the smarts and to pass the psychometrics, but most of all they needed to have that SAB X-Factor.

We created what were known as executive assistants. People would come into the business as executive assistants reporting to a director, a general manager or one of the Central Office functional execs and would be assigned projects.

They would complete their projects within 18 months and by then would have come to know the business and the business would know them. They were then deployed into one of the places where we could move a general manager upwards and here would be someone who had 18 months of experience to replace them. We created continuity.

In the 10 years from the time we launched into Africa, we expatriated 40 percent of our executives, 200 out of 500. We were able to do that only because of this approach. We were able to expand or contract as the need dictated.

Graham would send a note down to whoever was managing director at the time, saying we had just bought a brewery somewhere and we needed a managing director and directors of finance, marketing, production, sales and maybe a district manager. They need to be part of the A-team, ideally able to speak the language of the new country and be there by the following month.

(Although when Craig McDougall went to Moçambique as general manager, he said: 'Forget it. You can all learn English. I'm not learning Portuguese.')

Not long after that the same call would come through about similar needs somewhere else.

There was never the rebellious child who might say: 'As soon as you turn around, I'm going to stab you in the back.'

I came to Breweries from academia. I was a professor and was used to dealing with professors in the sanctuary of the cerebral. Breweries was such a beautiful experience. It was not a cerebral sanctuary. The people were as bright, if not brighter, than the professors. They had big round gonads and they used them. They were resilient and out there until all hours of the night if necessary.

Breweries had its own culture. The guys there attracted other guys like themselves to the company. There was no room for wilting daisies.

There's a story about culture I often quote to people. We had begun a project on functional integration. We had a team of two general managers, Mike Short and Tony van Kralingen; two human resources people, Alan Clark and me; and Richard Davies who was HR director at the time. This working committee would report to the board.

We worked with Gemini Consultants. We deliberated, interviewed, benchmarked, and everything else required and, after three months of investigation, presented our findings and recommendations to the executive committee.

Graham Mackay sat at the head of the table. The directors sat alongside. When we finished the presentation, all the directors deferred first to Graham. He said: 'This is the biggest load of bullshit I have ever seen.' We all knew our batteries had been pissed upon from a very great height. But after much deliberation, three hours later, he said: 'You're right. I'm wrong. Go for it.'

That encapsulated for me the Breweries' culture at the top level. In other companies the MD would have thanked everyone, said leave it with us, and then quietly rejected it. Graham had the balls to recognise he was wrong and to say so.

Breweries was always about honesty upfront and straight down the line. It had that level of directness that cut through so much shit. It was such a joy.

After my first day at Breweries, my wife Vanessa asked how it had been. I said it was fine, but I felt as though I had been back in primary school. I told her: 'I got there and went to Richard Davies's office. Like any good boss, he took me around and introduced me to people. If it happened once, it happened about six times. Everyone said: 'F..., you're tiny.' Nobody said welcome or that they were pleased to meet me. All they said was that I was tiny.'

I don't think of myself as tiny. I know I am two foot nothing. But it showed me, and anyone who worked there for any length of time, that it was a thick-skinned operation. I loved that.

I remember when I was HR manager and went to see Maurice Egan, the head of production at Prospecton Brewery. He was short and to the point: 'This is what I need. Have a nice day.'

I forgot about it.

A week later I got a call: 'Bluen', he said in his Irish brogue. 'Egan here. I thought you were better than that. You're nothing but another HR clown. You said you'd get back to me by today and you haven't. What are you doing? If I don't get it from you in a day you need never come back here.'

He let me have it. It was the best thing that ever happened. I realised I had dropped the ball. I told him I was sorry, and I never dropped a catch again. That was the beauty of the organisation. There was no room for pussyfooting around.

It employed people who had a psychological sturdiness. They were people who were solid and could take it.

Here's another example.

In the early days of performance management and integration (PMI), there was a meeting between Rob Childs and his team, and Richard Davies and his team. It was heavy. It went on for two and a half hours. There were no holds barred, the gloves were off. People were bleeding. It was messy, ugly and horrible. It was playing the man, not the ball, sort of stuff.

In any other company that would be the thin edge of the wedge. Ops and HR would go their own way and never talk to each other again, building a permanent rift between them. No one in that company would understand or remember how it had started and it would have moved them further and further apart.

At the end of this meeting the two directors said, simultaneously: 'Meet you in the pub at five o'clock.' We went to the pub, sat around talking shit, having fun and laughing … and it was over. That was the beauty of Breweries.

The Smell
of the Place

Mark Bowman told me that none of the listed companies with which he had been involved, and they were all class acts, compared in any way with SAB.

Mark

In SAB we were very self-critical. We never thought we were very good. We were sometimes arrogant in South Africa, but we were never completely satisfied that our business was good enough.

I think our people practices were very powerful, and we were at that stage able to attract very high calibre people. SAB was an attractive place to work, for good reason – it offered very attractive careers.

Just at the time when, in your early career, you began to get on top of your job and started getting antsy, they sent you on to another job. The experiential curve was powerful. I quickly went from management trainee to running a production warehouse and dealing with union issues, where I was completely clueless.

A guy called Paddy Tobin was the depot manager of Ottery Depot in the Cape, and he suggested I join a disciplinary hearing as a management representative. I had never been to a hearing in my life.

A truck driver had illegally sold a pallet of beer to a customer off the side of a truck. The driver admitted it, and everyone knew he was guilty. At the end of the hearing, the driver said he had been with the company for 20 years and supported a family, etc. and off he went.

Paddy turned to me and asked for my view. I said I felt he had done a bad thing, but the fellow had made a terrible mistake and I thought we should give him a chance. Paddy said thanks. They called the guy back in and summarily dismissed him. The driver wasn't surprised, the union didn't object.

The only person surprised was me.

And then I realised how little I knew about the way the business was run. You need to have very clear guidelines about what is acceptable and what's not.

A lot of people were prepared to help me. A guy called Marcus Liedtke took me under his wing and showed me how things worked. There were lots of people like that. They recognised if you were willing to learn, and they helped you out. There was a special camaraderie.

I went into IT, though I wasn't suited to it, but it was very good training for me. It taught me about managing people in different ways. Then I was offered the role of district manager at Chamdor in Gauteng; quite a powerful position.

In five years, that was my third role. I reckon that's the best role I ever had in my life. There was nothing else as formative in SAB than working in an environment like that.

You were in a privileged position, working in a township; I had never been in one in my life. I was responsible for our customer base in this township and within a month or two of being there, I could drive around and I knew everyone. You came with this SAB aura. You felt completely confident, customers respected you, and people welcomed you there.

This was in 1996, just after the election. There were still trucks being burned. There was still violence and South Africa hadn't settled down. Despite this I always felt confident and comfortable.

Comparing executives in other companies in the UK, I would always say that as an SAB executive you would experience one or two employee strikes. I don't know if anyone who has worked in Europe has ever experienced one strike, never mind a violent one, but the business carries on; sometimes you had to physically climb up into a truck and make deliveries yourself because the drivers were out. It was all hands on deck. Management in other disciplines ran the brewhouses and the packaging lines without operators, cleaned the tanks and the floors, and emptied the dustbins.

You had to deal with the issues of South Africa where the diversity of challenges was dramatic in that massive transition. You had a tough schooling that made people very resilient.

SAB in a broad sense was not a perfect business. I had a privileged position because I came up through the ranks, maybe quite quickly. But in South Africa if you were in a high growth business, you got those opportunities.

There's nowhere else in the world that people would have had the opportunities we had. The business was growing quickly, so they had to throw you into the deep end. Because someone had to go off to Africa or Europe, you could get that role, and that created opportunities for growth. It accelerated the career curves of most people in SAB, and you expected to get a new position every two or three years. In Europe I discovered that people couldn't assume that. They had to wait for the person above to retire.

KEN HITCHCOCK

There was an emotional X-Factor in the leadership of SAB that was powerful. Steve Bluen always talked about the battery of psychometric tests and how we recruited people, and there was always 'the what' and 'the how'. The how was very powerful in SAB people.

We were like minded. We were restless, we wanted to get things done, get them fixed, didn't suffer fools gladly, aimed for perfection, were prepared to give feedback, to suck it in and take it, and then to move on to the next challenge. When there was a problem, it was up to you to go and do something about it, but if you didn't, to your detriment you weren't going to be reminded about it.

When I was working my way through SAB there were two things I always thought: one was that if you were not improving, you were going to be overtaken. That just kept you in the game.

The second thing was that if you wanted to be promoted and to grow in the company, you had to continually understand what you were doing to differentiate yourself from others. How did you stand out?

An interesting thing is that most of my friends today are from SAB. Most people will have friends from school, where you live, university, and maybe work. But most of my mates come from SAB. I have a couple from university, none from school, and none from where I've lived because I moved around so much. The enduring friendships I have are through SAB.

It was a bit weird because often I was the boss, or they were the boss; but people were mature enough to say, 'That's okay, but today I'm not your boss.' Or 'Now I'm your boss, but after five 'o clock, we go for a beer.'

CLIFFORD RAPHIRI

Each region had its own characters. Alrode had MZ Pienaar and Denis Nyengwa in training. Chamdor had Eric Peebles. Eric was a packaging engineer at Chamdor and did a lot of the early projects in the building of the plants for new product development. He came from Isando to Chamdor and later went on to Central Office. Eric raised a problem for us. He reached 40 years of service, but there was no policy on what to do. We knew how to recognise 20 or 25 years of service, but not 40 years. A new policy was written for Eric.

For people who were unsuccessful in SAB, it wasn't necessarily the end of a successful career. Many of them went on to do well somewhere else. They were all bright people. Among those who stayed there was a common passion to succeed. Achieving results bonded people.

People didn't tell you to work hard, you saw them working hard around you and you naturally knew you had to work hard. It wasn't preached, it was shown. Many people stayed on because they were learning so much. What reinforced it was when you spoke to people outside the company. You met so many who wanted to work for SAB. There was also lots of fun. The work created results. Getting to the results brought a lot of pain, but the pain forged bonds that lasted forever.

IAN PENHALE

What stood out was the people, a wonderful set of human beings, still my friends today. I can phone them, and they are there for me. I don't think anyone else in other companies could have that bonding type of culture. Look at the reunions, an example of the guys getting together, to this day, all around the world.

MAURICE EGAN

What was special about SAB, unlike most companies, was that you made lifelong friends with many of your colleagues. There are very few of my non-SAB friends who would have said that about the companies they worked for. They finished the day and went home at six in the evening. We used to just carry on working. It may have been over a couple of pints or maybe several. We probably got the best work done in the bar after hours.

PINE PIENAAR

After SAB, what I miss the most is the friends and the sociability, when after a hard day's work, you could sit in the pub and enjoy the camaraderie. I made good mates in SAB, and we are still in contact. We don't see each other too often, but when we do, we feel as though we're still working for SAB. They're proper quality relationships. They're people with integrity. They're people you might not have seen for five years but you feel you can still give them a hug.

Clifford

You continue to apply the experience you've gained over the years. It's not a case of cutting and pasting what you did, it's more about the application of principles and processing you may need in a particular system. It doesn't have to be identical to SAB's but there are some underlying principles. You must have the discipline and some control to know where you are at any particular time and have key performance indicators that are relevant to the company. You must look after the talent pipeline. Those are things you did in the SAB way. In modern business they do it in their own way.

NEIL HOBKIRK

SAB was one of the best places I ever worked in because they knew how to execute. I have worked in a lot of places since, but I can say with confidence that there is no other company that has been able to rival that … here's what we're going to do, here's how we're going to do it, and then gets it done. It was like a magic formula. There were no politics.

I think that's the key. I wonder how many wars would be avoided if people could just sit down and drink a beer together. The product itself connects people.

What struck me about the company when I joined as a young person was this idea about excellence. We used to talk about excellence all the time. World class, be the best … and it permeated everything that everybody did.

There was an expectation and a demand for excellence.

They hired you because of your talent, because you had potential, not because you went to Michaelhouse. They spoke about it a lot – talent and potential. That was what they hired.

David Williams once told me: 'You know, Neil, you are so fortunate as a young person, because big companies can do big things, and you're being given these opportunities as a young person to run these enormous undertakings and really fulfil your potential in doing that.' For me that was another theme: being given the chance to do big things, really big things.

SAB was a very progressive company, in every way: progressive policies and practices, progressive politically. It was an enlightened business. Because it was enlightened it created in its people this sense that anything was possible. You could go on a voyage of discovery and if you didn't know something, you would find out.

The other thing that SAB did so well was that it showed huge respect for its longer-serving people. It treated them exceptionally well. These folk were heard, their lessons were internalised, and they were a community within the organisation who took the organisation personally. They felt free to walk up to any senior person in the business and say: 'Listen, I'm concerned about this. We learnt about this, or about that. We've made this mistake before.' And they were taken seriously.

JACQUI HOBKIRK

If you made it in SAB, you were respected. Even as a young woman in the business, I never experienced any sense that because you were a woman you were a lesser being and you didn't have much of a voice. I never felt as though I had to hold back. The sense was that excellence is about bringing strategy to execution. The fact that you could push a button and have anything distributed to anywhere in South Africa in two weeks – I've never had anything like that again.

I think there was a sense of belonging, no matter who you were. I never felt out of step with SAB. I felt that we were all together.

I was running Redd's with guys who were all 10 or 20 years older than I was, and they let me run the project. There was no back-stabbing. You just said: 'Guys, this where we're going, let's do it,' and we did it. Age or gender never came into play.

We did know how to have a party or two, where there were some shenanigans. I think that happens when you have young people who are engaged fully with what they're doing and who also socialise a lot. People are going to connect because they're spending 70 percent of their time there. They've been well screened, so you're going to have people who have an affinity with each other, intellectually and socially.

When I get a CV now and a see it's from SAB, I immediately interview that person. I have a girl who works with me at the moment who is from SAB and there's just an immediate connection. And loyalty. You get me, I get you, and we have the same ethic.

I've searched to find the same thing again. I've been in quite a few companies, and I've been looking for the same thing: that SAB magic. You felt so much a part of it. You wanted to get up in the morning. You didn't want to go home. You would work 24/7. Even now, I keep contact with the people I worked with 20 years ago.

With SAB you were a genuine team, all in it together. Even if there was conflict, you had this inner belief that there was a bigger purpose than you, and your job was to give your best, with your mates, and get the best outcome for the business. It was a brotherhood and a sisterhood. It was a cult of the right sort.

ROBIN GOETZSCHE

On reflection, I think SAB took average, hard-working, fun-loving okes and helped them earn some wealth for themselves. I don't know if that will ever happen again.

The company was generous to us with salaries, the way they incentivised and developed us, so in a way it was like winning the career lottery. The right time, the right place. I couldn't have asked for anything better. I always reflect on that. I would have loved to have gone for a bit longer. It's interesting that what I found in all the other stuff I've done, you just don't have the same passion for it.

A lot of other South African businesses didn't like SAB. There was a certain envy. But wherever SAB guys have gone, they've been successful. In a way, the company brainwashed us; they told us, that's how you do it. And you did. You were trained, and you got it done.

ANDREA QUAYE

When I talk about my career, I talk about SAB. I haven't worked in many other companies; I was at Unilever and Cell C for a short while, but my time at SAB has been the bulk of my career; it's where I learnt my greatest lessons and where I made deep friendships.

My greatest lesson coming from SAB was that strategy was nothing without execution, and if you don't understand what happens at the coalface, you've got no place arguing or proposing strategy. That was my first, and biggest, lesson.

STEVE BLUEN

I had 17 magnificent years at SAB. People used to ask me about the adjustment from academia to corporate. I found my home at Breweries. It was the best thing by a country mile that happened in my career … to find people who were like me yet not like me. Having been a professor of psychology gave me a licence to be a bit different, and I chose to be a bit different. But here we are sitting in 2021, 11 years after I left the company, and I am playing golf with some of my mates from Breweries; not 'my Brewery mates'; they are my mates. And just about all my friends were from somewhere else in the value chain.

Empowerment
to Own and Deliver

Everyone who worked at SAB would agree that 'Making Beer, Making Friends' summed up everything about the company. We had fun, we worked hard, and we had a great product, as Barry Smith recalls.

Barry

I don't know who coined that slogan, but it was very accurate. It's about friendship and beer: it's a product for socialising. We worked hard. I think I put in lots of hours, but we all did, and it was fun.

Our people were intelligent and hardworking and paid attention to detail. We were relatively humble and down-to-earth, from Meyer Kahn down, empathetic and very resourceful. We had that *'n Boer maak 'n plan* attitude.

I was on the boards of Tanzania and Zambia, and those were not easy places. They were difficult. But South African guys just got on with it. Resourcefulness was part of our DNA.

The secret of SAB's success was not technical innovation (unlike Apple), but rather our unique culture – something which others find difficult to fully appreciate. I've given presentations at Stellenbosch University and at the Gordon Institute of Business Science on the success of SAB and when I told them it was about our culture, you could see the guys look at you as though you were crazy.

Culture was defined as management processes, standards, values and behaviours (which are a function of the values). I think it was that: our attention to detail; the way we did things; our integrity. Culture can be defined and documented but is difficult to emulate. It's all got to do with your DNA.

We were also ahead of our time. Everybody talks about BEE nowadays. But we already had an equity programme in the '70s. When I joined, I was general manager of the Western Cape, and

I had a target of the number of people of colour I had to have in my team.

We were to all intents and purposes a monopoly – Meyer Kahn had described us famously as a 'temporary sole supplier' – but we were an empathetic company with our equity programme, our HR practices, and our fairness. We paid people generously. A lot of that emanated from Joe Horner who was head of HR when Pete Lloyd was managing director.

STEVE BLUEN

SAB's first employment equity strategy was launched in 1971 in the deep, dark era of apartheid, long before 1994 when equity became a priority for the government.

I keep coming back to the quality of decision-making by SAB leadership. It wasn't a moral or political decision; it was a business decision.

They said we make beer. Who drinks beer? Beer is drunk by blue-collar workers, our primary target market. The colour of our blue-collar market is black. Those are our customers. That's who we must look after. We can't just look at beer drinkers as a bunch of whiteys. We need to start using an employment equity approach. That came about 23 years before apartheid ended.

By the time everyone was clamouring to appoint a black non-executive director to window dress their numbers, Breweries were already far down the track on that. I remember interviewing a director general from the government, who came and said he would like to work at Breweries.

I asked him: 'What position would you like to occupy?'

'I would like to be a general manager.'

'Do you have experience in the beer industry?'

'No, but I'm a leader.'

I said: 'Let me tell you about Clifford Raphiri. He is one of our general managers, who happens to be a black man. Bright as a button, he started at the lowest of the low levels, worked his way up, and progressed through the ranks to the point where he is now a general manager, 20 years later. He has an MBA and 20 years of Breweries experience.

'One of his duties is to take people like you on brewery tours. When he walks past a filler and hears a noise that doesn't sound right, he calls the operator aside and says: 'Check your readings. They seem to be out.' He can hear it from 20 years of experience. Can you do that? No.'

It keeps coming back to that common denominator of great decision-making. Brains at the top of the business; thinking things through; seeing around corners and down the track.

Trevor Wilson, a guy from Canada, had an equity continuum: level one was 'there is no such thing'; level two was 'we do it because it's the right thing to do'; level three was 'we do it because, for political reasons, we have to do it'; level four was 'we do it because it makes for a sound business case'; and that's where we were at.

We said 85 percent of our market is black males, so why are we sitting here with a bunch of whiteys trying to go into Soweto to sell beer? If you want to get a sales manager in at that level, you have to grow them through the ranks.

It wasn't just about our equity initiatives; it was about all our initiatives. The term was 'grow your own timber'. We developed our own people. There was a science to it. We said we want to get to figures such as, for every four promotions, three should be from within, and one from outside. You need outside influence to create new thinking, but you also want continuity and corporate memory.

That was the whole issue of where we were coming from: just doing the right things, the best things we could.

When there was going to be employment equity legislation, South Africa based its legislation on the Canadian model. Richard Davies and I went to Canada and interviewed people there to find out what it was all about; to see what they did and how they did it.

Canada has an interesting situation: its alcohol tax is huge.

But these were the kind of things we had to do: we knew where the legislation was coming from, and we needed to be ahead of the game.

SAB gave you some licence to operate freely. One of them was that you could be told you were messing up – or you could tell someone else – and no one would collapse in a heap on the floor and die. Tomorrow morning the relationship would be back on an even keel.

It was all part of a high-performance culture. That was the critical feature of the culture of SAB. It was a culture of high performance and high engagement. It was not a case of just deliver the numbers. And the company looked after you.

The leaders at an operational level, not necessarily at a strategic level (Graham was in a class of his own), were great human beings.

What was also surprising was the amount of money the business would spend on developing its people.

We became members of the American Society for Training and Development (ASTD); we had all the benchmarks of the top global companies, and we were right up there with them. We never, ever, benchmarked against mediocrity. It was always against the best in the world. The fact that we had 98 percent of the local market meant nothing. It was more important to know where we were in comparison to the best in the world. Our training days, our training spend, all the KPIs for training, were up there with the best in the world.

When I was running human resources development, we were involved with 11 different universities round the globe – from local universities to Heriot-Watt and others – to get the best for our people.

There was also action learning. We took guys and put them on these programmes around the world, doing mind-expanding things with other people and bringing their experiences back.

We sent people to top universities on executive programmes like mini-MBAs. We would send the guys to the course at the schools best suited to their careers.

They would go for a month and take their wives for the last week. The business spent fortunes on the development of its people.

The beauty of performance management was that if you performed, everything was open to you. You got the money, in salary and bonuses; and you got development opportunities, exposure, and promotion.

Usually, human resources is seen as a nice 'touchy-feely' thing. But we translated every aspect of that into numbers, so you had three pages of key performance indicators. As I said to everyone when we were developing it: 'If we are going to be part of this business, we need to be sure we talk the language of the business world, which is numbers: absenteeism, percentage equity, percentage trainees, numbers in each quadrant, and so on. We had the numbers, and everyone was talking about them.'

It was line-owned. It wasn't run by HR, for HR. I used to do 27 people balance sheet visits a year. Every visit was with the relevant line director.

It was conducted by the general manager, not by the HR consultant, so the general manager could talk about his people in much the same way he would talk about his finances, sales, market or production. They had that much in-depth knowledge.

They could talk about their people with personal insight and detail. For example: 'We wanted to move so-and-so, but his mother-in-law is suffering with hip problems and the family needs to stay near her.'

When we started working with ABI, and Velaphi Ratshefola was new there as operations director – he had only about three months' worth of exposure, compared to the normal 10 years – he went in and told his managers about each of their guys. They looked at him in amazement. At SAB we said that's what we expect of our leaders; they know their people, not just those who report to them directly, but all the people all the way down.

Calibration was part of the whole performance management process. There was the ability for high level strategic thinking but also a deep dive into knowing that someone's son lived in Durban with his mother, and he was having a hard time, or whatever.

A Commitment
to Performance

Commitment in the '90s to that set of activities that was called performance management was probably one of the most powerful forces that drove the success of SAB.

The ever enlightened and inquiring Graham Mackay led a team of company executives to the US to investigate how this process might enable the company to ensure it could meet, effectively and efficiently, its goals.

They engaged with Pat McLagan, a guru of organisational change in business and high performance work cultures, and returned to cascade it through SAB.

SAB was one of the first organisations in South Africa to adopt performance management. It became legendary.

McLagan lived in South Africa from 1992 to 1998 but began working here in 1983. She was in South Africa long before it was obvious to others that there would be a change in government. She saw that apartheid was in its death throes.

Working with several high-profile companies in the run-up to free elections in '94, she realised that business organisations in South Africa were playing a huge role in bringing about a peaceful change.

In a global economy, no 'closed' ways of operating could succeed. South Africa was killing itself because more than 70 percent of its population was disadvantaged, and the system was keeping them disadvantaged.

She worked with corporations to transform their governance and management systems and leadership practices, and with labour representatives to help them into a more functional participation in some of the changes.

She worked with illiterate people to help them develop the skills of participation, and with management to help them think about how they would lead.

In SAB, the result enabled creation of a supportive climate and the alignment of processes to its values. Performance management became part of the company's DNA. Underpinned by the values of the organisation and how its people engaged with one another, it became the way to do things. All employees were expected to practise communication characterised by respect, honesty and constructive feedback.

The company sought feedback from business partners and customers and reviewed individual performance by a collective management team. Human Resources provided the tools and support.

At SAB, line managers owned the process. They had regular goal review meetings with individual employees and their teams, using a standard format that supported a coaching approach.

Personal goals looked specifically not just at 'what' the output was, but also 'how' it would be achieved. It called for development of management and self-management goals.

It balanced the 'what' with the 'how', recognising that a person's style (as a manager or a team member) had the power to enhance or weaken performance.

The 'SAB Ways' became a proven approach to performance management and reward and ingrained a unique performance culture at SAB.

Soon after the acquisition of Miller in 2002, Graham was reported as saying: 'Substantial work is being done to enhance the performance culture within Miller in line with our practices.'

Mobilising and invigorating the organisation and its people to instil a performance culture was one of the four components of a turnaround plan at Miller, along with building brands and shaping the portfolio, getting sales and distribution right, cutting costs, and increasing productivity. The company believed that creating a performance management culture throughout SABMiller was critical to reversing the downward trend in sales in the short term.

A change in culture involved engaging the hearts and minds of all their employees. It went beyond business and touched the employees at a personal level, giving them a feeling that whatever they were doing made a difference.

It instilled a sense of pride and broke down hierarchical barriers.

The thinking was: 'We work for a brewing company. We need to be proud of what we stand for, of what we do as a company. We need to be knowledgeable about what we do.

'We need to have a more open, engaging, challenging culture, and that's what we're working towards. We are not afraid to speak up. We feel confident to engage in debate and to be part of what's going on.'

It was also about enabling change. Employees began to realise that they need not resist change.

Over the years SAB had focused on building its people's capability. For the future, the company set out to decrease its high dependence on recruiting, developing and exporting South African talent specifically for our overseas operations. Its people strategy, particularly for people with top line capabilities, was to develop a global talent pool through training and management development programmes.

MAURICE EGAN

Around July 1991, a group of us took Pat McLagan on a visit to the Kwa Maritane game reserve in the Pilanesberg. On a game drive, Kobus Burger was in the back of the vehicle. As we came around the corner, we were confronted by a bull elephant in musth. In her broad, swanky midwestern American accent, Pat asked: 'Ranger, how do you tell the difference between a male and a female elephant?'

Out of the side of his mouth, Kobus Burger said: 'The penis is a dead giveaway.'

Barry Smith was part of the EXCO team when Graham said: 'Let's sit down and define our mission, vision and values and where we want to be.'

Barry

The mission was to be a world class marketer and brewer of fine quality beers while behaving in a socially responsible manner (we specifically chose the word 'marketer' because we weren't great marketers). The country was changing, and we were at the forefront of the change. Our vision was to be among the top five brewers in the world by any measure by the year 2000.

When you talk to people about mission, vision and values, if they can't tell you what they are, they mean nothing. They're just words on a poster on the wall.

Our values were uncompromising quality; excellent customer service; open and frank communication; continuous improvement; honesty and integrity; and dignity and respect. It took us two full days to define them, and it was a great time for me.

I was ops director at Northern Provinces and Free State when Graham told me: 'I want a line manager to implement performance management, otherwise it becomes an HR function and that's the last thing I want.'

I had a team: Chris Barrow as the strategy guy, Mitch Ramsay as the communication man, Roy Bagattini as the process guy, and a lady who did the training. So we had the strategy; a communication plan that the whole organisation could buy into; the processes to set it up; and the resource for doing the training.

In each division or department, we identified performance managers who would come back from initial training and lead the process within their particular function. About 20 SAB people went to McLagan's HQ in Minneapolis-St Paul for induction.

It was a major driver of our success; not so much the process itself, but more the underlying philosophy that you set your own goals. We were a company that believed in continuous improvement, and we strived to reach the goals we set. You could walk into a brewery and pick up immediately that this was an SAB operation.

Our vision, mission and values provided the right direction and were inspiring. They were not simply a poster on the wall.

ANDRÉ PARKER

Personal accountability was brought in to drive a performance management culture. It really said 'You're accountable. You're the boss of your own job.'

To me that was probably the main ingredient of what made us successful and enabled us to move into Africa, drop a couple of okes off there, and tell them to get on with it. They were happy working on their own. In fact, they preferred it.

They were happy to take on extra responsibility and they didn't need someone in head office to tell them what to do.

When we come to look at the lessons we learnt, we probably overdid the head office stuff towards the end. I became involved in setting up a Guide to Excellence, the sales standards guide, which was loosely based on what Anheuser-Busch were doing for their wholesalers in their 'dimension of excellence' programme. I was working with Pete Savory at that stage, and he insisted that I go to the US once a year to check on what was happening. We always wanted to compete with the best, not just be a successful South African business.

In the dark days of apartheid, we couldn't do much, but we managed to stay abreast of what was going on in the brewing world. Because of that, I think we attracted really good talent. In later years, when we encountered some of the western brewers, our people were far superior to theirs.

In the western world brewing was seen as a staid, old-generation type of industry. Bright young people were becoming merchant bankers and the like. Brewing didn't attract the best talent. In South Africa, though, it was seen to be the opposite, and we attracted the best.

JOHAN NEL

In the early '90s, my human resources consulting company worked with SAB on a large project that engaged with all 13,000 employees in South Africa in a value sharing process in preparation for the country's democratisation.

How would they personally contribute to raising SAB to one of the top five, by any measure, by the year 2000?

That devolution created alignment but, more importantly, made sure that people were clear about what was expected of them and that there were consequences if they performed well and consequences if they didn't. It brought a step-change in the quality and calibre of SAB people.

Top performers were rewarded handsomely and thrived. Poor performers were weeded out. We took the whole concept of a high performance, accountable culture to the next level.

The first of our values was that people were our enduring advantage. The second was that accountability was clear and personal. They were very simple, but they meant a lot and became the ethos of the organisation.

The implementation of performance management and world class manufacturing became the platforms for taking the company into Africa and the rest of the world.

We had been reasonably good at taking people out of SAB to go mainly to African breweries in developing Third World countries. The sequence started by enhancing manufacturing processes; making the beer better and more consistent; reducing costs; and delivering on the promise to the customer of quality beer.

Performance management then allowed us to begin exporting professional management across the company, not just creating a consistent manner in which we ran the companies, but ensuring that in whatever nation we were operating, the company culture remained the same.

That culture was based on the values and management processes that we believed in deeply. It enabled us to respect the uniqueness of every culture in which we operated; the norms, values, governance processes and diversity of every country. But we said that in the workplace, the values we espouse will be the same across the world.

In many places, we didn't have money. Breweries we took over were struggling after the devastation of communism and post-colonial problems. Some companies might have been tempted to take over such an operation and denigrate its past, telling its people how badly they performed and how incredibly clever the newcomers were, arriving as the new owners to show them how to step up into the new world.

Instead, we went there to honour and celebrate their history, bring them on our side, and agree that together we could build a better place; to remind them that they had been through changes and survived. Our attitude with governments and shareholders was: 'Let's do it together.'

It bought us credibility and a licence to succeed. Our attitudes and processes helped us win the trust of our stakeholders. It was an attitude rooted in truth and honesty. We made it clear that things had to be significantly different and better, but we showed how we could fix them together.

I spent about four years at the helm of HR in South Africa. What stood out for me was the massive scale of the change.

Working for Norman Adami was a unique learning experience. He would ensure that you had 20 important change projects in progress, stretching the staff and the business enormously, and then would have another ten for you the next day.

He believed in priorities and pervasive change, but he could also juggle multiple projects in his head at the same time with a belief that they could all be managed simultaneously. Why take ten years, when you can do it in three?

I was also impressed by the capacity of the system and the amount of energy for change in sometimes conflicting situations. SAB was retrenching and re-educating a large number of people, retraining the entire staff in different work practices, and changing the culture from one led by manufacturing to one led by brands. It was a significant change in attitude and skills.

The capacity and enthusiasm that people showed to do their jobs, and to understand that they came with adjusted goals that had to be achieved at the same time, were phenomenal. Never was the performance of the business allowed to decline. That can-do, must-do attitude was vitally refreshing.

SAB stood out, against every other company that I worked for, for the superior quality of its people – a legacy of the people in the seventies – engaging in recruitment practices, psychometrics, screening, incredible care in selections, both for the intellect and qualification of the individual, and for their ego, strength, charisma and character.

I would work with middle management and supervisory people in SAB who were superior to the executive committees in other businesses, not only in their passion but in raw talent.

SAB had, over years and years, built this exceptional quality of expertise, and was able to embed in it a culture oriented towards achievement and accountability mixed with a huge dose of spirit, fun, laughter and camaraderie. That was the vital differentiator. It was unashamedly a people-led organisation.

Because of sanctions and the weakness of the rand, SAB had been outside the trend of globalisation in the '80s and '90s. So what qualified it to say it was going to be in the world's top five brewing companies by any measure by the year 2000? It could be viewed as ambitious, even arrogant.

What made it feasible was its depth of talent. SAB was able to acquire businesses and resource them with talented individuals who had been through the beer wars, had experienced significantly changing productivity levels in their breweries, had grappled with the idea of becoming a brand-led organisation, and had tackled professional and repeatable management processes.

That was all largely due to Graham's determination to put an effective performance management process in place.

People would have goals and be accountable. You could devolve authority right down the organisation, so that you were trying to win not with the efforts of a few hundred managers, but with the efforts of every employee. That's very powerful.

Of course, when you export people, you face becoming weak at home. Then your cash-generating machine could begin to unravel and become vulnerable to competition. We were able to counter this because, in the move towards democracy in South Africa, we had accelerated our affirmative action programme. Taking people out of the country created an enormous space to bring much more black talent into the organisation.

(This was not a response only to events in 1994 in South Africa. SAB had had black advancement processes in place since 1971. This was truly visionary.)

The space created had to be filled not just with black talent, though certainly a large proportion of it was, but also with women. The profile of SAB in the early '80s was a male-dominated white company. By the time of our sales conference in 2010, half the people attending were women and SAB was a showcase of diversity.

That was a wonderful achievement and a lesson in the way to run companies anywhere in the world. Wherever you go, diversity and empowerment of all the people is essential.

From South Africa, we took hundreds of executives into the international fold. From 2002 we moved people from Poland and Hungary to North and South America. It became a global, talent-led strategy.

ANDREW WOLFF

People who have never worked in another organisation tend to believe this is the way all companies are run. You set people's goals and ask them to do things. They come back at the end of the month or in the specified time frame and the job's done.

When you scratch the surface, you see the depth of organisational culture and understanding. For instance, when I worked in the mining industry, the skills sets, understanding, performance management, accountability and attendant culture just didn't exist.

I told my boss at the time that we had a performance management problem, not just in the supply chain but in execution. But he was a mining engineer at heart and didn't want to mess with the organisational culture.

It really made me understand the depth of skills and the understanding that people in SAB had. What you committed to, got done. If you didn't get it done on time, you knew the consequences. If you didn't put your hand up in time to say there's something going awry, or there are some other resources that you need, you took accountability for not doing it.

I had a conversation recently with a consulting company based in the UK. They said the one thing about working with South Africans, and SAB specifically, was that when somebody stabbed you, they did so from the front, not in the back. You could see when the shit was coming, you knew why, and you knew you probably deserved it. In the UK, they said, everybody stabs everybody else in the back.

SAB was an exciting place to work. If you were capable and could deliver, you were given free rein. You felt empowered.

It was also like a family. At the end of the day, if you weren't going to sit around a dinner table, you would sit in the pub. It was like the TV series 'Cheers' – you could almost be sitting beside Norm, cradling a beer. It was like being at home.

PINE PIENAAR

For me, as the district manager in a rural market, the bi-annual performance review meant you knew exactly where you were. You were part of goal setting and part of agreeing how you would be measured, and you could debate the targets, and all of this was a great help. You could say anything, but if you hadn't performed, it was there in black and white.

Ndu Duduzi was an area manager who worked for me. After the first six months he achieved a performance rating of two (out of six). It was like I had hit him in the balls. I told him he could scream and shout or go and complain to somebody about it, but it was not going to change anything – he was a two. Those were his goals, and that's how he had performed.

From that time on, he underwent a huge change; he left the district manager position and went on to perform extremely well. The only reason for that was that SAB had integrity in the system. It was honest with people.

Some people had a blind spot and didn't respond to performance management, but those guys were usually fired. But if you embraced your goals, your tasks, and your performance measures, then you were fine.

What was also important was that we calibrated it. You couldn't say: well, that's just my view. You had to go back to the executive team meeting and tell them why you rated a guy a four or whatever. We looked at everybody's goals and measurements and asked ourselves if they were fair. We adjusted up or down based on the calibration and realised we may have been a bit tough on some and a bit lenient with others.

Ultimately, you were comparing apples with apples. There was very little favouritism in the system. It was about facts and figures, and that helped us. You knew that if you managed people's performance well, they performed well. In the following year you could see the step up in performance.

In my early days, there were no systems in Witbank. I got claims for meals and questioned them. I said: 'How could you eat at a restaurant at eight in the morning?' So I stopped signing the claims. Guys got upset with me. They thought I didn't understand sales. I focused on discipline.

We started off last in the rankings in the country, but after the first year we won the prize for the most improved sales team. The next year we won the MD's award. Halfway through the year, I was appointed District Manager (DM). That was two years after I had arrived.

When I think back, I think the DM job was the most challenging job, more so than even the GM. You had to be strategic, and you had to be hands-on. You looked after sales, distribution, credit, human resources, your own income statement, and the depots. I was effectively running the entire value chain.

We had six depots, and each had different teams in place. We operated over a geographic area of 78,000 km^2. I also looked after the brands. I needed to make sure that the image the brand guys wanted was correctly portrayed to the consumer.

It was tough, but the best job ever. I had the opportunity to move to Central Office, but I declined because I thought I had the best job in the country.

There was nothing better on a Monday morning than to find that your sales volumes were up. That you hadn't overspent. That there had been no truck breakdowns. That your housekeeping was good. That your debit book was in good shape. That trade execution was good. That you had good HR scores, and your people were happy. What more could you want?

You were managing a variety of things. If it went wrong, it could go badly wrong. If it worked well, it was the best job in the world.

In those days, I think ours was the biggest district in the country. We looked after depots in Groblersdal, Standerton, Ermelo, Dwarsloop and Nelspruit. We had a turnover of R2 billion and made R1 billion profit a year. We sold around 1.8 million hectolitres per annum. We had about a hundred people in the district, excluding the owner-drivers. We had three distributors – Groblersdal, Dwarsloop and Ermelo.

Around the time I left, we had a distributor in Dwarsloop, Tshepo Mohale. I appointed him as a management trainee, then he became a financial planner, and then I made him a depot manager in Standerton, a small depot. Then I promoted him to Bushbuckridge. That was part of the HR process; honesty with people throughout their careers. He said he didn't want to go to a large depot, or become a district manager, he wanted to be a distributor. He stayed there and eventually SAB sold the distributorship to him. Dwarsloop is now doing 300,000 hectolitres and he is still running it.

That was SAB. We honoured our commitments. If you are honest with people and people are honest with you, there can't be issues. Sometimes you don't like what people say to you, but at least it was honest.

TONY VAN KRALINGEN

Performance management was as much about making the organisation at senior level far more focused, directive and successful, as it was about making sure everybody in the organisation felt a sense of belonging in it.

When you do engagement surveys across organisations, invariably the bottom layers feel disconnected, disenchanted and dissatisfied and that they just have to work, keep their mouths shut, and carry on.

We treated people with dignity and respect. We would err on the side of being generous rather than being mean. Management was expected never to be mean-spirited. People felt secure and warm.

Many of my friends who worked at SAB and have gone to other organisations realise how spoilt we were and recognise the privilege of working for SAB. The flip side was that it made us a bit naïve because we thought everybody was like that. Many people have been disenchanted when they've left SAB, wondering why their new employers don't manage the way SAB did. They don't get the same warmth, rigour or discipline.

The process instilled in you that you just had to be better and better. Processes, disciplines and systems were always searching for improvement.

When SAB started world class manufacturing in the late '80s factory efficiencies were at around 50 percent. When you were running 24 hours a day, seven days a week, factory efficiencies should have been 70 percent and more.

We reached and topped 70 percent because we forced ourselves. Everybody, in whatever discipline, found things they could introduce to the business that made their part of the business better, and if they made it really good, someone else would pay attention.

The Guide to Extraordinary Achievement (GEA) came from André Parker and Pete Savory after looking at what Anheuser-Busch did in the US and asking why we didn't do it: set targets and benchmarks and see how our sales force could become better and better at handling sales issues.

The GEA, world class manufacturing, and management accounting were all disciplines and processes seen not as jobs or tasks, but as business challenges and processes that people could adjust and improve, not just instructions on the way you had to do it.

All these things we learnt, we learnt quickly, and they became competitive advantages. We were able to assimilate dates and issues, use our processes and make progress very quickly.

It caught some people on the back foot. A classic example of that was in Poland in the late '90s. Barry Smith was the MD and he saw an opportunity to free the country from where they were trapped by introducing a different returnable bottle in a different crate. By the time the competitors had wiped the shit out of their eyes, we had gained 10 percent market share. Poland was on a ten-year journey to great profitability.

A big part of that was the determination of the people to look deeply at how they could make the business better. It was encouragement rather than punitive demand. It was empowerment.

WAYNE McCAULEY

Performance wasn't negotiable. It was obvious if you were a performer. SAB was not the place for people who didn't like to be measured.

People who are self-motivated and determined want to be tracked. When you were falling short, it made you want to work harder to get the results, because you were in the company of performers. You knew exactly where you stood at any time.

Our five-year and three-year planning, and the way the whole thing cascaded down, were good processes. Sometimes we were guilty of over-engineering things. We tended to become too academic with some of the processes. But mostly they were strong, rigorous and fair.

People often wondered why it was that SAB was able to go into Africa and the rest of the world when few South African companies had been able to grow globally. We had a good operating model underpinned by strong processes, operating procedures, and people, all of which we were able to export to other countries. We were able to take expats who were familiar with them and could implement them straight away. It wasn't as though we just rocked up.

What we did well was that we never took the local brands away from the countries. That was important. We embraced the local people and the local stars. We understood what their brands meant to them, and we built on their brands. Slowly we introduced new brands at a more premium level. We had well documented operating models of policies and procedures. That's the thing that other companies miss.

In the years before we were able to compete overseas, we were competing with ourselves, and we kept on getting better at tracking and driving our competitiveness through internal awards, and that enhanced our business. When we were able to compete internationally, we were ready to do so. At one stage we had something like 300 expats.

The people processes in SAB weren't perfect; they were good, but based on what I've seen in other corporates, they were outstanding. We took that stuff really seriously and did more and more of it. We believed in honest feedback.

You had the mission, vision and values that drove the overarching intention, but underneath that was the strategic plan, underneath that the annual budget or operating plan, and then under that the team and individual goals. And a feedback loop that drove our performance management system. The whole thing was completely integrated.

The feedback cycle was pretty natural; it required training and consistent management to make sure it worked, but most companies don't do those things. They don't link the individual and team back to the performance plan, they don't provide feedback or, out of that, plans for individuals and careers.

The idea that the human plan and operating plan were completely interlinked appeared unique. A lot of guys came from other corporates and said they understood it, but somehow SAB worked it well. It was not onerous in the sense that it sucked all your time away from what you had to do in the market; it was a very healthy discipline.

I always had a sense in SAB that if you had a plan or a suggestion that made sense you would always get airtime and support. Even when I was a relatively junior manager, if you had a good idea, they would let you go with it, to a degree. Very rarely if you cocked up would they come and say that was a disaster.

KEN HITCHCOCK

In production, we were able to compare ourselves with the whole of ABInBev. We ran the supply chain in ABInBev and our production and quality were far better than theirs.

They tried to document production and regiment how it should be done, and maybe they were better at that than we were, but the production process was at the heart of what we were trying to do

– our belief system – whereas ABInBev made it like a mechanical resolve.

SAB was visionary in the way they took people like me – an engineer – and threw them into sales and distribution. They would take marketing guys and try them in a production position.

Unfortunately, this was not the case after the takeover by ABInBev in 2016, and I think we squashed a lot of careers by not doing that, instead of allowing people to diversify just a little and keep life interesting. We also took the South African out of SAB and made it a global company that was not necessarily run by South Africans.

The guys they brought in never really got to understand the grassroots of what made us successful. They just glossed over them. The strength of SAB was that everyone in a senior position had worked the system. They started not necessarily at the bottom but at operational level, worked at it, were successful, and grew from there. When they sat in leadership positions, they knew exactly what you were talking about; exactly what was happening on the ground. As we went global after 2016, we lost that.

Although Performance management was power, the career development bit sometimes got a little out of hand. We may have raised people's expectations too much because it forced us to have career discussions. It's not easy telling someone 'look, you've gone as far as you're going to go.' So why have the discussion? Just move on. But the absolute goals, targets, performance feedback, one-on-ones, team-on-ones, team-on-teams … that was power.

If you're on the wrong end of it, it can be quite unpleasant, but people took it on the chin, recovered, and moved on. They were the type of people you wanted.

Barry
Someone once told me: 'You guys in SAB measure everything that moves, and if it doesn't move you kick it so that you can measure it.'

People in the places where we did due diligence could never understand why we wanted all this information. We want to know not just the quality measure but what drove that quality.

Graham said we should never underestimate our management processes and our culture of measuring. You can't manage unless you measure.

At Efes in Turkey, I sat on the board, and they had all these charts, and you could pick up very quickly that they were not managing by those numbers. It was just paper on the wall.

As Andy Andrews used to say: 'Many South African businessmen end up pissing in their pants. It gives them a great warm feeling but at the end of the day all they have is wet pants.'

He also used to talk about South African executives who claimed they had very strong company values, but if the numbers weren't right, they were just meaningless words.

Wayne

Strategy was one thing, but execution was another, and they were never seen as two different buckets. Strategy was only as good as the way we implemented it. With a lot of companies, strategy is often parked in a corner and then managers never execute it.

I think a big reason for SAB's success was that we executed against the strategy. When times got tough, we didn't change the strategy, we worked out a way to win and how we would measure it.

Another big difference between SAB and other big companies was that we got things done – there was no ducking and diving. Once we agreed the strategy, we were going to execute it. We used different countries for better practices and so forth to embellish strategies, but they themselves stayed the same.

People who have gone to work for other companies always say it's not the same. In my short time at a telecoms company, I was surprised at how loose things were. I wasn't used to that. We said we're going to do X, but nobody ever asked the question whether X ever happened. They would want to move on to something else.

A lot of other companies made mistakes, where it was easier to do the nice stuff and not the hard yards. SAB did both.

MEYER KAHN

Three aspects of our own identifiable culture in SAB at that time worked in our favour. Some of the elements were unique.

The concept of excellence was indivisible. You can't brew a great beer with poor ingredients. You can't sell a premium beer in a scuffed bottle. All that stuff we took for granted in Beer Division.

But it's indivisible. Your receptionist can do as much damage with one phone call to one person as a truck driver might do by knocking over eight poles. Every job in the company must be at the same level, at the top level of excellence. Our accountants needed to win. We needed to be applauded for our annual statements. Our human resource management needed be top-notch. Every aspect of the business must come out tops.

It's like a pot of soup, is the way I used to describe it ... you can have the best meat, the best vegetables, but if you put in the wrong water, you've spoiled the taste of the whole pot. That's what the culture was all about.

That led to the belief that no job in the business was more important than any other. It may be different, but it's no less or more important. That is something by which I would stand and fall in every business I have been part of. The driver is as important as the MD and the MD is as important as the messenger. When you do all that, the pot of soup tastes magic.

To summarise the culture of the business, we took our business seriously, but not ourselves.

I remember saying that once in an interview in Business Day. You cannot believe how many people stopped me in the street and people who phoned me and told me that was the best lesson they had ever learnt.

11 Following
the Great Leaders

Leadership, as an integral part of people, was at the core of what made SAB great.

Its leaders throughout the organisation – from CEO to MD to general manager to sales manager and warehouse manager to the shop floor – was founded on that culture of performance management, empowerment and accountability.

Indeed, SAB churned out a brand of skill and dedication that over time benefited corporate South Africa as some of the greatest talent took their SAB grounding and moved elsewhere.

In management across the board, the culture was one of accountability, passion, delivery, and celebration of success. Recognition was as important as reward, if not more so, as success was seen as potential and the opportunity to fast-track individuals through the business.

The top leadership and architects of the five-year and ten-year future thinking were the geniuses in plotting the roadmap to achieving the status of the second biggest brewer in the world in less than two decades.

The standouts were Graham Mackay, the cerebral master; Malcolm Wyman, the financial guru and merger and acquisition lead; Meyer Kahn, the cheerleader and orator who had an impact on every person he met on the journey; and Norman Adami for his leadership of South Africa twice and his turnaround of the ailing Miller Brewing Company.

Leadership spread at every level through the 70,000 employees around the globe. Key players who made immense contributions included André Parker and Gert Goedhals for their pioneering approach in Africa and China; Danie Niemandt in Tanzania; Barry Smith for his impact in Poland and North and South America; Karl Lippert for his work in South America and in various other countries;

Alan Clark and Sue Clark in Europe in the tough years; Johan Nel in human resources best practice; Tony Van Kralingen in South Africa, Czech Republic and later global HR and procurement; Robin Goetzsche in Africa and later Russia and Turkey; Grant Harries and Richard Rushton in Colombia; Gavin Hudson in Colombia, Russia and Turkey; and Simon Harvey and Andries du Plessis in Nigeria.

These superb leaders number too many to mention but their leadership was pervasive and the secret to our success, our people and our leadership brand.

South Africans were on the move, marching into the world, hungry to succeed after living in a country where apartheid had haunted us for years, now being able to show true colours on the global stage, with a work ethic that I believe made us unique, and a level of brewing expertise and overarching general management understanding that made us who we were. With people centricity at the core of everything we did, we showed them. About the three men at the top, Neil Hobkirk put it succinctly.

Neil

You had the Scottish intellectual as the spiritual leader; the Afrikaans Jew as the architect; and the Lebanese South African smous (hawker), like a greengrocer with an IQ of 160, as the general.

For any organisation, to have guys of that calibre, all at the same time, leading an organisation ... we were blessed with tremendously enlightened, insightful, battle-hardened but caring people in a business/stakeholder/social combination. They all expressed it differently and for me it was the greatest privilege.

Meyer and Graham were a formidable team. Meyer was the big personality. Graham was the brain, thinking ten to 20 years in advance and not being dragged into the day-to-day stuff. Then there was Malcolm Wyman on the finance side. They were formidable. That was the powerhouse.

Graham was the visionary, but he needed the energy of a Meyer. Somebody called Meyer the cheerleader. He was always championing the business, out there motivating people, speaking to analysts ... he was good at that stuff.

Meyer gave Graham and Malcolm emotional support. His track record as an operator was not all wine and roses. (We ultimately had to sell OK Bazaars for R1.) When Graham convinced him to come on board, he was an ardent supporter.

Norman was the man you wanted with you in the trenches. He was a tenacious fighter. He gave the Americans a hard time. He was outstanding at many things, but his management style was something they did not want to have at the top.

Graham, Meyer, Malcolm Wyman and Norman were the quartet who made up SAB.

It's a pity for the world that SAB never had the chance to finish the job. Who knows, with that kind of culture, those principles, that whole belief system, what kind of a role it could have played in the world of business at large? Down the road as a proud South African company, who knows what it could have been? The great tragedy is that it never happened.

Norman articulated a view universal in the company now and in the past: Graham Mackay was the architect of the greatest ever South African business success story.

'I worked for him directly for 25 years,' he said. 'He was a visionary, very articulate and very bold.'

Ally

In my countrywide interviews with colleagues and friends for this book, the opinions voiced about Graham varied very little.

Graham was seen always to be years ahead. He would be thinking of what the company should look like in five to ten years' time. It would always be four or five things that would re-shape our future dramatically. He was never one to dabble in a whole lot of little things. He focused on the big levers. That was the genius of the man.

He had an enormous intellect, was extremely ambitious, and he had a deep belief in his own abilities. And he had a big ego. He wanted to be the top beer guy in the world. It was a frustration for him that he knew he was probably better than most of the people with whom we were engaging from the other top beer companies.

He was a man of enormous integrity and energy, but it was a focused, calm energy. He was deep-thinking. Many found him deeply engaging. Some recall happy times walking into his office and telling him a joke at which he couldn't control his laughter. He had a wonderful sense of humour.

Graham was the right man for the right time. While we were in acquisition mode, he was the guy with the vision, saying we wanted to be one of the top three brewers in the world. In any potential deal, he was the one who saw more of the opportunity and less of the risk and hardship.

Graham, as was Malcolm Wyman, was very calm and collected. You never saw either of them flustered, even in heavy negotiations. Graham had remarkable and uncanny strategic vision and he was an excellent communicator.

At any presentation, it was always likely that Graham would ask a question. You would think: 'Really, where on earth did that question come from?' Then you realised that he was thinking ten years ahead and looking at the big picture strategically rather than operationally.

He didn't necessarily have the answer. He asked a question and expected you to go and find it. He was very insightful. Yet he was never intimidating. He made you feel comfortable. He never belittled you.

Graham saw where we could add value. We had people to offer. We had management processes that enabled us to go into breweries and run them well. And we were able to benchmark. How much was it costing to do this or that? We could see immediately what we could improve on to make lots of money.

SAB was in the right place with the right offerings at the right time.

Graham truly believed that people were our enduring advantage and that he could go out on a limb, and the guys would rise to the challenge.

Several saw him as a genius and felt a sense of disappointment when they met some top ABInBev executives. There was just no comparison. There was a void the size of the Grand Canyon.

CLIFFORD RAPHIRI

For someone who was chairman and CEO of such a big company, Graham wasn't an intimidating leader. You never went into a room with him with knees shaking. He was personable, without an ego, but very stylish. He wore the best in suits. He was always the best dressed person in the room. Graham always walked slowly to the stage. Grant Harries joked at a sale conferences when Tony walked up to the stage: 'There's Tony doing a Graham'.

TONY VAN KRALINGEN

In the '90s, SAB was well into thinking about expansion, maybe into Moçambique, Zambia, or Zimbabwe. Graham and Pete Lloyd asked me to lead a small team to see if we should buy in Argentina. A banker in Argentina was keen that we invested because of the strength in Argentina of Ohlsson's, selling about a million hectolitres at the time.

We were under the misconception that it was great brand value. Tobin Prior, Mike Hoy and I went there for three weeks. We came back recommending that we didn't go into Argentina for two reasons: the peso was linked to the dollar; and we understood what it was like to own 98 percent of the market. At the time, Quilmes had 94 percent. There was a little brewery in Buenos Aires and another in Salta, which we could have bought.

We also found that the reason we were doing so well in South America was that Ohlsson's was packaged in cans and there was no can capacity in South America at the time.

It made you think: What did SAB have to offer? Most other South African companies, when they went abroad, would go to the western world. We didn't. Graham, Pete and Meyer saw that our capability was in the darker areas on the world map and in a sense, we went to switch on the lights. That's what our people did.

In many of the places we went, we switched on lights. We helped those economies grow. We did what we did best: built breweries, capacity, capability, and brands in markets that were surprised by this. And we did it without money.

It shows how remarkable the SAB story really is. When we went to Hungary, Tanzania, Moçambique and China, all in the early '90s, we sent SAB people into places other people wouldn't want to go.

We didn't have money. We didn't export our brands. We exported our people and our methodologies, processes and disciplines. We chose people very thoughtfully, and when we were assessing expats, we focused also on the spouse. If the partner was resilient and strong in those places, then the expat had a much better chance. It was an important assessment whether a wife was likely to support her husband and make him successful. If the answer was no, they did not get the job.

When you committed to SAB, it was more than committing yourself, it was the commitment of your whole family to the lifestyle that was SAB, and it was enduring. When you worked at SAB you were involved all the time, wherever you worked. My wife Sharon says she was as much part of SAB as I was because she lived 35 years of it.

So, when we went abroad, it was with people only. We did not buy things of great value – they became great value.

Malcolm Wyman in his farewell speech, said: 'When we bought Tanzania, it was losing money. In 2010, it made $150 million.' That was a great example of what we did. We converted ordinary businesses into businesses that were the envy of most companies in that country and for many companies outside.

We bought them cheaply and put a few people in, not too many. When we went into countries we never looked down on their people. We were never the 'clever South Africans'. We didn't hire people who were arrogant or believed they were superior. Meyer says we hired honest triers. We were all quite humble and all wanted to be better.

I recall in my early time in the Czech Republic, I spoke to one of the Czech ladies about the audit. She said:

'Why are you talking to me like this?'

'Like what?' I asked.

'You're treating me as an equal.'

'Well, you are. Why would I treat you as inferior?'

THROUGH A BRICK WALL

'Every other multinational I worked for treated me as a junior. This is a different experience for me.'

I wasn't even conscious of it. Ninety percent of other SAB people would have done exactly the same thing. We weren't taught to be arrogant or superior. We were taught that if you treated people like equals you would get the best out of them. We also saw our suppliers as partners for life, not people to be exploited.

VINCENT MAPHAI

Graham was a powerful leader. We wouldn't be where we are if it wasn't for him. I did think Norman was a strong leader and likely successor.

I reflect a lot on SAB and the learnings that come to me. The one thing I learnt about was loyalty. Norman and Meyer would die for SAB.

STEVE BLUEN

Breweries guys were big, strong, alpha males, full of fun, natural leaders, in for a good time, and they believed in the product.

Graham was very different from that. He played squash but didn't present himself as a big jock. He was an intellectual, less extrovert than Meyer, and he was running the show. He did it all so cerebrally.

As a collective, the leaders of SAB were clever, in the cerebral form like Graham or the street-smart form like Meyer and Norman. What that translated into, and I use the words deliberately, was 'substantively excellent decisions'. They were not process people who needed a *bosberaad* to think about what to do next. They said let's go to the bush, have a drink and we'll do this and that. They had vision and substance.

The moves into Africa and into Central and Eastern Europe were ballsy decisions, macro decisions about substantive directions such as I never saw anywhere else. That's why the decisions were so great.

Graham said SAB would be in the top five brewers in the world in five years. We were getting to a point of consolidation. The top two soft drink companies-controlled 80 percent of the market. The top ten brewing companies-controlled 10 percent of beer.

'We can either do breakfast or be breakfast,' he said. 'We will do breakfast.'

I remember board meetings with Graham. He would fly in and answer questions about what was happening in South America, this in Miller, this in Europe, in Africa and China, and paint a global picture. In the next breath he would ask why the sales of Hansa quarts were down by half a percent in Polokwane.

That's what was meant by leaders: people who were worthy of the title. I met so many leaders who were not worthy of the name. They drove the fancy cars, sat in fancy offices, and earned fat salaries, but they didn't deserve the title.

During debates, in the boardroom or anywhere else, the unwavering focus on the business case prevailed. We will do what's best for the business. Norman would fuss about the detail.

The other thing about Breweries leadership that I saw lacking elsewhere was the readiness to 'have your back'.

There were times when I stuffed up royally, and other times when I would be under attack. I would go to Richard Davies (Tony van Kralingen to some extent but Richard definitely) and other guys, and they would have your back and say: 'Give it to me, I'll handle it from here.'

I had a situation where one of the directors wanted me to change a psychometric report. He wanted one of his people to be appointed. I said no. He said my report was wrong.

I took it away, had another look at it and told him it was right. He said: 'You don't understand, I want to bring this guy in as the next ops director, and I can't do it with your report. You must change your report.'

I went to see Richard immediately and told him what happened. I said: 'You will have my resignation before I change one word in that report. Do I have your support?' He said: 'I don't want to hear another word about it. Just leave it with me.' I never heard another word.

It was an occasion where it would have been easy to tell me, well, change it and move on, but no. His decision was ethical, principled and good governance.

Ally

On a lighter note: Graham had a passion for Pilsner Urquell. Whenever he came to South Africa, he would be onto our general managers about the stocks of Pilsner Urquell (PU) or the lack thereof. Like with most things, the wave would flow downhill, and most sales guys were running around to ensure that the brand was stocked wherever Graham went, both on business and socially.

There was a stage that we instituted 'Project Hermanus', named for Graham's passion for holidaying in Hermanus on the Southern Cape coast. It was a hotspot for us to get PU properly stocked in every bar, bottle store and spaza.

PU was not a big mover and was prone to ageing. We would regularly uplift large quantities from the trade. We decided that the most cost-effective way of managing our CEO's expectations was to follow him around, a bit like a blue light brigade with comms to all the on-the-ground networks to quickly move the brand from the vehicles or surrounding off-trade outlets into the restaurants and bars where Graham was going.

It was an operation that became slick and something to witness. I don't think Graham was ever aware of the logistics and resources following him in hot pursuit to ensure that his favourite lager was at arm's length. As an engineering graduate from the University of the Witwatersrand, Graham had developed a great circle of fellow graduates that met each year for a reunion.

One particular get-together was hosted at The Baron on Main in Bryanston, Sandton, and the sales team had rallied to ensure that copious quantities of PU were on hand for the twenty chommas congregated there.

I was unaware of this reunion and was quietly having a Thursday evening beer with my mate and agency partner, Marc Spriestersbach. We noticed the panicky focus on a large table and later saw Graham enter and take a seat at the head of the table with his back to us.

The table was covered with ice buckets, drip mats, bar mats and centrepieces all carrying PU branding. I'm sure Graham's mates at the reunion were suitably impressed.

I knew the owner of the Baron, Theo, and at one stage in the evening I asked him to arrange to have 20 Castle Draughts delivered to the table. I asked the waitron serving the table to tell Graham, at the head of the table, that while he passionately supported PU, he should be drinking the brand that made him and his company famous in the first place.

We were hiding behind a pillar. Graham nearly had whiplash as he searched for us, knowing exactly who would be responsible. He found me later in the evening. We laughed and hugged.

He was a special person on another level and although very cerebral, had a personal touch as well.

SAB folks found Graham unquestionably erudite and super capable. Many of the SAB swashbuckling types were great at making statements, but the true depth of the man was that he asked the very insightful questions. The minute he became ill, the company went pear-shaped. Undoubtedly, he died too young. The company was never the same thereafter.

Garth Saunders recalls an investment analyst meeting soon after the company had bought Miller. It was turning into a disaster. Norman and Gavin Hattersley were sitting in Sandton with all the British financial analysts.

Meyer told them about Miller being a very sick patient in surgery, but not to worry, Dr Hattersley and Prof. Adami were there, so the patient was getting the best care.

While the SA analysts were rolling about on the floor laughing, Meyer turned to Graham and asked: 'What's wrong with these guys? Do you think they paid for their seats?' He was the only guy who could get away with that.

Meyer had that special magic that could pull these guys around and was even better at rallying the troops. He was a raconteur, inspiring and very clever. With Graham's intellectualism, it made a good combination.

Clifford

I had lots of stories afterwards about the number of small businesses who went to Meyer for help while he was chairman of the company. He assisted them to start up and mentored their leaders. It was how he got to know Jabu Mabuza and Ashley Mabopane, who were running a small business on the side. He did a lot to help people.

People would come to him to offer sophisticated presentations with slides. He would say: 'We're talking R10 000. That doesn't warrant a slide. Give them what they need.' The impact of that was significant.

There were occasions when we tried to rationalise things. He said there's a simpler way of doing it. Meyer helped to teach people how to do the simpler stuff.

ROBIN GOETZSCHE

Pilsner Urquell sponsored a golf event for top businessmen at Leopard Rock, outside Pretoria, and invited Meyer. I played with him.

I think both of us buggered our golf clubs because there were so many rocks. It was the most horrific golf day ever. After the game, Meyer got up to make a speech and said: 'We operate in more than 50 countries globally, and I've been to most of them, to China, Hungary, South America, North America; but on this golf course today, I have never felt so far away from home.'

PINE PIENAAR

I had just become district manager in the north when he played golf in an SAB golf day at Glendower. He was quite stressed because he was drawn to play with Meyer. On a short hole, Meyer went into the water while I finished about two feet from the pin. He turned to me and said: 'When last did you wear a jacket? Do you ever spend any time in your office?'

My golf promptly fell apart.

What was important, though, was that Meyer could come down to that level and identify with the people in the regions. He was not out of place sitting on a plastic crate and drinking beer with our customers in the trade. That made him such a brilliant man.

JOHN COCHRAN

I remember Meyer in his heyday at a sales conference at the Wild Coast Sun in the Transkei, when he asked everyone who was non-SAB, including the sound people and the entire production team, to leave the room and close the doors.

Then he let rip. He told us that this was the sales force of SAB, not South African Railways, and we did not carry passengers.

What a turn of phrase that was. He could talk the fear of God into you, but at the same time remain a boykie from Brits, a real human being. His leadership was visionary. There was a mentality about those kinds of men; they had balls of steel, and a vision, and went out and fulfilled it.

GRAHAM EDMONDS

Meyer used to mesmerise me with his speeches at the sales conference. In one speech I remember well, Meyer said: 'You can't make a chicken salad from chicken shit.' I felt that this was a great lesson.

Meyer was the inspirer, the motivator, the straight shooter and the cheerleader. He was highly competitive, and his great talent was that he could relate to people. He could arouse a lot of passion and competitiveness in people.

He was an unpretentious individual. I think that gave the people the confidence to believe they could also do great things. They saw this chairman of SAB who was very down-to-earth, an ordinary guy who spoke in an ordinary way, yet he was the big boss of the company.

SAB people were unpretentious. They weren't prancing around in self-importance. Meyer's influence rubbed off on them. It gave them confidence that an ordinary guy could do extraordinary things. His style was very different to Graham's. Yet they made a great team.

Ally

The SAB leadership and executives got on well with partners and employees. They were down-to-earth, empathetic, created positive work environments, mixed with staff at all levels and clearly added value. First name terms were used always – Graham, Meyer, Norman, Rob … it was really personal, and hierarchy was not important.

It was part of our culture to go into guys' offices and talk to them. New employees had never seen this before. Success was a great motivator. We developed a momentum and had good references from whomever we worked with.

Just as they did with Meyer, many SAB staff saw Norman as one of the finest managers and leaders of the time. His standards of business and leadership were exemplary not only to do the right thing, but to build an ethos of a company that cared for its people and appropriately rewarded performance.

If you bust a gut and did what you said you would, you were looked after handsomely. But he championed, as did Graham, having folks improve their competence and capability, move around, take on other jobs and expand expertise. He even encouraged extra studies, which the company would fund. Not too many companies in those days were doing that.

There were people from Wits, UCT and international universities knocking our doors down to find out how that was done. It was pioneering, not just in South Africa but in the world. It was just such a wonderful chunk of time to be involved, from about 1990, ticking away until we listed in 1999.

People showed an immense respect for Norman, for the business he built. Getting into the nuts and bolts of the business, everything was important to him, down to the last detail. He wanted to know about it. People appreciate it when they feel they are not just a number, they're a person. Graham and Norman epitomised that.

Norman was always a bit untouchable but, man, he just had a way of getting things done beyond the measure of anyone else.

In the US, employees had stations serving coffee and dough-nuts. Norman decided costs had to come down.

One of the first things Gavin Hattersley told them was: 'This is over.' That kind of thing was a culture shock for the Americans.

Norman and Johan Nel would go in really early at about 5.30 a.m. and meet the ladies coming in to clean the offices. They got to know them. One day one of them went into Johan's office asking if she could tell him something. 'Of course,' he said.

She said: 'You know, since you guys came, it's the first time for many years that somebody has called me by my name and taken the time to talk to me.'

Clifford

Norman was a hard task master. But in my entire experience of working for him, I can never remember Norman ever giving the guys on the shop floor a hard time. The brewery could be doing terribly but Norman always walked the floor to motivate the people. He would talk to the managers later in private. He would take on the leadership but never take it to the floor.

JOHAN NEL

Miller was supposed to be such an advanced, liberal company. The top guys had not been to a brewery for ages. Norman went on a tour of the whole of the US including the Milwaukee Brewery where head office was located. And he went to the brewery at different times of the day so he could see every shift. As he walked through the brewing and packaging operations he was introduced to various people. On the way out, he remembered the names of every single person he had met.

He also stopped to speak to a guy and say he had seen something on a particular line, and he commented on it in some detail. It was just a different world for those people to see someone with that grasp of the detail. And that level of respect for them as individuals. That was when we really began to turn the corner there.

Clifford

André had his own unique style. Norman was in another corner. Graham was quietly observing, umpiring. Barry Smith had his own quiet way of impacting conversations. It was all fascinating to experience. Each of them was different. They were managing different parts of the business, each one with unique features. You couldn't say who was better than whom.

Ally

André Parker was extremely dedicated and focused with impeccable integrity and personal values. But he also wanted to run his business independently. He didn't believe you could equate a business in say, Ghana, with Miller. Why would a global organisation try to impose the same systems, or systems costs, or the same processes, on those businesses? One is top in the First World and the other has problems with electricity outages, education and a lack of tarred roads. You can't treat them the same way.

André was extraordinary in protecting his people and his organisation, saying: 'We are all with you on wanting to be a global company and having high standards, but please don't expect the impossible from my people; we are just trying to move.'

SAB had been around a long time. But the African businesses were fledgling or broken businesses. André was great at employing the right strategy for businesses in a different environment in a different time.

Barry Smith stood out as a man with one of the highest levels of integrity I have ever come across. He had that exceptional focus and the ability to lead by example from the front.

SAB leaders were seen as different people with different styles, but you could talk to any of them: Meyer, Graham, Norman, Tony.

People to whom I spoke saw Tony as a very respectful person who also epitomised what SAB was. He was always interested in people. Robin Goetzsche was inspirational and able to manage difficult situations.

Grant Harries was a fantastic, engaging guy. He won respect for his style, for never having to shout or bully or project a small-man syndrome. Wherever he went around the country, he was a success. And he got things done through people. He didn't have to bang desks and throw cell phones at walls. He was a giant in a small body.

Wayne McCauley commented: 'I can't say I ever worked for a terrible boss or a guy I didn't like or didn't respect. That must tell you something.

'I looked around the business and there were a few people I didn't really respect, but they were the exceptions to the rule, and that was testimony to the process of how they selected people for the senior roles.'

12 A Pioneering
Spirit

After the birth of a democratic South Africa, it was politically acceptable for SAB to set foot on the global stage. The group sold most of its non-core South African assets, preferring to buy brewing assets internationally, including in sub-Saharan Africa.

DANIE NIEMANDT

Our core competencies as a low-cost beer manufacturer with a robust set of systems and processes that had been proven in South Africa, and its unique mix of First World and Third World characteristics, stood us in good stead internationally.

Our South African market was mature, and we needed new sources of growth.

Due diligence in Tanzania showed a substantial pent-up demand for beer that Tanzania Breweries was unable to satisfy. It was importing more beer than it was able to brew itself. Other factors added to the appeal of investment there.

Our core skills enabled us to fix, relatively easily, a combination of underinvestment in assets and people and poor management processes.

The government's ditching – under pressure from the World Bank and the International Finance Corporation – of President Julius Nyerere's disastrous African socialist experiment in favour of a free market economy, greatly improved prospects for the Tanzanian economy's recovery.

Though this was one of SAB's first forays onto the global stage, the relatively low cost of entry limited the downside potential.

Because the venture was a joint one with the Tanzanian government, the government was an ally rather than a potential obstacle in transforming the business and it softened a hostile Tanzanian business environment prevalent at the time.

It was also a strategic benefit to gain a foothold in East Africa where the British brewer, Guinness, had already established interests in neighbouring Kenya and Uganda. If it acquired TBL as well, Guinness would have dominated the region, effectively locking us out for good.

In late 1993, when the Tanzanian government privatised its bankrupt, state-owned brewing company, SAB paid $20 million for a 45 percent stake and management rights.

South Africa's minister of finance at the time, Trevor Manuel, stipulated that we could move out of the country but couldn't take out cash. For every acquisition, Malcolm Wyman had to organise offshore finance to pay for it. If we took any cash out of SA, it had to be with the minister's express permission.

Danie was seconded as managing director for the first five years of the joint venture to nurse the new business back to health.

He had built a successful 20-year career at SAB, initially as a human resources practitioner and later in general management. Apart from the necessary experience (his human resources exposure turned out to be a particular bonus in the many people-related issues he faced), he had earned the respect of those who worked for him and of his team of battle-hardened expatriates.

Danie's team were excellent, not only in doing their jobs but in interacting with the local employees and teaching, coaching and mentoring them.

Self-sufficiency was an important attribute, especially in those days before mobile phones and the internet and was a strength in Danie's makeup.

When André Parker first went to Tanzania and entered Danie's office, Danie was using his telephone as a doorstop. 'It was a clear signal that no communications worked. We got the message and bought some satellite phones because the landlines just didn't work. Telexes didn't work either. Even the satellite phones would go off air on a Friday afternoon,' André remembers.

Danie faced numerous additional difficulties. The brewery was in a shocking state of disrepair, as were the country's utilities and infrastructure.

Over-employment in the company (there were more than 4,000 employees, more than twice the required number) and costly supply and distribution agreements (both hallmarks of the socialist system) had to be dismantled, despite local opposition.

The government was initially extremely suspicious and defensive about SAB management's turnaround plans. Only when it began to see results did it become most supportive.

Danie was forced to attend about ten board meetings in the first year to try to explain what we were doing and why. There was a very vocal group, including some local newspapers, who saw the deal as nothing but foreigners stealing 'the crown jewels'. Rectifying this misconception took an enormous amount of management's time.

Ally

Several colleagues and I flew into Dar es Salaam in the Citation Ten company jet one balmy day in October 1997 to be met by a wall of heat and 100 percent humidity as we walked across the runway to greet the Tanzania Brewery management team on the ground.

We drove in a Toyota HiAce van through the city of Dar in peak traffic and after two hours arrived at our hotel, the Agip, for check-in.

Agip was a brand of fuel as far as I knew and was not a renowned hotelier. My assessment was not far wrong. The hotel was a dive. I climbed the stairs to my room on the fifth floor and was literally drenched in sweat by the time I reached it.

Room 515 was scantily decorated, and the windows had no insulation. Air flowed in freely from outside. The air conditioner was not working, the temperature was around 38°C, and the humidity was still at 100 percent. I took a cold shower (which was actually lukewarm) using a bar of soap that was smaller than the ones you get in the chalets in the Kruger Park.

I dressed in clean clothes and walked downstairs to be met by my colleague Steve Goodey, who was also sweating after a shower. We decided to call our chairman, Mr Jabu Mabuza, who was also Managing Director of the Southern Sun Group at the time, to find out how everything was tracking.

'Good day Mr Mabuza', Steve said. 'We're calling to see if everything in your room is okay. We understand the bed is a little too soft so can I suggest that we send up a spare door that we have in our workshop that will make the bedding a bit more solid? We also suggest fumigating the room in case the mosquitos get in while you are out this evening.'

Mr Mabuza was about to explode when the two of us, unable to keep our composure any longer, burst into gales of laughter. He had told us upon entry to the hotel that he could see this was a dive and that it was unacceptable for the chairman of our Tanzanian business to be accommodated in such a dump. As head of the Southern Sun Hotel chain in South Africa, he was obviously used only to the best. While he appreciated the humour from Steve and me, he was hardly delighted with the arrangement.

Transport arrived to take us to the 'Njama Tjoma', a downtown restaurant serving goat meat. Things were not going according to plan. The driver informed us that he had to fetch another colleague at the nearby Sheraton, a hotel that had been recently built and was in the six-star league.

The colleague turned out to be Antonio Rossetti, our exports manager, who was ensconced in the luxury of premier accommodation in Dar es Salaam while the chairman was shacked up in the Agip. Antonio entered the vehicle fresh from a six-star shower in an air-conditioned room and as always splashed with a good dose of cologne, to be met by the wrath of the Mabuza tongue.

The conversation that evening between Jabu and Danie, our MD of Tanzania, was tense. You could cut the atmosphere with a knife. Which was more than we could do with the tough-as-a-tackie goat meat.

In the opening address the following day at the TBL board forum, Mabuza informed the board that although he understood that our intention was to show our partners how thrifty we were in booking accommodation at a below-reasonable rate, he would not attend future board meetings unless he was booked into a decent hotel in the same league as Rossetti had been. Needless to say, he woke up in another room the following morning as if the mosquitos had carried him across the corridor.

The hotel eventually became the New Africa Hotel and Agip decided to stick to petroleum.

Soon after taking over management of TBL, the company was hit by a large number of lawsuits emanating from pre-joint venture days (mainly from ex-employees and suppliers) for payments either outstanding or claimed to be so.

A number of claimants were chancers, other claims had some substance, but all required time and management, especially since the last thing we wanted to do was to go to court where, in those days, you could well lose despite the obvious merits of your case.

Despite the thorough due diligence we had carried out, cash flow during the first year was atrocious, as Danie's team had underestimated the restructuring and operating costs, especially the once-off ones.

Danie had been assured there were only some 3,000 employees. In fact, there were another thousand or so casuals who were, because of prior mismanagement, entitled to full employee benefits. He had to go begging for cash to pay salaries and wages during the first few months, and to curtail some very expensive expatriate benefits.

In the early days, we ran into corrupt practices especially in clearing goods out of Dar es Salaam port, and had to rebuff these and inform government accordingly, where necessary. Our unambiguous stance against corrupt practices simplified matters for Danie's team – they had no choice but to say no.

To ensure fair play between the two partners in the early days, the International Finance Corporation (IFC) and a consortium of international banks were invited to take a minority stake in TBL, including a seat on the board. This helped eliminate initial suspicions among the partners and laid the foundation for a unified JV that survived for many years.

The chaotic state of TBL at the time of SAB's entry required it to rely heavily on a team of experienced expatriate managers seconded from South Africa. An initial team of 22 had to rebuild, from scratch, the TBL organisation, its people (including retrenching many people surplus to requirement), its physical assets and its brands.

Danie's view was: 'When required, don't put only one person to do it – put in a turnaround team.'

A happy coincidence for us was the fact that our affirmative action programme in South Africa had created a group of experienced managers who could be seconded to businesses such as TBL, opening opportunities for previously disadvantaged candidates at home in SA. These secondees proved to be an excellent fit in transferring basic knowledge and skills to TBL staff.

Fortunately, local staff responded well to SAB systems and processes, resulting in TBL recovering sooner than expected. While there were some baddies and some big problems, the Tanzanian employees responded really well to the initiatives we put in place.

Danie's team fixed staff ablutions and canteens before worrying about management offices. He improved safety and working conditions, got basic employee communications going, and initiated training as soon as he could.

The training and development of local staff was critical to establish a unified workforce that took ownership for business results and became off-site ambassadors for TBL, giving further credence to TBL's claims as being 'truly Tanzanian'.

Local employees rose to the challenge; the subsequent expatriate complement shrank to single figures, despite massive growth in the business. Danie's mantra was: 'Focus on the employees – get them to understand what you're on about and involve them.'

Danie and his team went out of their way to 'think and act local' in their interactions with community and government stakeholders. 'You may disagree with them, but do it in the right way,' he advised. They also tried to ensure that they didn't become a closed SAB expat community that worked and played only with each other.

The people who went in there were really pioneers. They were used to internet connectivity and all that went with it, but from Tanzania they were allowed to telephone their families for 20 minutes every Sunday on a satellite phone. Their resilience underlined the fact that SAB's strength lay in the export of good people.

ANDRÉ PARKER

When we went to Tanzania before '94, it was a hellhole. I relied on so many people, like Danie, Craig McDougall and Roger Smith. These chaps went there with their families and got on with the show. They were fantastic guys who were not put off by how tough it was. Many of them had to bundle the kids into boarding schools at a very young age.

But I think our expats loved every minute of it, because they had this freedom to build something, which is very rare in a guy's working career. Very few expats came back to South Africa. Once they got into expat mode, it was their life. They certainly wouldn't fit back into corporate culture.

In Tanzania, Danie soon found out that cash was king. Our approach to acquisitions was that a new affiliate had to be self-sufficient for its cash requirements from day one. The parent company would not inject more cash into TBL. Danie learnt to focus on cash flow, and although profits could be great, without cash flow you didn't sleep.

Fortunately, this approach bore fruit. Danie said: 'Interestingly enough, the IFC was right in what we all thought was a very optimistic forecast about cash flow and profits, and our cash flow was positive within 12 months, and the bottom line was black within 18 months – although we had reckoned on about twice as long to get there.'

The downside of this 'pay as you go' approach was that TBL battled to keep up with the growth in demand for its products, frequently running out of stock during the peak summer months.

Apart from taking the SAB ways of operating (systems and processes) with them, the expats also arrived with SAB's vision, mission, values and business philosophies, all of which contributed to shaping the 'new TBL' around these critical issues.

SAB was clear about its intention to add value to TBL's product offering through improved quality, packaging, availability, brands, and consumer choice as a means of enticing the consumer to pay a reasonable price (not cheap), and so generate cash at decent margins. It was able not only to reward shareholders appropriately for their (high risk) investment but to finance the aggressive capex programme that TBL needed to be robust again.

SAB's 'tight/loose' business model (HQ sets the rules and then empowers the affiliates to operate freely) was perfect to meet the challenges it encountered in Tanzania, but the proven approach had to be overlaid with the need for local knowledge and responsiveness. 'If necessary, amend them, but try to keep the basic processes and systems that work for the group in place,' Danie advised.

In fact, he and his team simplified the SAB processes to develop a business approach for TBL that all staff members understood and shared.

They embraced technological advances to accelerate the turnaround process. Later advances made in the areas of mobile phone and internet technology were a great help. New brewhouses built in Dar es Salaam and Mwanza were fitted with state-of-the art, automated PLC systems from Europe.

In the beginning the business focused on the middle and upper classes, although later, efforts to reach into the economy segment were also explored.

They tried to aim traditional beer (made from sorghum and maize) at consumers at the bottom of the economic pyramid but found that price competition from informal home brewers was tough and it eventually sold that business.

In 2007, a PricewaterhouseCoopers survey done with Nation Newspapers, TBL was voted the 'most respected company' in Tanzania, for the fourth successive year.

At a ceremony run by the Association of Tanzania Employers, it was the overall winner in the category of human resources, won first prize for training and development and occupational safety and health, and won second prize for the fight against HIV/AIDS, for corporate social responsibility, and for employee relations.

With time, SABMiller increased its shareholding and, when government sold a large slice of its holding through a listing on the fledgling Dar es Salaam stock exchange, about 20,000 individuals bought shares.

It was no exaggeration to say that SABMiller transformed TBL from a broken-down, state owned enterprise into a profitable, modern, publicly listed company, to the benefit of all shareholders, government, customers, consumers and the Tanzanian community.

In later years, Robin Goetzsche went to Tanzania to help with a marketing strategy. At the time, the brewery was producing between 250,000 and 500,000 hectolitres annually. There was no distribution system. Beer was collected at the gate.

Robin

Part of the deal was that, in addition to buying the breweries in Dar es Salaam and in Arusha (neither of them very effective), we would build a brewery at Mwanza on Lake Victoria.

The trick used by SAB, initially as Indol Africa and then as SAB Miller, was to cobble together plant that we had recovered cost effectively from breweries all over the world. A lot of equipment came from breweries that had been closed in Eastern Europe.

In the early days, the beer was hardly drinkable because of poor housekeeping. We worked on perfecting quality and started developing a brand portfolio modelled pretty much on SAB's; Safari had a masculine positioning very similar to Carling Black Label; Kilimanjaro had a 'pride in its origins' positioning like Castle's in South Africa (although it drank very much like Hansa Pilsener); while Ndovu, meaning elephant in local Swahili, was a premium brand in a green bottle with a neck foil. Then Castle Lager was introduced as a premium international brand.

Ally

East Africa was a great frontier for SAB in the '90s. We had a pioneering business with great brands: Safari Lager and Kilimanjaro Lager, iconic on the African continent.

Then there was Tusker Lager, a beer from Kenya that had monopolised that market for more than 80 years and had also become something of an East African icon.

When consumers wanted a Tusker, they asked for 'Ndovu' – the Swahili word for elephant – an icon that was part of the heritage and status of East Africa's favourite beer. A proud head-and-shoulders of the largest mammal in Africa on the label represented strength and other powerful connotations.

As Tusker Lager made inroads into Tanzania and impacted on our local franchises, we went about ascertaining if the name Ndovu had some form of registration in East Africa. It didn't. We set about designing a new pack, a green bottle featuring a bull elephant in black and gold. It was premium and standout.

To maintain the confidentiality of our project, only a select five from brewing, procurement and marketing, and the MD and I, knew what was happening.

We brewed a great tasting beer and developed a marketing programme to profile our new Ndovu brand. We had the labels and point-of-sale printed in South Africa and hired a cargo aircraft to move the shipment of materials one Friday evening to Dar es Salaam under cover of darkness.

I travelled on the aircraft with our new brand assets. We transported all the materials to our brewery in Dar and set about filling and labelling the first run of Ndovu, with only a handful of people in attendance. We lined up the pallets for the new lager on our wet depot floor for the entire weekend.

By Monday morning we had a stockholding sufficient to flood the market.

The entire brewery team across the value chain arrived at work that morning to be treated to the launch of the new brew, the best-kept secret in the business and in Africa. By Monday evening, our distribution system had delivered vast quantities of Ndovu Lager to our substantial network across the region and was moving towards the Kenyan border. By Tuesday, when Tanzanian beer consumers asked for 'Ndovu', they received, to their surprise, Ndovu.

This assured immediate trial for all Tusker Lager drinkers, so we hit the target audience first time. Ndovu Lager became a hit and lives on to this day as a premium lager in Tanzania.

It was reminiscent of the '70s Colt 45 and Stallion 54 case study in South Africa, showing that we weren't scared to learn from previous success stories.

JOHN COCHRAN

Then there was football's COSAFA Castle Cup. Ally and I flew around Africa with eight tons of broadcast equipment, landing on runways that were a bit short in chartered Russian Antonov planes flown by pilots of dubious repute. I am not sure if they applied any rules between bottle and throttle.

I remember one time when Ally and I flew out of Namibia's Eros Airport with all that equipment. On Saturday we had broadcast the game in Windhoek and were then flying to Botswana for the Sunday game, with these Russian pilots and their cigarette-box calculations. According to Jaco van der Westhuizen on the ground, we missed the fence at the end of the runway by a metre. There we were, oblivious, lying on the back of the cargo door, hung over and ready to face another day of football in Africa.

In Kenya, before we had our brewery there, we were exporting. It was a tough market, and the Kenyans were not fond of us. We had a COSAFA Cup game there, as they were a guest nation. Our competitors at Tusker had managed to lock the stadium so we couldn't get our equipment in on Saturday for the Sunday game. Eventually we found a way to get in but had to set up throughout the night. We had to deal with this type of incident often. It was tough.

Robin

The business grew nicely with good margins and developed strong links with the Tanzanian government. With government members on the board, we had a very helpful excise regimen. When TBL launched Castle Lite at 33 percent premium, it did phenomenally well, gaining close to 12 percent market share and 20 percent value share.

Eventually, we did a deal with the British multinational beverage alcohol company, Diageo plc, such that East African Breweries handled our products in Kenya, and we sold theirs in Tanzania. We did a remarkable job for them with their brands, Tusker and Guinness, but their efforts with our brands, particularly Castle Lager in Kenya, were poor.

In 2010, Diageo decided to go on their own by buying the start-up brewery at Mwanza, Serengeti Breweries, which had about 10 percent market share in Tanzania, and selling their local brands in Tanzania.

It led to an acrimonious divorce that ended up in the International Commercial Court in London. By the time the issue had been resolved, SABMiller Africa had a swing of about $500 million in our favour, based on what we had to do to buy them out, and vice versa.

As part of the deal, the 26 percent they owned of Tanzania Breweries was listed on the Tanzania stock exchange. That unlocked the share value, which hadn't been trading very much, and the value went up a hundredfold. It was wonderful for the Tanzanian shareholders, who included a number of employees who had held shares for some time. The business went from strength to strength. We took a lot of best practices, like retail price management, out of South Africa and extended our footprint.

Of the Diageo brands, Tusker on its own had about 16 percent market share and Serengeti had about 10 percent, so their entire portfolio should have settled at about 30 percent. Fairly quickly, we had them down to about 15 percent.

Inevitably, we began running out of capacity: we put additional lines in Dar es Salaam brewery and in Mbeya in the south, built a state-of-the-art brewery that was operated only by Tanzanians. The team there raised the brewery to the point where it was consistently number one in machine efficiencies out of all 80 breweries (excluding China) that SABMiller operated.

Many of those Tanzanians also had the opportunity to work in South African businesses when SAB and SABMiller Africa became one. It was a feather in the cap for the development of local talent.

We were also fortunate eventually to obtain the licence to brew Peroni, then only in South Africa and Tanzania, as our super premium brand, which had good exposure among tourists to Zanzibar and the game parks.

Driven by a strong focus on costs, clever management, and high efficiencies, and by really using the assets at maximum efficiency, the Tanzania business achieved ultimately the highest margin EBIT to revenue business in the whole of SABMiller, more even than that of Colombia, which had a higher total profit but a much bigger business. For an African business to be able to deliver margins like that was extraordinary.

What was also advantageous was that we also had a wine and spirits business in a joint venture with Distell, and owned a brand called Konyagi Gin, which contributed about 12 percent to our profitability.

It proved that if you put the right systems and processes in place, you can be successful. The success of SAB was those systems and processes, backed by the fact that we exported experienced operators around the world. We weren't exporting money, or necessarily acquiring businesses.

Where we did acquire businesses, we got very good value and we leveraged and improved them. We bought Tanzania Breweries for under $40 million and when I left in 2014, the business made $240 million dollars of EBIT. Imagine that as a return on investment. That's incredible.

In my first year in Tanzania, we were putting in a new packaging line in Dar es Salaam. All the packaging equipment had come from Krones, and we were going to launch Castle Lite, so we had all the Castle Lite bottles ready. Then a fire broke out.

I was called at midnight and rushed to the brewery. The wind was blowing. The brewery, the whole empties yard, and the stairs were on fire, and there were three different fire departments there. And we had to get the new equipment out.

The forklift drivers were shit-scared of the flames. Then David Magwasa, who was part of our sales leadership team, walked through this tunnel of fire and led the forklift drivers to pick up the containers with the spare parts and bring them out. It was an unbelievably brave decision. I've never seen a guy do that. To see the forklifts follow him in through the flames and bring the containers out was just incredible.

A lot of the pioneering guys, the likes of André Parker and Danie Niemandt and the John Harris's of the world really did the hard yards, and you have to admire them.

Challenging
Convention

After the collapse of communism and the fall of the Berlin Wall in 1989, SAB identified Eastern Europe as a primary target market and made its first purchase in the region in 1993, entering the Hungarian beer market.

Rolling Rock was a beer unknown to most South Africans.

It was brewed by Latrobe Brewing, a company founded in 1893 in Latrobe, Pennsylvania, as part of the Pittsburgh Brewing Company. Forced by prohibition to close in 1920, it was bought by brothers named Tito and reopened in 1933 selling pilsners.

In 1939, it introduced Rolling Rock beer, which helped it become one of the largest brewers in the US. It was also the beer that sparked SAB's expansion into Europe and further afield. Meyer Kahn related how that came about.

Meyer

We invested in America long before anyone knew about it.

Company management teams consider moving out of their home market for two main reasons.

One is that when your market share is so high, the law of diminishing returns begins to apply. The second is that managerial ego wants a company to go out and play against the best in the world.

For years, countless files crossed my desk from analysts detailing beer businesses for sale in the world. All of them had been turned down by every other brewer in the world. One day one of them looked a little different: that was Rolling Rock. We decided to go and have a look at it.

Ken Williams, Pete Lloyd and I went to Latrobe. The company had just come out of a six-month labour strike and the place was a mess beyond belief. The beer was fairly light but drank well. We decided to try to buy the business and make it better. But to buy it, we needed money.

Exchange control prevented us from taking money out of South Africa. The only money we could get was by milking the rest of our South African investments. We eventually borrowed $3 million from the Bank of North Carolina.

To buy the business, however, we had to gain approval from the Tito family. In Boston those WASPs are not as smart as they think they are, and not as rich as they think they are, but are treated like royalty. We flew across to meet them.

After 24 hours in the air, we disembarked to find my suitcase was not there. I was wearing jeans, a dirty, smelly T-shirt, and a pair of tackies. Now I'm going to be interviewed by the Tito family.

Somehow, we passed muster, offered $5 million, we had $3 million as our equity and borrowed the rest against the assets of the buildings and the brewery.

Our engineers went in and set production right and we concentrated our efforts on the college campuses. Sales turned around and began selling nicely. From 400,000 barrels (about 478,000 hl) within a year we pushed it to six, then eight, and eventually a million barrels, all on the campuses. We never disclosed our South Africa connection.

Then another business came on the market, called Sunny Delight, a so-called breakfast juice. The closest it came to fruit was that once a year we put a bag of oranges in the back of a bakkie that drove around the plant once.

We later sold the beer business at a multiple of 10 to a Canadian brewer, Molson Coors I think, and Sunny Delight to Procter and Gamble. We walked away with a nett $145 million and gained permission from the Reserve Bank to buy a Canary Island business which we used to park the money.

When the Berlin Wall came down in 1989 that was the money that got us into Hungary, Poland and other parts of Europe. It was in effect the start of our European and international expansion.

Ally

Two years later SAB invested in Poland, which became responsible for the greater part of SABMiller's early profits in Europe. We acquired Lech, a pilsner with a rich history in Poland, and Tyskie, from the brewery located in the Upper Silesian town of Tychy.

BARRY SMITH

I was told he had to manage both businesses. We had a Polish chief executive, but Gary Bull and I were basically running the business. I spent six months in Tychy away from my family.

The two companies had about 19 percent market share but were beginning to lose ground. I was really worried, and I didn't know what to do. The plan was to merge the companies. At the time, I had to report to Gert Goedhals and he said: 'Why can't you run the two separately? Just run them well.'

In hindsight that was definitely the best thing to do, because of the economies of scale. Fortunately, Graham said we should do it, and we did.

We thought now we are going to be a national business and we did a full national brand portfolio.

In those days, the whole industry shared a common returnable bottle. Inevitably they were scuffed. When the peak season came, everybody was meant to return bottles, but nobody did. You just sent your guys into the bottle stores and collected all the returnable bottles you could.

If you sold 100 full bottles, you brought back 300 empties. Nobody invested in bottles, so you ran out of stock. Came peak, nobody had enough bottles and you lost sales.

With Gary Catell, I decided we needed a proper bottle. I went to London, and we sat with our big bottle manufacturer at the time, an international company, and shaped a new bottle.

The industry also had common beer crates. We knew if we introduced our bottle, we would need a crate to retrieve them in. A Dutch company came and set up operations for us just outside Tychy and manufactured crates that fitted only our bottle.

Overnight, the new bottle just took off.

Also at that time, we weren't allowed to advertise an alcoholic beverage. What we did was to put a line in small print on the side of the bottle that it was non-alcoholic. Everyone did it but we pushed it. In the ads, you would notice the non-alcoholic line, but by then the impression had been made.

We went on national television with the Tychy brand and some phenomenal ads. Here was this beer from Tychy, akin in South Africa to a beer from Vereeniging. Tychy was a mining town where miners were particularly thirsty after a shift underground.

The first ad showed a group of people drinking beer in Ireland and later realising that their favourite beer was actually brewed in Tychy. The Poles loved it because it gave them an identity.

After that we flighted something similar with beer drinkers in a Czech pub. The Czechs, thinking they made the world's best, are impressed by this fantastic beer and demand the waiter tell them which new Czech beer it might be. 'No', he says, 'it's Polish.'

And the big guy who was dominating the conversation suddenly pipes up: 'My mother-in-law's Polish!'

The market was growing by about 12 percent a year and we must have played a big role in that because suddenly the beer category just jumped. Beer came in attractive new bottles, with appealing labels and good marketing. Eventually the other brewers changed their bottles, but we had stolen the march.

We went from 18 percent to 27 percent market share in three years – in a post-Communist country where people were becoming more marketing oriented and the economy was growing. People were becoming influenced by consumer marketing.

Our major competitor, Heineken, held about 43 percent of the market and we held 18 percent. By the time I left Poland after about four years, we had 27 percent and they were down to 32 percent.

I was very proud of our success in Poland. We made money. We had volumes climbing and no real competition pulling the price down. At the time when we had Russia and Hungary, we were making 110 percent of Europe's profits. They were making losses and we had to subsidise them.

We had to sit with accountants at the end of each year and make provisions, claiming we would lose 10 to 20 percent of our bottles in the year. That way we kept our annual profit down. In fact, we were retrieving 98 percent of the bottles issued.

It helped us to manage our profit, but we were a little scared. We didn't know the market and lacked the distribution network we had in South Africa, where we could control bottles right to the consumer. In Poland we were working through distributors. But the bottom line was that we really did make a lot of money.

People tended to believe our success was all thanks to the bottle, the Euro bottle. It was then used in Kenya and in Tanzania, I think.

I remember cautioning them: 'You need to understand the context in Poland and its market. It wasn't just the bottle. It was a whole combination of different marketing inputs.'

When you change packaging, people tend to think you have changed the product. In Poland we had local Polish shareholders who started asking what we had done to the beer. I told them: 'nothing.' They refused to believe me, saying it tasted so much better. It was all in the mind. And when you're holding a beautiful bottle, it will change the taste dramatically.

14 Africa is not
for Sissies

In the early years, SAB had always looked across the fence into our backyard and longed to move into Africa. We operated initially in our neighbouring countries in Lesotho, Swaziland, Zimbabwe and Botswana.

We were an African company and although each country on the continent was different, there were similarities.

The people of Africa were special, and I have to say that in all my travels across the continent, we were always welcomed. A humble approach stood us in good stead to work together to create businesses that became the darlings of each country in which we operated.

SAB's major advance further northwards into Africa began with the success story in Tanzania.

André Parker, John Kirby and their team had built a remarkable business. From a tiny base where they had celebrated hitting $10 million of EBIT in 1999 or thereabouts, it grew steadily. By the time we exited the country that figure had grown to $900 million. In almost 20 years, it had grown from almost nothing to the same size as South Africa's beer business.

MARK BOWMAN

I succeeded André Parker. We bought Tanzania for under $40 million and at our peak we were making $250 million a year in EBIT. Africa was just so perfectly suited to it. We sent our experienced old hands into Africa to fix dysfunctional facilities but by the time I arrived there we could change the model a little.

Instead of just fixing what was broken, we began investing in new equipment and building two or three new breweries a year in East and West Africa.

Graham and Malcolm Wyman said let's double down and do this thing properly. So we built new breweries to a standardised template, which allowed for easier maintenance and for breweries in Africa to start operating to a decent standard, averting a sense that there was only a certain level you could reach because education and skills were lower.

We said you can't put in a $100 million facility and operate it at 30 or 40 percent utilisation. You must operate it according to world-class best practice. We involved our suppliers, Krones and others, and got that brewery operating to almost the best standard in the world.

There were no expats, only Tanzanians, running a brewery in the deep south of Tanzania to the highest standard.

It was a tribute to the way SAB had evolved, starting with the old hands, bringing in newer, younger people, and some expats at an earlier stage of their career, then cross-developing locals back into South Africa. With local training we set a new bar for how we would run the business.

If you were, for instance, a commercial manager in Uganda, you had no idea of what excellence was unless you had worked in another environment. So we did a lot of 'industrial tourism'. It was frowned upon in some circles but was always very valuable.

We'd send people from Africa to Latin America, for example, to see how they were running their sales. Each of them had to come back with two or three ideas to make a meaningful impact in their markets.

When SAB listed in London, we were considered a strange animal from the Third World. Slowly the market came to respect us as they saw the growth potential. We fulfilled that potential because it was a good business that was well run. We did make mistakes as we went to these new markets but mostly, and importantly, we adapted to those markets really effectively.

As we spread across three of four continents and 30 or 40 markets, the learning process began to accelerate. The business began improving much more quickly. The natural competitiveness that was inbred in the management layers, plus the ability to say things like 'by the way, the guys in Colombia are doing a wonderful job', and then to go to Colombia to see it and copy it, brought us acceleration that helped us enormously in Africa.

Though we had the advantage of growth, markets were becoming more competitive. We had to drive our margins through better efficiencies, even in many 'rats and mice' markets.

We also learnt to understand the dynamics in the markets and the idea of driving value. The SAB model, to price below inflation in the long term, drove a natural efficiency. Budgets had to be good every year. If you priced inflation into everything, you would never get better. If you price at 90 percent, everything flows from that. We did that in SAB for 20 years and that made us almost impenetrable to competition.

We did the same in Africa. We drove up our competitiveness and our volumes, because relative pricing became more affordable. Efficiencies started to go up. As the scale increased we became even more efficient. It became a virtuous cycle. The idea of affordability to drive value was very powerful.

Being a force for good in Africa is something of a risk. We were naturally a force for good because we were such a big taxpayer. In African markets we were the number one or two taxpayers in the country because of excise and payroll taxes. Tax collection was inefficient, and we could normally engage with government proactively and positively.

Then we started to do things like brewing sorghum beers and cassava beers, which opened new avenues for growth and employment and new ways to add value to the countries in which we operated.

The idea of a malt-based beer is very European. If beer had originated in Africa, it would have been made from sorghum or a root or something that was prevalent here. The beers in Africa were all imports as a result of colonialism of some sort. We adapted to using indigenous resources.

ROBIN GOETZSCHE
I was an ops director in Africa and looked after 14 of the businesses, excluding East Africa, for two years. The move to Tanzania was 'pioneering stuff' from the outset and set the tone for more to follow.

We managed to really move the needle in that business just by introducing the best practices that we had been lucky enough to learn in SAB.

We had a portfolio of beer brands similar to SAB's, with Safari positioned around masculine appeal and Kilimanjaro occupying the 'pride of origin' space in our portfolio.

Then we launched Castle Lite in a smaller bottle at a 33 percent premium, and it just flew. It reached about 15 percent market share by volume and about 25 percent in turnover. It was a huge success, as was Nile Breweries in Uganda, where we managed to gain market leadership ahead of Diageo.

The Africa business then, in the mid-2000s was like SAB had been in the '80s; very decentralised, very entrepreneurial. You were allowed to take risks and do things.

ANDRÉ PARKER

In Angola, nothing seemed to work. The one hotel where you could stay in Luanda was terrible. One of the greatest assets we owned was the corporate jet, enabling us to get in and out. In lots of these places, commercial airlines were very iffy and irregular. You could cover a lot of ground with your own jet, and you could leave before you had to stay another night.

All these places improved drastically, but when we bought an African business, we said that from day one it had to be self-sufficient. We were fortunate. We had closed down Butterworth in the Transkei and United Breweries in Garankuwa in South Africa and held on to a lot of used brewing and cellar equipment, so we had equipment to take into Africa.

It was old but robust, well-maintained equipment. That was phase one of fixing the breweries. In Tanzania, for example, we took second-hand equipment and fixed it.

As soon as the breweries began generating excess cash, we put it back into the business, replacing antiquated assets. When we made the beer even half drinkable, sales just exploded. So there was lots of expansion.

In most of the African breweries we started with government as our partner because there were no business partners to team up with. Many countries had just emerged from the socialism era. The happy result after years of improvement was that government sold their shareholding by listing on their local stock exchanges.

So today, local investors in Tanzania and Moçambique own shares in the brewery. That's a good free enterprise story. That's how it's supposed to work.

We never had to pour in more money from South Africa to help them as they grew these businesses. They funded themselves. We also reported in US dollars, so we kept the accounting currency hard, which meant that in Africa we were quite profitable.

You could question the strategy. Because beer is quite heavily taxed in those countries, it was more expensive in these territories than it was in South Africa. It was positioned as a semi-premium product. Would we not have been better off if we went with much more competitive price points?

At that stage, country risk was quite an issue. Going into Tanzania was a risky move, so shareholders were looking for some reward quickly. In countries like Zambia and Botswana, where we could, we used Chibuku, a packaged sorghum beer, as an economical offering where they had a taste for sorghum.

In many of the countries, we had Coca-Cola bottlers as well. All these markets were pretty small and self-contained, so you had to fill up your truck when it went out.

We learnt as we went along. There was no book on this, no blueprint. But we had space as the rest of the world had pretty much ignored Africa until then.

Guinness and Heineken had a good position in Nigeria in the west, but many businesses were too scared to enter the markets that we did.

We had a pioneering spirit but were sensitive about our origins. The racial aspect was uppermost in the approach of all our expats and their families. We were respectful and humble, and we went the route of 'think global but act local'. We never flew a South African flag at a brewery. It was always the local flag.

We looked for local partners. We took in the necessary number of expats and then reduced them over time. We always put the local brand first. We resuscitated all the local brands and introduced Castle and later Castle Lite as premium offerings if there was room for them.

It was not the way the normal multinational company would do things. They would go in with their own brands and their own formula and dictate that this was the way they would go to market. We turned that upside down, maybe because we didn't know any better, but probably because our South African background made us very sensitive to *local is lekker*.

Mark

Angola was, in a sense, a failure. We were a bad business and to some extent trapped by Coke. They were putting pressure on us, and we were importing cans at a loss. We were bringing thousands upon thousands of shipping containers into a market that couldn't deal with containers. We were paying $3 million a month in demurrage costs because our containers were getting lost. The place was chaos.

It was also a cynically corrupt country. You couldn't get anything done as a legitimate business. Our local partners were somehow part of the system and were corrupt as well. We couldn't trust them. It was frustrating because we put excellent people in there and they would immerse themselves in a problem. Then four other problems would creep out. So they would pull back from one problem and tackle another. We were not actually in control of our business. You had a sense that the business was controlling us. It was nerve-racking.

One year, we took a big loss. I thought my job was on the line. It was a big business. We put a lot of money into it, and we were losing a lot of money. The currency was tanking. It was extremely difficult.

We built a brewery because we had an ongoing fight with Castel. We had agreed we would combine efforts in Angola but when the time came, they didn't want to combine a profitable beer business with a marginal soft drink business. So we said we would build our own brewery. We already had a brewery in the south, so we built one in the north. They said do what you like, but when we did, they were massively unhappy about it.

It put our whole relationship under huge stress, to the point where it nearly ended. It forced our hand to sell the Angolan business and they gave us their Nigerian business in return. They didn't like Nigeria, oddly enough, because no one spoke French there. So they were happy to give it up.

I was relieved to be out of Angola. SAB execs had many meetings with different officials and were never comfortable with any of them. There was a game going on that we weren't part of. Castel knew the game and could play it. We couldn't go near it.

Then the currency collapsed, and they were left with a massive amount of money trapped there. It was less our operating problem and more theirs. So it was better for us to leave.

The arrangement turned out to be a master stroke. We remained a shareholder in the combined business, but they could run it differently and they took our $18 million of EBIT in Angola to $150 million the next year. We shot the lights out.

DUANE BIRKHOLTZ

Unlike most expats, I never actually joined Beer Division. After completing articles to become an accountant, I wanted to travel but my passport didn't allow it, so I went to work in Swaziland and became the financial manager of Coca-Cola alongside the brewery operation.

The company used to send expats into smaller operations like Lesotho and Swaziland, where you couldn't really cock it up that badly, and if you made it there, you would be moved to the bigger operations.

I spent time in Botswana with the late John Harris, who had started about a month before. Johan de Kock was the ops/commercial sales and marketing guy, and Alex Pretorius was doing distribution.

Before John started, he had come down to Swaziland for a Coke conference. All the bottlers were there. I hadn't really met him. He told me to come for a beer. All I can remember is that Harris, de Kock and I scrummed everybody in the pub, all over the tables and chairs, and caused chaos.

John had come from Beer Division where he had a lot more resources, and he would tell guys he wanted this, and this, and this. We would have to tell him we could do all these things but not all at the same time. He had been there about six months when we had an EXCO meeting, and he was pissed off because nobody was doing the 20 things he wanted done. We had a heated debate about it for about three or four hours. At the end of it, he said he had heard everything, now we could have a beer. We began drinking.

The following morning, my wife woke up and came looking for me. I had made it into the spare room, the first room I encountered in the house. We hadn't eaten anything. We had sat and drank until midnight.

To John's credit, he had then tempered his approach to: 'Ok, what can you do?' That was the thing with Breweries: you delivered what you promised. The rule was: 'I'm not going to tell you I'm going to do X, Y or Z, when I know I can't.'

The way the budget presentation worked was that Craig McDougall and Gert Nel would call us. They had a simplified Excel spreadsheet with various figures on it. They had a view of all the countries and would say we need 12 percent profit out of Botswana. You would go and work at it and then present it to them. We said we could make the 12 percent. The presentation started at 9.00 a.m. and finished at 10.00 a.m.

After they phoned us, John put the phone down and told the EXCO: 'That's the easiest budget presentation I've ever had. Let's go and celebrate.' By 11.00 a.m. we were in the bar drinking.

John was a character. He would overreact to everything. Everything was either completely red or completely black.

We had monster storms in Botswana. A big wind had blown over a pot plant in reception, which was in my department. He crapped on me about that. He would completely lose it and then an hour later walk into your office and invite you to play golf on Saturday.

At one stage, John decided unilaterally to put up the price of Hansa Pilsener by 5 percent. Volumes and revenue increased. But it was classed as semi-premium, no longer mainstream as it then was everywhere else. Head Office told us to drop the price back to what it had been.

John was a heavy smoker. De Kock and I would go into a meeting there with him and Pretorius. It was like being in a fog. When I got home at night, my wife would ask if I'd been to a pub. I said: 'No, I've been in Harris's office for three hours.'

During his tenure, we moved from the brewery closer to distribution into offices well kitted out with a smoke detector and sprinkler systems. It wasn't long before John was in there smoking and it triggered the system, which sprayed water everywhere. He phoned the health and safety people to come and disconnect it.

Shortly after John's untimely passing, Lon Mtongana came in. We had finished our budgets and had them signed off. The pula was then devalued by about 20 percent. It meant all our input costs went through the roof by 20 percent and our rand profit plummeted.

I did a rough calculation and phoned John Kirby. I told him that around 35 percent of our profits were now gone – and that was if we didn't lose volume, which could easily happen with increased prices. He asked me if I was sure. An hour later he phoned and said: 'We're coming tomorrow.'

The next day the jet arrived, and we had to redo the budgets with a profit forecast of zero. We came to doing our short-term incentive bonuses and I told McDougall that we had no chance of getting anything here. It was out of our hands.

I said: 'We aren't going to hit our sales volumes. Everything imported is going to go up'.

He said: 'Unlucky!'

At the end of that year was the smallest bonus I ever got in my life. KPIs were just not attainable.

One of the things we did was borrow money in Botswana and put it on call in South Africa at 8 percent, so my forward cover was zero. I phoned Cedric Becker, the treasury guy, and told him what I could do. He said it's not possible. I assured him I could do it. You could do things like that in SAB. If you came up with an idea, you could do it. Botswana was making money and producing cash, so we could do things.

We also had Chibuku reporting to us, but it was Wes Tiedt's empire. Chibuku, a packaged sorghum beer, made more money than the whole of Swaziland.

A Chibuku brewery was quite easy to set up and could make good money. Then a competitor came in with one or two brands. We called a meeting to work out what to do, but Wes was confident he had it sorted.

We agreed to meet again in a week. By then he already had the packaging and was launching four new brands. I said: 'You can't just launch stuff. Have you got all the registration requirements and trademarks and whatever?' He said he had all that stuff in his desk drawer. He had it all prepared way before.

The competitor came in selling at P1.70, compared to our selling price of P2.0. Wes launched four brands at P1.70. The competitor wanted 30 percent market share but was getting about 6 percent, which wasn't enough to keep going. Three months later they closed down and the brands were gone.

Ally

As we began to build a foothold in Kenya, Antonio Rossetti and I had jetted into Nairobi to meet Karume Investments, a potential distributor for SAB. We were planning to build a new brewery in Thika, 56 kilometres outside Nairobi, and were looking for a distributor to help us to purvey our brands, imported at the time, to begin to establish some traction for the future.

Driving through the city of Nairobi is not for sissies. After Lagos, it's the most hectic hustle and bustle traffic jam city in Africa.

I had been to Nairobi shortly before and was collected from the airport by the Holiday Inn shuttle to transfer to my hotel in the city centre. The driver was a friendly chap, and we began to converse about the world in general. He realised I was from South Africa and asked: 'What are those shiny things in the centre of the roads in South Africa?'

'Oh', I said, 'those are tigers' eyes.'

'We have similar shiny things here,' he said. 'They're giraffes looking out of potholes.'

The roads have several lanes, but neither lines nor rules. Antonio and I eventually made it to the high-rise Intercontinental Hotel. We left the cab and made our way towards the hotel entrance. A burly, friendly fellow wearing a top hat and tails adorned with badges and mementos, greeted us at the entrance and welcomed 'Mr Rossetti' by name. I realised Antonio had, as always, established a good rapport with people wherever he went.

Thinking nothing of the greeting and his connections, I checked in at reception and headed for room 1048. Swinging a cat in that room would be a challenge. I had to climb over the bed to get from one end of the room to the other and into the bathroom. I showered and gave Antonio a call.

'Did you perhaps reserve a meeting room for us?'

'No need', he said, 'come down to my room and we can meet here.'

'You must be joking,' I said. 'We'll all need to sit on corners of the bed and face inwards to discuss our potential partnership.'

I headed for room 1002 to discover a palatial suite with a lounge, kitchen and dining room table the size of a boardroom.

Karume got a very good impression of the two fellows from SAB, driven not just by their spritely personalities but, I guess, more so by the elegance of the suite in which we hosted the meeting.

Antonio told me that he paid the same rate for his room as I paid for mine. It's not what you know but rather whom you know.

Kenya was a 'hiccough on the road to Cairo'. We chose the wrong partner. We tried to smash our brand into the face of Kenyans who maybe weren't that keen on South Africa. There was arrogance, perhaps, in our approach.

We gained 9 percent of the market, but we couldn't break even. Companies like Heineken would work in a market at a loss for 10 or 15 years but still keep going. It was a pity that we never cracked Kenya.

While SAB was king of the Tanzanian market, with a share greater than 85 percent, next door in Kenya, Diageo had been a monopoly for more than 80 years and dominated that lucrative market with almost 100 percent share. Tusker was the bull bellowing in Kenya.

In 1997, we began to explore Kenya with more purpose and while Karume Investments was distributing a small quantity of Castle Lager and Castle Milk Stout, we decided to develop the greenfield brewing operation at Thika.

We worked to establish a focused business model and built a new brewery with a small expat community to begin our journey into Kenya. I worked with Stuart Scott, and, under the leadership of Roger Smith, we developed two new local beer franchises, Trophy Lager and Ranger Lager.

What we didn't realise at the time was the pronunciation of the dreaded 'r' in Kenya: our two new franchises became known as 'Tlophy' and 'Langer'.

Be that as it may, having experienced first-hand student riots near our Holiday Inn and teargas as part of the daily atmosphere, we got off to a start in a time of turmoil in Kenya.

We trained 150 operators to work in our new brewery and embarked on a fairly aggressive marketing campaign with Ogilvy Kenya as our partner.

Our entry into the market included Trophy and Ranger plus locally brewed Castle Lager and Castle Milk Stout.

We were most proud of our portfolio and particularly the brewing and packaging quality we achieved in the early weeks.

Part of our strategy was to introduce cold beer in Kenya, as previously consumers had only off-the-shelf beer that was 12°C at best, and mostly warmer. We bought and installed 200 fridges to get going.

Kenya Breweries (KBL) out-muscled us with about 2,000 fridges and some bullying tactics, particularly pressuring bars and outlets who stocked our brands and ripping down our point-of-sale material. Such deliberate spoiling tactics were new to us.

We had a share target ambition of twelve points after two years in the market. We managed to achieve only nine share points. Given the market conditions, that was an achievement in itself.

We decided to offer Diageo and Kenya Breweries a deal in East Africa: if they closed their Moshi plant in Tanzania, we would close our Thika brewery and relinquish local brewing in Kenya.

This was to my way of thinking an easy way out, a commercial decision that worked at that time, but ultimately the worst decision for our beer businesses on the African continent.

We had bust a gut to get to 9 percent and were beginning to get critical mass in certain areas and build pockets of loyalty, which could have turned the market in our favour. After KBL had monopolised the Kenyan market for more than 80 years, it was never going to be easy. Patience to play the longer game was key, in my view.

As it happened, one of the agreements reached in closing our respective breweries was that we would continue to distribute Tusker Lager in Tanzania and Kenya Breweries would continue to distribute Castle Lager in Kenya.

We were later to find out that any staff members in Diageo who were found drinking Castle Lager in the KBL operation were disciplined and banned from consuming it at all.

We also discovered that KBL had been operating with Serengeti Lager, our key competitor in Tanzania. It led to the breakdown of the entire East African agreement and an eventual fallout between us. The gloves came off.

Sadly, the fallout came too late. Thika's brewing equipment had been redeployed into other breweries across Africa and it was too late to re-establish a brewery foothold back in Kenya.

The key learnings for me included that sleeping with the enemy is never an option. We had rented Heineken and Amstel in South Africa and it came to haunt us later.

We now went into a wimpish coalition with Diageo and expected a different result.

However, we applied the good lessons we learnt from this experience in our continuing march northwards.

Robin

Building our brewery at Thika in Kenya got us a bloody nose; a lesson for us in moving into somebody's backyard. It was not a lot different from East African Breweries which had Kibo Breweries in Moshe, where we did the same to them.

It's very difficult to break into a market where an established player has very strong brands. That talks to the strength of a brand portfolio.

The learning from Kenya was that we went in with Castle Lager and Castle Milk Stout initially and the Kenyans saw those as South African brands. The Kenyans have quite a strong patriotic view and disliked South Africa. They saw it as the big bully on the continent. In Tanzania our strength was that we had local brands.

You also need a lot of patience. It was a lesson we learnt from Heineken when it was our partner in South Africa. They had a 10-year view of building the business, not a three-year vision. It takes time. If you rush it, it just doesn't happen. A new brand needs about seven years to build a consumer franchise, with a strong marketing investment behind it, let alone making sure the proposition works and you deliver the quality. Perseverance is key to building brand equity.

Moçambique made $80 million a year. For us, operations like it were rats and mice but people would give their eye teeth for businesses like that. In a normal world, an $80 million business is as good as you're ever going to see.

Ally

In Africa generally, we assumed that not everything was going to work perfectly everywhere, and that it would take time. But if the proposition was right, why would it not succeed?

Africa was growing. It had lots of young people. They were all urbanising. While they drank few of our beers, we had to assume there was a desire for them. The maths was simple. Per capita consumption was just 10 litres per annum. The global average was 35. And there was a strong desire among all of those 10-litre drinkers to get up to 35 if they could move away from the home brew. Plus, GDP growth was 5 or 6 percent.

Brands were a huge premium in African markets. What was termed a mainstream brand was an expensive purchase per serve per dollar. In the US, beer's cost has little relevance to the consumer; in Africa it's a big purchase decision. A dollar for a beer is a big expense when you're earning $2 to $3 a day.

For us, it was about getting some of the people to the entry level of beer and then to mainstream, which was effectively premium.

In Moçambique in 1995, SAB acquired both the Laurentina and the MacMahon Breweries, which became known as Cervejas de Moçambique (CDM).

We reinstated the Maputo brewery after it had been closed for some 30 years. It was home to rats as big as cats and most of its equipment was in need of serious repair or upgrade, if not replacement.

In the true spirit of SAB, we restored it to working condition and began to brew 2M, a beer named in tribute to former French president Marie Edme' Patrice Maurice, Comte de MacMahon. In 1875, in a dispute with Britain over which of the two countries should be with possession of southern Moçambique, he decided in favour of Portugal.

2M was a crisp, flavourful and fruity light lager originally brewed in a 550 ml bottle that bore no label and was identifiable only by its crown. It looked a bit like a hand grenade. My good friend Craig MacDougall told me that there was no need for any marketing input: the queues outside our brewery in Maputo were lined up for more than two days waiting for beers to come off the production line

Around late 1996 the brewery began to catch up to the demand and the lines outside the gate began to dwindle.

It was then that Craig gave me a call and suggested I fly to Maputo to offer the benefits of my prowess at marketing, which was hardly his passion.

My immediate insight was that a label would be a great starting point for our marketing journey. I set about briefing a design that captured both the heritage of the brand and the spirit of the people of Moçambique, at that time a country with perhaps the lowest gross domestic product per capita earnings in the world.

We came up with designs for both 2M and Manica, our brand brewed in Beira in the north of Moçambique, and after a few iterations and some research, settled on a design. We prepared final art and went to print.

In my view, this was to be a journey of epic proportions to build from scratch a brand that had really been a commodity, but which had been quenching the thirst of Moçambique's people and visitors from South Africa for more than 30 years. We were ready to bowl over the consumer with our new packs.

Or were we? After printing and airfreighting the labels to Maputo and Beira, I was excited to see how the pack was being accepted in the market. About ten weeks later, I asked a friend who was heading for Maputo to buy a few bottles of 2M so that I could see how locals might perceive it.

I found the bottles still had no label and were identifiable only by the crown and the 550 ml bazooka resemblance of the bottle.

I decided to pay Craig a surprise visit and one Tuesday stepped into his office unannounced. He was taken aback, his face lined with guilt and embarrassment. He had decided to hold off on the label for as long as possible to save an additional twelve dollars per hectolitre on label costs for the shareholders.

The rest is history. I did not leave the brewery until the labels were running. Today 2M is a standout brand that represents the vibrancy and spirit of a nation on the rise; a colourful brand that speaks to the spirit of Moçambique and its people.

Zambia, a market with a structure and consumer dynamics not dissimilar to South Africa's, became another jewel in our African story under Mick Marriot and later Roger Smith.

Mosi Lager, which depicted the country's seventh wonder of the world, the Victoria Falls, was an icon in Zambia and Zimbabwe, a refreshing 'pride in provenance' brand that took its name from *Mosi oa tunya* – vernacular for 'the smoke that thunders',

I made a point of drinking local beers on my journey to countries to work in marketing to show support for their pride notwithstanding my passion for Castle Lager and Castle Lite, and always looked forward to enjoying a Mosi with the team when we met in Lusaka.

The powers that be in the early days told me that Castle Lager would not work in Zambia, but I did some research and discovered that Zambians had an allegiance to South Africa. Many exiles in the days of apartheid had lived there. The brand reached a 30 percent share in months and eventually went on to become the market leader in Zambia, and very profitable.

We later introduced the COSAFA Castle Cup which became an annual event that helped countries in Southern Africa not only to compete against one another but to develop their national football teams to compete globally.

It also cemented Castle Lager's links with the passion point that is Southern African football and built brand equity as a powerhouse in Southern African countries.

In Ghana, we opposed Diageo and Heineken combined. We went from a weak number three to a pathetic number two and were making a loss.

We bought a water business to generate some cash flow and then turned it all around and became the biggest brand in the country with Club Premium Lager. We started making $30 million a year there and built a new brewery.

In Nigeria we had established a footprint. We had our old brewery, the new brewery, and Castel's Ilesha brewery. Suddenly we had true scale.

When we went into Uganda and were based in Jinja, we had about 35 percent market share with Nile Special and Club in competition with East African Breweries' Tusker.

By the time Nic Jenkinson retired from Uganda we had reached about a 55 percent market share.

Our brewery there was built effectively in one line: silo towers to utilities to raw materials to brewing to packaging and to the warehouse. From their offices, management could see the entire process. It was very efficient.

My colleague Stuart Scott and I flew into Entebbe, Uganda one Monday evening. Aircraft damaged in the Israeli raid on Entebbe Airport in 1976 still lay burnt out on an old strip alongside the current runway, a testament to the devastating human atrocities the country had suffered. We had no idea what to expect and were perhaps not that well prepared.

We were met after customs by a team of formidable looking bodyguards who escorted us to two black four-wheel-drive armour plated Nissan Patrols in the car park.

Our journey to Jinja, source of the Nile, took close on three hours and we discovered only later that the jungle around us was the most dangerous 100-mile strip of road in Africa. Killings and kidnappings were targeted particularly at *mzungus*, white businessmen like ourselves who were willing to risk the journey.

Close to midnight we arrived at a very modest guest lodge on the river and checked into our rooms. Throughout the night, we could hear the river's torrential rapids.

Breakfast in the morning was more modest than the room. We settled for toast and a banana and headed to our newfound business that brewed Nile Special Lager from the waters of the Nile.

There we met the members of the Madhwani family, who owned some seven percent of the GDP of Uganda, and set about reviewing the current marketing strategy and the opportunity to bring some of our brands, like Castle Lager, into Uganda.

We were later to discover that the local shareholders were less than inspired by our South African brand franchises and were to continuously boycott these brands from the outset, in favour of local brands that had been developed on their watch.

Our hunger pangs grew through the day. We were offered little beyond the Rwenzori Water that our new partners owned.

After a long day, we returned to the lodge for a lukewarm shower before a meeting with the managing director, Henry Rudd, at a local recently completed pizzeria. Henry, cousin of British actor, Hugh Grant, was the ultimate host and looked like Hugh in many ways. In fact, we could have made a movie that night.

Henry was delighted that a new pizzeria had opened. The cuisine in Jinja was rather limited. We placed our order for a salami, a mushroom and a four-cheese. 'Sorry', we were informed. 'The pizza oven is not yet operational – goat meat is the meal of the day.' We declined.

Instead, we consumed copious volumes of Nile Special at 7.5 percent alcohol by volume from 500 ml bottles, a big leap up from Castle Lager at 5.0 percent.

There was a stage in the conversation when Stu and I heard a loud thud. Henry had fallen between us in the middle of an epic story, headfirst onto the floor. We picked him up and, after dusting himself off, he continued his story as if nothing had happened. Henry was never short of words; he was an entertainer of note.

Another long day passed before we returned in the late afternoon for the three-hour journey to Entebbe, once again running the gangster gauntlet with an entourage in tow. When we eventually boarded our plane, I thought Stu was going to swallow his bread roll in its cellophane wrapping.

From the outset, Castle Lager was destined for failure in Uganda and showed that local belief and conviction were always key criteria for success.

On future trips to Uganda, we took our own non-perishables to ensure our sustenance, and the odd gift for Henry to accompany his Nile Special.

South Sudan became independent during Robin Goetzsche's tenure there, the newest independent country in the world. We launched a product with a similar approach to Hero, called White Bull, and built a little brewery in Juba. Sadly, when the civil war escalated we had to mothball it.

Namibia, to the north-west of South Africa and the most sparsely populated country in the world after Greenland, was from 1884 a colony known as German South West Africa and survived several stages of colonisation in the late 19th century until gaining its independence and its name change to Namibia in 1990.

German culture and traditions remain. It's a slice of Germany in Africa. German heritage is nowhere less evident than in the Ohlthaver and List families, who owned and managed Namibian Breweries and other lucrative business ventures.

For decades, SAB tried in vain to acquire a brewing licence. Eventually it was allowed only to import non-returnable bottles to the country, in terms of a law passed to protect Namibia Breweries and backed by Sam Nujomo, the president of the day. He was given seven farms to ensure that the brewery was protected.

Over time, SAB managed to gain some sales traction by launching a less profitable non-returnable bulk pack in a market similar to South Africa's, where more than 80 percent of beer consumption was from bulk returnables.

After conducting a usage and attitude study in the country in 2000, we realised that in truth Castle Lager was a bigger seller in the city of Windhoek than Windhoek Lager itself.

We decided to test German humour. We secured a prominent billboard on a bridge between a residential suburb and the industrial area where Namibia Breweries had their plant.

Our campaign began with a billboard depicting a magnificent 'pack and brag' shot of Castle Lager with the headline 'Windhoek's Lager'. The reaction was akin to World War Three. A photo of the billboard appeared on the front page of the Republikein, Allgemeine Zeitung, and other publications. The battle lines were drawn.

The case was referred to the Advertising Standards Authority. After ten days, we were asked to remove our ad.

We still owned the site and proceeded to post a second billboard in the series. Again, it depicted the shot of Castle Lager. The new headline: 'Windhoek's Bitter'. The spin-off was again dramatic, and many publications featured the now famous billboard on their front pages.

Back to court and a further 10 days before we were asked again to remove the advert.

We moved on to the next posting in our sequel. We had entered Castle Lager in the World Brewing Competition at Burton-Upon-Trent in England that year and, not surprisingly, won the award for the World's Best Bottled Lager. Our third post in the series thus featured our pack and brag shot with a headline: 'Castle Lager voted best Bottled Lager in the World'.

This was a little more difficult for Namibia Breweries to contest, but 20 days later we were again asked to remove this advert on the argument that Burton-Upon-Trent might not necessarily have represented the world cup of brewing contests.

The billboard rental agreement was still in our name, and we moved to chapter four of our campaign with a magnificent visual and the headline: 'You can't make a great beer from sour grapes.' The media frenzy continued and the exposure within the small community of Namibia had tongues wagging.

The final straw would have been when we replaced our fifth posting with a visual of a wooden table sporting a Castle Lager bottle and glass, superimposed with the headline: *Maak seker daar is a Castle op die Tafel* (make sure there's a Castle on the table). Tafel – meaning 'table' – Lager was the flagship brand of Namibia Breweries. It went down like a lead balloon among the opposition.

Norman Adami, managing director at the time, suggested we hold back on that billboard for a while. He was worried that I would end up in a Windhoek jail.

Before we had presence in a lot of African countries, Antonio Rossetti was the company's exports manager, selling beer into many sub-Saharan African countries.

ANTONIO ROSSETTI

I went to places like Rwanda, Kenya and Angola regularly, and to Mauritius, Madagascar, and even to the Isle of Mayotte in the Comores. I saw places that I had not even known existed. I was there before SAB really arrived. It was a privilege.

The people I met were often suspicious about alcohol. They saw it as something often used to hide other dubious things.

The toughest but most interesting market was Angola. It was like a sponge. Whatever you put in there just disappeared. At one stage, we were selling more than a million hectolitres of Castle Lager there annually.

Angola was probably the toughest country in which to travel. It had just come through a civil war and there were soldiers everywhere. They would confiscate anything they thought might have value. They took my phone away unless I paid a $100 bribe.

Wayne McCauley went to Africa around June of 2014.

WAYNE McCAULEY

Wow, what a time! I had a dual role. I had seven Southern African countries in which to set up their sales and distribution strategies. I had established a sales and distribution team and we had our MDs in the countries. Mark Bowman's leadership made a big difference. He was really a long-term player and had an exceptional level of maturity about him.

I loved the time there and really enjoyed working for Mark, a keep-it-simple, straightforward, very decent human being, with exceptional vision.

We were on a difficult assignment. The country MDs had strong autonomy and marketing were there to build processes to help them, not to take over. It was a delicate balance. I think we did that exceptionally well by understanding the people.

The thrusts we implemented were about penetration, where to go via wholesalers and where to go with direct delivery, and we knew exactly where we were at any time.

I think we were adding great value and that was done in two years. We built up huge capability and I think Mark acknowledged it ... both on the brands side and in sales and distribution.

I loved the people and the countries. I had a great respect for the conditions they were living under. And in that environment, where you feel you are adding immense value and you're all working exceptionally long hard hours and travelling away from home, the camaraderie was something I had never before experienced.

We had freedom but at the same time were building something great. Mark gave us that latitude and we always respected it. I don't believe that we went off the boil even for a second. It was sad that it was just too short.

When Andrea Quaye left Unilever, she told herself there was one company she wanted to work for, and it was SAB. The HR department said there were two positions: one at Beer Division, the other in Africa.

ANDREA QUAYE

The African role was a lot more defined. André Parker was the CEO at the time, and it was a very pragmatic environment. It was really about consulting and helping the countries.

I worked on several segmentations and a few new product development projects and learnt a lot about execution. I travelled two or three times a month, but this was not as much as the others.

Moçambique always stood out for me. The people there were really dedicated. The brands they built, like 2M, did well from the beginning. Their marketing wasn't highly strategic or very clear, but they managed to build great brands.

2M was built on painting walls and creating the 2M world. That's why it is such a successful brand.

A lot of best practices came out of those countries. In Tanzania, Safari and Kilimanjaro were brands that really stood for pride in origin. There was so much of that, and it was colourful, expressive and vibrant. You just didn't over-think stuff. It was simple.

It wasn't about the TV ad; it was about how you executed in the trade. With so many constraints a lot of creativity came out of those markets.

We were welcome there. I remember travelling to locals' homes and being welcomed by their wives and staying with them. They were really kind people.

Uganda's drawback was just that drive from Entebbe to Kampala. We would stay over at the hotel in Entebbe at the lake, with the thinnest mattresses I have ever slept on. Some of the African hotels we went to were terrible.

Ally

If you stood still in Uganda for too long, you would start growing because everything grew in Uganda. Nile and Club were beautiful brands.

Andrea

I remember travelling also to Ethiopia, Algeria and Morocco with Henry Rudd. We were looking at a merger or acquisition opportunity there, buying a water business, and we met the Castel group. Every day we would go out to lunch. There would be 20 or 30 of us sitting around this white tablecloth and we'd be served wine. We were a beer company looking to buy a beer business or a water business, but we were served wine.

As the lady in the party, I would be seated alongside Monsieur Castel. They loved that I could speak French. They used to call me 'angel' (with the French pronunciation). Obviously, they had forgotten my name and I was nicknamed Angel. If you speak to Henry Rudd now, he'll call me Angel.

Neil Hobkirk joined the African journey only much later, towards the end, but found it had definitely embraced that culture of SAB.

NEIL HOBKIRK

You could see the culture imbued in all of those countries. All that purpose, those principles, that excellence that had been unbelievably successful in Africa.

SAB believed in Africa before anyone else on the continent, because we came from Africa, and we understood its potential. We worked and grew up in emerging markets. In SAB, we spent most of our spare time in the townships.

It was 70 to 80 percent of our business. So we were all completely familiar with that environment, its flow, its dynamic.

Across Africa, there are obviously different languages and cultural nuances, but the fundamental African-ness is real. You had all these South Africans going to live in African countries, sometimes in the most atrocious conditions to begin with, and in some of the most difficult operating environments in the world.

I've spent a lot of time in Nigeria over the last five years. In running a business there, you have no idea what you're dealing with. I think the devil lives in hell and rents out Onitsha.

Operational conditions, just in basic infrastructure, were unbelievably difficult; just getting a truck from here to there, going to do a promotion. Some of the places are quite dangerous.

When we were running our business in South Sudan, it was a war-torn and very dangerous country. So was Moçambique in the early days. Nigeria is still pretty dangerous in many parts of the country. Our guys just went there and hit it out the park.

The whole of SAB has just been one wonderful experience for me, with some pain and disappointments along the way, but in the main the whole thing has just been the most unbelievable journey. It changed me as a person and transformed my life financially.

We used to get on that plane and fly around Africa. It was the best time of my entire working career, those two years. We knew we were going out to embrace a continent, with all its people and all its cultures.

I had the feeling that I was sitting on the front seat of history.

Snow
in China

China: officially the People's Republic of China. The world's most populous country, with a population of more than 1.4 billion. It spans five geographical time zones and borders 14 different countries. Doing business there was not easy.

ANDRÉ PARKER

It was a bliksem. We had immense challenges there. It was really difficult, and we had to throw some of our rule books out of the window.

We entered China as a 49 percent partner with a government-owned company, China Resources Enterprises (CRE). We were the only overseas brewer successful there and we made that company the biggest brewer and brand in the word (even though it made less money than Botswana).

China was a like a different planet. You couldn't speak to the customers or the CEO. Everything required an interpreter. The Chinese were bright. They were lots of little Norman Adamis. The CEO, Yuma Wang, was just like a Chinese Adami; a hard guy who knew all the detail of everything. You didn't interfere on his turf.

I remember attending a meeting with him one frozen morning in Shenyang up in the northern rust belt. We arrived to find Yuma ill, so sick that he was sitting at the conference table with a drip in his arm. He was smoking.

Because it was such an unusual and difficult joint venture, Graham remained on the board of directors, as did the chairman of CRE, and came to China religiously to attend most board meetings. Mostly, though, he let us get on with the job.

One morning after an evening of many toasts of *ganbei* and downing a lot of terrible, liquidised burnt rubber stuff called *maotai* at some sort of banquet, Graham's wife Bev had to prop him up against the wall to dress him.

Like Africa, China was more than one market. It was very regional. The country has massive cities, and every city is almost a market on its own. In the beginning, we had three breweries. By the time we left we had more than 50, dotted all over the map. If there was a city without a brewery, we built one there.

We made bugger-all money. It was all being reinvested. But when the footprint had been established, we began to reap rewards.

We followed a unique approach to brand building. There was no research to it. Our original brand was Snowflake, and we decided every brewery would make and sell it. To meet local preferences, we allowed numerous variants, like Snowflake light, medium, heavy and dark, all with different alcohol contents. They used to drive us mad. Dave Carruthers came across from time to time to teach them about branding. He would dissolve into a mess at the after-work drinks.

We had a real clash of cultures there. I remember flying 12 hours to Hong Kong for a one-day meeting and flying 12 hours back because of some crisis. The Chinese needed and wanted us basically for the technical stuff, the brewing manuals and the like. But they were Chinese. They learnt quickly and adapted.

They would buy a new German state-of-the-art brewhouse. The next one they would make themselves, not particularly well, but by the third or fourth attempt, they would have something pretty close to the original for a third of the price.

That was what made it great working on the strategic stuff with Gert Goedhals and Graham. Gert would sometimes say: 'Let's consider for one minute that they might be right, and we might be wrong with our brand strategies.'

We tried to win a place for Miller Genuine Draft in the market there, but they had a different MGD in the east from the MGD in the west, and we had to adapt to their ways as we did in Africa. They were clever, independent-thinking people, and while we used the best of what we knew and our experience, our eyes were opened to the need for local expertise and ultimately to have locals running the business. That's what made us successful in China.

We sent some good SAB people there – Roy Bagattini, Chris Barrow, Johan Krige – but it was really difficult going out with a rep without understanding what he or the customer was saying. You couldn't even read the brochure on the brand.

We had long meetings in smoke-filled rooms discussing conceptual stuff which, the Chinese tell you, doesn't work for them. It was best just to go with what they said. You could tell them this is the way to do it, and we would bring them to South Africa to see how we did it, and they would accept one or two ideas. Then they would simply revert to the way they thought it should be done.

In the human resources arena, when you talked about pension schemes and share options and medical aid, their eyes glazed over. They had none of that. It was a pretty autocratic, top-down sort of operation. Performance management was never a viable prospect. Processes like that were much easier to implement in Africa.

We were a big user of McKinsey. Some would say we overdid it. I would say we didn't use McKinsey much in Africa, but I think our use of McKinsey expressed our desire to be up there with the best, and world class. They brought us a lot of good stuff. Particularly in the isolation years, it was good that we got that sort of input.

GARTH SAUNDERS

I the due diligence for the first brewery bought in China. I told Malcolm Wyman in China: 'I have no idea. If you want to buy it, buy it. I can't tell you.'

I think there were issues, but they were impossible to work out. I fell asleep in every meeting. We asked the guys how many bottles in a crate and twenty minutes later they'd tell you the crates were brown.

I went to the GM there. I said: 'I'd like to see the title deeds of the land.' He said there were no such things in China.

'How do you expect us to buy an asset?'

He said: 'Come back, come back tomorrow.'

So I went back tomorrow and he said: 'Okay, here's a letter.'

I read the letter. It said this is the name of the brewery and it is entitled to the property that it stands on for the rest of its years. It was signed by the GM. I said: 'But you signed this.'

'Yes', he tells me, 'but I'm the government's representative.'

That's when you know you've been outplayed. But we bought it.

MAURICE EGAN

I did due diligence in Shenyang. There were two of us. I was to do the technical bits and Philip Hall was to do the financial piece. We were flown to Hong Kong and stayed at the Hilton.

We were among the first into China since the Americans had gone into Manchuria in World War II. When we landed in Shanghai, they had never seen round eyes. The kids in the street were touching the hem of my clothes.

While still in Hong Kong, the McKinsey folk who were the integrating consultant, warned us: 'Enjoy your meal here because by the time you reach China the food is going to be a little bit dodgy. You're there for three nights and we'll meet you back here.'

So we went. Shenyang has a population of about ten million. It's a big city. You couldn't see it for the smog. Every now and again the ground would shake from the occasional earthquake. It was just a mess.

Phillip and I had decided to do this together. We flew in an Air China propeller-driven aircraft, white knuckled, with about four other passengers and two Chinese hostesses. For whatever reason, they decided to put us in front of two Chinamen, who after half an hour started to evacuate their nostrils into the vomit bag. Blurrgh.

I just lost it. I stood up and said: 'F... you two. You don't understand English, but move, move!'

That's what you saw in the streets of Shanghai. You had to step over these pavement oysters. In restaurants, they had a typical South African braai grid roasting either a little Chihuahua or some other small dog. That was what they were doing in 1993.

At the brewery, we sat in a meeting without air-conditioning. The place was hot and the Chinese all smoked. When they felt hot, they'd roll their shirts up like a Bentley belt above their tits and they'd be smoking away, and the translations would be going on, and you just knew this wasn't going the way you wanted it to go, and they were just telling you shite.

As you walked around the place you saw that there were three times the number of people there than were needed, and the numbers they were sharing with you were silly, because the lines weren't running or, if they were running, they were running too slowly, and people were getting in the way of each other.

Then disaster hit. I got the runs. I had to excuse myself and go to what they called the bathrooms. Picture a dormitory with stalls, no doors. The stalls are essentially up to your hip. You could have a lekker chat, if you spoke the language, to the lassie next to you. There was no separate male or female.

There was a hole in the ground. You're desperately worried as you dropped your rods that your passport and wallet could fall in the hole and never be seen again. That fixed my runs. I don't think I even farted. I hit the Hilton Hotel three days later and exploded.

Those were pioneering days. We bought the brewery in the end, despite our recommendations.

By the time I went to work in Woking, just outside London, we had 100 Chinese breweries. We were buying breweries with CRE at a rate of one a month. We had a hundred breweries in China and 106 elsewhere in the world.

The thing about China was that it was a long, long game. You had to be there because the belief was that the economics would come right, but maybe in 20 or 30 years. As the population became a little affluent, they would be able to spend a few more renminbi on beer.

Most brewers – Lion Nathan, Coors, Heineken – were there and making about a dollar a hectolitre. You needed to make three dollars a hectolitre to make it viable. That was the magnitude of it. They all went in on their own and tried to force their homegrown brands down the throats of the Chinese. Inevitably, they all left.

Our joint venture strategy made Snow the biggest sales volume of beer the world had ever seen; around 100 million hectolitres plus per annum.

There were variances though. Even with one Snow there were variants because the Chinese would just copy, paste and move on. There was no love for the past when it came to embracing the old labour and manufacturing processes. They just grabbed, took and improved as they ran forward.

André

While grappling with challenges in China, we gained additional learnings in the massive sub-continent of India. We bought Shaw Wallace & Company Limited, abbreviated to SWC. It was an Indian liquor manufacturer headquartered in Wallace House in Kolkata, West Bengal.

We cleaned up the business and built the odd brewery there. Richard Rushton spent five years there.

It was a tough place for expats but there was brilliant Indian talent. Talk about acceptance of new processes and performance management, man, those boys ran with that stuff. They were English speaking, well-educated and bright as buttons.

We just needed to kick it on for bigger volumes against, in those days, still a lot of anti-alcohol sentiment. Some states banned alcohol totally. Others taxed it out of existence.

The real issue, though, was corruption. I had to tell the people in London at one stage that we would not be able to do anything in India without a facilitator. You can't get a car licence without paying somebody to stand in a queue, or for someone to stamp the document. We did things through facilitators who were often ex-army generals. That's what they did. They had the contacts. The whole of India worked like that.

John Mancer, our non-executive director, understood it and at one stage came with me to India. We asked ourselves if we could do business there and live up to the ethics we profess to have. We worked out a system where, because we couldn't pay a facilitator in cash, he had to give us an invoice, which had to be auditable, and we would use him to do something positive, like advise us on local conditions, lobby for us, or help us to see the local minister. They didn't take big amounts, but they relied on the odd handout here and there.

The real issue in India was to grow the beer market. It was still quite small when I left.

Ally

It was very complex. To sell beer in a state you had to build a brewery in that state. And produce labels in that state. We brought in Foster's and some of our other global brands.

André

So the business was profitable in a small way, but it didn't live up to the potential that we thought a billion-plus market would give us. I think it's still a small beer market.

16

Bavaria Magic
in Colombia

In 2005 SABMiller, by then the world's number two brewer, moved into Latin America in a merger with the Colombian company, Bavaria SA, controlled by the Santo Domingo family.

SIMON HARVEY

I was lucky enough to be a member of the due diligence process ahead of it, we were looking at four countries: Colombia, Peru, Ecuador and Panama. The due diligence group, mostly South Africans, was split into two. I was in the Colombia and Panama team. Robin Goetzsche and Ian Penhale were in the Peru and Ecuador team.

Goetzsche was laughing at Penhale and me (neither of us was South African). On our first day we had training on what happens if you're kidnapped. South Africans were a little more worldly about that sort of thing.

Three companies were showing interest: Carlsberg, Heineken and SAB. We were the last of the three to visit Colombia. Two groups of eight of us flew in on two different planes. We didn't want everybody on one plane. I remember going through Miami customs at number five in our queue.

The first one goes through, and the customs guy says you have been randomly selected for a search, the second one was told you have been randomly selected for a search, and so it went. By the time it got to me I said: 'I suppose I have been randomly selected for a search?'

He said: 'Don't get cheeky with me, son.'

'Why are six South Africans going down to Colombia?' he asks. Imagine what they might be thinking about us. We had gone in the guise of an IT company, intending to look at the systems structure inside Bavaria. That was our cover.

What probably gave us an edge in the negotiations was that the Bavaria management team realised we weren't the same as the teams that had been there in the month prior.

On our first night in Bogota, like typical South Africans, we went out to a restaurant. The Heineken people never went anywhere other than from the hotel to the brewery. They didn't go into the trade. We didn't want to go to the formal trade; we wanted to see the mamas and papas to understand how alcohol was consumed on the ground.

When the decision was made, Julio Mario, father of the Santo Domingo family, said he chose SAB because of the company culture, and I think that was true of a lot of acquisitions.

For eight weeks we shuttled in and out of Colombia, to and from Miami, and probably did look a little like drug mules. Every time we came into Miami, you were taken into the back by US customs. Why had you been to Colombia? Why had you been there three times? Etc.

Then you drop the pretence, you go in with the real story. You don't want to be found lying to US customs.

The crown in the deal was the Colombian business. When we bought it, it was making about $3 million or $4 million per annum. After four or five years, Karl Lippert and his team pushed that up close to a billion dollars, as a single business. It was astonishing how they were able to take over our processes and procedures.

Those were the reasons we were successful in our acquisitions: people and processes. What we were really good at was going into a company and making the brewing process and the route-to-market process pump, on top of all of the issues.

In eight weeks, we had to understand the business and build a business case for the following three years to allow the mergers and acquisitions team to make an offer. We were working 12 to 18 hours a day, Saturdays and Sundays. We learnt a helluva lot. We worked hard and played hard in a non-hierarchical organisation, and we believed in the product.

On the third night in Bogota, we were invited to dinner with the Bavaria directors. We had to go with equal numbers. We went with five and they brought five.

In a fancy restaurant in Bogota, they ordered five whiskies. They believed that senior people didn't drink beer. We ordered five beers. For us, it was all about our brands.

BARRY SMITH

A guy called Craig Stewart came across from Coke to Latin America for a while. We were having dinner in a hotel somewhere. We were new there and Rob Priday claimed he could speak six languages: English, Afrikaans, German, Polish, Spanish and …

He was about to mention the sixth when Craig interrupted … 'Ja, but you talk the same kak in all six.'

GRANT HARRIES

Colombia was by far number one in the world. Being MD came with a lot of stress. Every 10,000 hectolitres lost was a million US dollars off our EBITDA, so we would have weekly updates and as soon as I saw sales going that way, we'd call the team in and cut our cloth accordingly so we could keep up with the results.

It was very sensitive for all the analysts. They were my first-hand friends. They'd phone me monthly, if not more often. When things were not going well, we would have to make some adjustments or tell people it was not going to be a good month.

One month we lost 100,000 hectolitres, so that's $10 million. Boysie (Boyce Lloyd, Managing Director Honduras) was in Honduras at the time. He said: 'Jeez, Grant, with those numbers you've just blown three months of Honduras's operating profit.'

Hence it came with a lot of big responsibilities. Financial guys would be phoning from London, Alan Clark would be calling. The whole world would be phoning just for reassurance. But to be fair, when it was going well, they also phoned.

In 2015, Colombia delivered $1,3 billion EBITDA. Full marks go to Karl Lippert and Richard Rushton who put everything in place. I just had to leverage that.

We applied some good enhancements but, as Karl used to say, it was like trying to get an elephant to dance. The locals weren't very good at getting things done and I'm a guy who needs to get things done, not to analyse and paralyse.

Once we were 70 percent or 80 percent along on implementing what I thought was a good idea, we would go ahead with it. The system struggled because they weren't used to getting such an easy 'go'. They would say, let's go and do some more work on this. I said: 'No, we can work on this forever, let's do something real now.' I think that helped, and we got a lot of things done.

We had five South Africans on our team. We all lived in the same suburb behind an entry boom. One of the guys said: 'You all live there. I'm going to need a visa to come and visit you. It's like little Pretoria.'

I met a lady who was in government there and we were out one evening. She said: 'I suppose you corporate guys are wanting to get rid of the *Chiccas Aguila* (a team of pretty girls employed to promote Aguila, the local beer). That can't be so good for your guys based in London.'

I said: 'Yes, I was getting a little anxious about it.'

She said: 'They're part of society; you can't get rid of them. They've been around for years; they are revered, and we all love them.'

I said: 'I'm going to quote you,' and I got her name.

At the time of the FIFA World Cup in Brazil, we had a suppliers' convention attended by 500 people and we were handing out various awards. The *Chiccas Aguila* were there and the compère announced that the first one who could tell us the first names of the girls would win a miniature world cup football. Every single woman stood up and told us their names.

The latter stages of the *Chiccas Aguila* was a reality TV show through which the public voted for their favourite girls. The presidential election had been held three months before. Voter turnout was 37 percent for the presidential election. For the *Chiccas Aguila* it was 68 percent.

What I always loved about SAB was our involvement with sport. The only place we didn't do so was in Russia. We weren't a big enough player. We wouldn't really have got the benefit.

In Honduras, we owned a football club. We sponsored the Honduras and Colombian national teams, and we were involved with all the leagues. In Colombia we did some sponsorship of cycling with a malt-based soft drink.

We also supported communities with various projects like tree-planting initiatives in the jungles of Peru and Honduras and setting up nurseries in jungle areas. Those were big projects.

GAVIN HUDSON

In 2011, I was in Cape Town when Norman Adami called, telling me to fly to Johannesburg because he wanted to talk to me. I thought I was in trouble. Norman had this habit of phoning at odd times, like a Sunday evening, to ask how it was going with the trade and customers. I learnt afterwards that he had phoned those customers earlier in the weekend and asked them the same question. Norman told me there was an opportunity open and asked if I was prepared to move to Colombia.

The Colombian culture was very much a beer-drinking one; they also drink a lot of whisky and Aguardiente (a drink made from sugar cane and anise that has an alcohol content of 29 percent by volume). Unlike South Africa's 'rainbow nation', Colombians are all Spanish, all Catholic, and they look after their own.

The country has old-age homes. Old people are well looked after, whether they're your family's or someone else's.

Bogota stands on the Equator 3,000 m above sea level and has two types of weather. It's either raining, or it's about to rain. Daily temperatures hardly vary from 16°C to 19°C, but 40 minutes' drive away, down in the Amazon jungle, it rises to around 35°C.

We had a very sociable EXCO, with many internationals. The South Africans included Adam Swiss and Grant Harries. The guys supported each other, and we did a lot of good work together.

When I arrived in Colombia our market share was around 63 percent. When I left in 2015, we were up to around 75 percent. The light beer market, with Aguila Lite, had grown in a similar way to the Castle Lite story.

The famous *Chiccas Aguila* became real ambassadors for the brand. Everywhere we went the *Chiccas Aguila* were there. Everyone in the company got to know them. They came to head office. They opened every show and were at every football game.

In SAB we knew that this type of advertising or promotion didn't sit well with our friends in London, and they did try to stop them, but there was too much backlash from the community. They toned them down for a while but I'm not sure if they've stopped them completely. The legacy remains, though.

When I left South Africa, SAB was fiddling with telesales but hadn't consolidated anything. When I arrived in Colombia, we had 2,500 people working for us, in different regions with different processes, and we were struggling with orders, because we were looking after 450,000 customers compared to 35,000 customers in South Africa, maybe even fewer.

We had reps calling on 50 customers a day. The local outlets, known as *tiendas*, were relatively close, so a rep would go out on a bicycle or a scooter or literally walk the street. They weren't doing any merchandising or point-of-sale work; they were just taking orders.

We had around 12,000 order-takers who weren't really adding value and we were looking at premiumisation and introducing a light beer.

I presented the telesales concept to Karl Lippert and then to Richard, and after the fourth or fifth attempt finally convinced them. I had been to Mexico and found the software guys who could do it, essentially converting banking software. We launched it with a big risk, as we were going to take all our order-takers off the road.

We converted people from order-takers to reps. A lot of people were nervous about it, and we had a massive turnover, but we persevered. At an EXCO meeting I presented details of the progress to the EXCO and needed the go-ahead from Richard to implement a second phase.

Unexpectedly, he dug in his heels and said we would not go ahead. This was after he initially agreed. We had pulled the trigger and I was asking permission after the fact. I said he had given me his commitment and support and we would be doing it anyway. It was the only time I saw him throw his toys.

One of the technical team told EXCO he firmly believed that it was the right thing to do; he had been shown the progress and we had done the work. Every one of the EXCO members said they supported me. Richard left the meeting for about 20 minutes. Finally, he came back and said: 'Let's carry on.' That was the end of the discussion.

We implemented it, saved a huge amount of money, and improved our market and premium share. It wasn't long before it was rolled out across the globe and became a global benchmark. We grew our customer base and our revenue significantly.

As Bogota was seen to be the drug capital of the globe, many expats living there were from drug enforcement agencies in Australia, the US and the UK, all high-ranking young guys who were there to find out when drugs were moving to their countries and so stop them from entering. We made many friends among them, and we showed each other different sides of life in Colombia.

One year we took them to an October beerfest in Bogota attended by between 2,000 and 3,000 people, and invited them to join us at about 11.00 a.m. in our VIP tent.

By three in the afternoon, they were flying. A fellow named Paul Watt, who stood about six foot seven, was particularly inebriated. We had one of the most famous bands in Colombia playing at this event and he had met one of the female members in the crowd. When he saw her on the stage, not realising they were setting up to do their show, he bounded onto the stage to say hello.

As he did so she began singing. He found himself part of the act in front of thousands of fans. She played along and tried to make him part of the act. His colleagues never let him live it down.

The Colombians loved putting you in touch with successful and famous people, especially if you were senior in the company. We had this beautiful lady, Amini, who played pop music on a saxophone.

I think it was Grant Harries's birthday. We had built a new office in Colombia. The MD (they used to call him el Presidente) had his office on the top floor, nine storeys up, probably 100 to 150m^2 of office space with a view over the whole of Bogota.

One afternoon, after hours, they set up a surprise birthday party for Grant. The whole EXCO was invited, and we all knew what was going on, but Grant didn't. We arrived there and out came the beers with snacks and a birthday cake.

Amini arrived with her band in tow and gave us a private show to celebrate his birthday.

That was just how they rewarded the leadership. The *Chiccas Aguila* arrived, and everyone had a good time. They made a lot of effort for the important occasions, like farewells, birthdays, and things like that.

I spent a huge amount of time in the trade and in such a big country with so many customers I always felt I wasn't getting to the deep rural parts of the country. The roads were often terrible, if they existed at all.

People were scared to travel too far into outlying parts because there was always the risk of guerrilla activities. My security detail would never take me deep into the countryside.

Soon after I arrived there, I bought a motorbike, much to the disgust of the leadership. I was warned on a few occasions that I was contravening the security protocols.

But every weekend I was out somewhere on my machine.

Eventually I started riding with the corporate affairs director. Then I started a small group of bikers from amongst the guys who rode bikes to work, some bikes bigger than others. Every other weekend we had an outing in a group of 30 or 40, from floor sweepers to security guards to reps. For me it was wonderful to meet such a cross-section of people.

It eventually reached a stage where the corporate affairs director and I decided we'd like to see Colombia in its entirety. We put together a production with a film crew. There were six of us on bikes and we travelled literally to all four corners of Colombia. The film was less about the bikes than about the remote little villages that seldom, if ever, saw people from the cities.

We spent about four months doing it. Sometimes we'd ride to a destination, park our bikes at an airport, fly back and work for a week or two and then retrieve our bikes and go further. We put together a whole programme and visited the poorest of the poor in the most remote places you can imagine, on roads that were passable only on bikes. Everywhere we went they showed us tremendous hospitality.

DUANE BIRKHOLTZ

I was in Colombia from 2011 until 2016. When the move came to Colombia, I was working for the transformation team putting in Project Triumph and IT projects, at that stage trying to implement them in Ecuador.

Accounting had all been done at the head office. We then regionalised IT so that all IT contracts were done centrally. Then we moved into outsourcing and built a shared service centre at the airport. I never worked at the brewery itself.

With two small children, my wife and I didn't want an apartment, so we moved into a house in Bogota. Later Gavin Hudson moved into 'little Pretoria', as did Adam Swiss, Grant Harries and Janice Hallot.

We were at Santa Anna, between an army base on one side and an old village called Usquen on the other. There was only one road in, so it was almost like a gated suburb. Around us were all the politicians and army generals, so security was very good.

When the end came, the company wanted Harries and me to stay and we had three months to work; Harries to consult and me to work. The wives all left in November and we were there until December. The last two men standing.

We were like an old married couple. One night, our quiet night, we went for dinner and had six draughts and a bottle of red wine. That was a quiet night.

When ABInBev came in, the Colombians were devastated. If you talked to the guys at Bavaria, they were SAB people. They loved SAB and it was ingrained in the culture.

Our Brands:
our Lifeblood

The journey of brands goes back to the early days when marketing gurus around the world loved to work on cigarette and beer brands because of their sheer scale and nature.

South Africa was no different and we saw the emergence of strategic and creative geniuses from inside SAB and in our partner agencies.

Neil Hobkirk and I reflected on some of the giants of the advertising world.

We agreed that we had two great gifts who created a legacy of substance and power in our brands.

The first was Peter Savory, a friend of advertising legend David Ogilvy and a former journalist. He understood the power of communication. He was connected even while South Africa was disconnected for the reasons we know well. He used to visit David Ogilvy in his chateau in France. He and David, the guru of advertising in the world at that time, really hit it off.

These almost spiritual brand marketing personalities imbued everything in brands and brand marketing with perspective, substance and depth, and with advertising that would sell.

Linked to Peter was a genius, Bruce Starke. Technically he was the most capable marketing person we had ever met, anal as he was. He was truly an ad man; a marketing technician, hired from an advertising agency and strategically, conceptually, and insightfully brilliant.

We were taught very well without going on training programmes. We were infused with knowledge from these people.

We had this era of the greatest advertising people that the world has ever seen – and advertising agencies used to make a lot of money in those days after hiring the most creatively talented people.

South Africa had phenomenal advertising men like Brian Searle-Tripp and Roger Makin. We would walk into meetings as young Turks to be exposed to confirmed gurus, recognised as giants in the world.

We were surrounded by titans at every level. The work that came out of it was 'The Taste that's Stood the Test of Time'; 'Down a Lion. Feel Satisfied'; 'Biermanskap, Leeu Plesier'; 'Crack a Carling'; 'More Refreshment, More Reward at the End of the Day'; all some of the greatest advertising lines yet.

Carling Black Label was a great example of taking a social movement and really climbing inside it to transform a brand completely. SAB did so at a time when it was revolutionary and courageous to put your brand at the vanguard of the trade union movement and present it as the reward for the working class hero.

And even though we had so few brands, the differentiation was powerful. Lion vs Castle and Black Label, while Hansa began rattling the cage as the David of beers potting a few stones at the Goliaths and drawing distinctions between lagers and pilsners. Willie Sonnenburg was the guy who did the Hansa 'Accountants' commercial. Later came the Robin Putters of the world, then the Ashley Bacons and the Mark Fishers. They were the doyens, the second wave.

They were all respected. I don't know if the advertising and marketing world is respected today in the same way. These were the people driving the ideology of the company and influencing the ideology of the country. You don't have that same gravitas today.

There was a special relationship between SAB and Ogilvy. There was something in the DNA of the two organisations that said we're going to be around for a very long time and do things properly together.

TONY VAN KRALINGEN

I've thought a lot about brand marketing in the '80s and early '90s. It talks to how naïve we were at the time. We had three big brands that over the years would take the lead or swap positions. They never stayed number one for too long.

I took over Black Label, which had been number one in the late '70s and was disappearing fast; it had 14 percent and carried on dropping. And I had Amstel and Ohlsson's. The second brand group was Lion Lager and Hansa. The third was Castle Milk Stout and Castle Lager.

There were three group brand managers at the time: Hugh Noble, Jamie Semphill, and Tobin Prior. I had an assistant, John Olsen. That was the brand marketing team. We reported to Bruce Starke.

We called them mainstream brands and segmented brands. It was only in the late '90s that we thought about our portfolio in a more sophisticated way. We talked about core brands, premium brands, and brands with a different flavour.

When we started going international in the mid '90s, we worked out quickly that we were as good as most of our competitors in cost management, efficiencies, production and distribution.

In SAB there was always a cognitive dissonance; we were never happy with who we were. We always wanted to be better, to challenge ourselves. We went abroad to see who was doing what. All of us travelled abroad, before the company went international, to look at other operations.

In 1989, Robin Goetzsche and I took two agency guys and went to Miller, Anheuser-Busch, and Coors, the three big names in the US, and to their agencies, and tried to work out what we could do better.

The marketing guys would hate me for saying it, but the engine of SAB in the '70s, '80s and early '90s was its operating excellence, underpinned by sound management accounting. We trusted the numbers we were given, and that management accounting along with our distribution and manufacturing capability provided a solid platform when we went abroad to compete. We always had management accounting processes to manage any untoward intention or activity. Great governance was part of the ethics of the company.

At that time, the brand guys had to go to each of the regions to sell their ideas and get buy-in. It wasn't often that they got a thumbs-down. It was more a consultative process so that brands could think about whether they were on the right track.

If you didn't listen, your promotion would probably not go well. If you listened and adjusted, it would probably succeed. In a sense it limited our creativity because we were always held to account by people who wanted volume quickly, so it narrowed what you could do. They couldn't see creative ideas because they wanted short-term big volume. That meant that brand building relied on above-the-line advertising only.

Lion dominated rugby and Castle dominated football, cricket and darts; the rest of the brands had nothing. They had great opportunities to build awareness. When I took over Carling Black Label from Johan du Toit, it had country music. Ohlsson's had road running.

One of the things we never came to terms with was that if you give a couple of brands the big sports, they would be the ones that were always seen, making it very difficult to build other brands.

Hansa arose out of some confusion in the market in the late '80s. But it was very difficult for any smaller brand to get enough airtime to be seen. That was the sponsorship limitation. Because the sales guys wanted volume now, they wanted the big brands. They were the brands that would give them their incentives, their rewards and their monthly or quarterly bonuses.

When you came with ideas for a smaller brand, it was really something of a curiosity because they felt it would not give them enough volume.

In the '80s, our history with brands was brilliant. If we look back from 2016 wondering how sophisticated we were at positioning and brand management, and how integrated we were with through-the-line positioning of brands, one could say that what we did in the '80s we left a lot to be desired.

Unilever was ahead of us in the day. I once had a conversation with Laurie Dippenaar, who was then the chairman of First Rand and Momentum, about the different directions businesses were taking in building their organisations. He said they were always envious and admiring of two things in SAB: 'Although you were dominant and a temporary sole supplier, you forced your brands to compete with one other. You didn't decide how they would play. You gave responsibility to individuals and let them have a go at each other.' The point was well made and probably a tribute to Peter Savory and his brand management concept.

'Secondly', he continued, 'you're a monopoly, yet I cannot get over how passionate your people are about working for this company. Why can't banks get that loyalty and passion? It feels, if one didn't know better, almost false; that you are told to be like that. It seems too good to be true.'

When I was marketing director, two things were important. One was a failure to see the potential in Castle. I thought it was a squandered opportunity to create a brand portfolio that would resonate with brands at a mainstream level. Secondly, using Castle Lager and Castle Lite to grow into Africa was an opportunity that was missed for too long.

ROBIN GOETZSCHE

When I started at SAB, I arrived on the agreed date to find out I was the brand manager of Carling Black Label and Hansa, I had been expecting to manage Amstel. It was a helluva shock for me because I didn't even know who drank Carling Black Label.

But it was a much bigger job. In fact, at that time, in 1987, SAB did 14 million hectolitres and had 14,000 staff members. We gave away more O&G (a monthly 'Office and Gratuity' beer allocation to every employee) than we sold Hansa. Then we did that 'sheep and accountants' ad. Consumers didn't get the logic of 'Oh, it's different from the lager,' they just thought accountants drank Hansa, so it must be larney.

Hansa grew like hell, and Bruce Starke was instrumental in taking Carling Black Label to the blue-collar worker segment. He was a very clever, insightful marketer. That brand went from strength to strength.

I remember when Tony was the brand group manager on Castle and I was the brand group manager on Lion, and we had to upgrade the labels.

For Castle, the team asked consumers to redesign the labels and then choose the best one. Graham Mackay and Meyer Kahn were very nervous about this. Graham called Tony and said we had to come and present our label changes to him and Meyer.

Tony goes first and outlines his whole programme about how we haven't changed the beer, etc. Kahn says to me: 'So now what are you doing on Lion?'

I said: 'We're just changing the label.'

'But aren't you advertising it?'

'No, Castle is doing that for us.'

'No, you will advertise the change of label and you will air it on every TV station.'

There were three TV stations in those days. So we had this 15-second ad where the label changed from the old one to the new one, and we flighted it three times after 11 p.m. on each of the channels.

Then Tony and I went on a benchmarking trip to the US. Every time we phoned home, Castle had lost 5 percent share. It was wiped out. The consumers rejected it. It was an interesting case study at the time.

We were lucky that Lion and Castle we were not from different companies.

Ally

John Cochran, who was one of my soldier colleagues in marketing in the early '90s had earned his stripes in the sales environment and understood how the beer business worked. What stood out for me was his zest for life and his ability to work with people.

Together we did some exciting and memorable campaigns on Castle Lager that appealed to the psyche of a nation and united South Africans during a delicate time in our history.

John

Ally had told me: 'There's a job in Jo'burg. It has your name on it.' A Sharks supporter who lived in Cape Town, offered a job in Jo'burg? Horror of all horrors. Move to the Big Smoke.

I relocated with my pregnant wife, walked into my office, and next thing I was managing the biggest brand in South Africa. A baptism of fire. With Ally's tutorship, we stopped drowning and found our feet and developed some innovative stuff together. Great years. It was an honour to work on that brand. I think I need a tattoo of Castle Lager on my body somewhere ... a badge of honour. Taking the brand into Africa, working with the export team to gain a beachhead, buying a business, building a business: they were all pioneering.

Ally

In the late eighties, Hugh Noble was the custodian of Castle Lager in South Africa and, with a team of creative gurus, dreamt up the Castle Lager Tavern Tour of Europe concept.

Essentially, we searched for like-minded ambassadors of Castle Lager and South Africa to go to Europe on a trip in search of a beer to match the taste of Castle Lager. To qualify, prospective contestants were asked to perform an act that epitomised their passion for Castle Lager. Events staged around the country culminated in a national final where five two-person teams were selected as ambassadors for Castle to explore Europe for seventeen days.

The concept captured the hearts and minds of South African beer drinkers and was so successful that the promotion ran for eleven consecutive years and became, in my view, the most creative promotional concept in fast-moving consumer goods marketing.

We sang...

'He must have been an admiral,
a sultan or a king,
and to his praises we shall always sing.
Look what he's done for us,
he's filled us up with cheer,
the Lord bless Charlie Glass,
The maker of Castle Beer.'

I had the privilege of inheriting this innovative concept from the previous leadership and was tasked with continuing the great legacy. I came to manage and lead three Castle Tavern Tours from 1990 to 1992, creating some of the greatest memories in my beer career, while building some deep friendships that, to borrow a phrase, 'would stand the test of time'.

The selection process in itself was arduous as we toured our seven regions to attend the regional finals for consumers who were prepared to entertain and creatively show their passion for the flagship brand of South Africa.

The creativity and approach were ahead of their time, in fact almost two decades ahead of Idols.

Creative lyrics and staging led to an adjudication panel selecting finalists to appear at a central venue to qualify ultimately for a berth on the tour.

The first of them traversed Holland, Belgium, Hungary, Ireland, Scotland and England, with a stopover in Nairobi, Kenya, en route.

Dressed to the nines in tour blazers in 'drinking colours' and other matching apparel, the team gelled and became lifelong friends who reconvened annually at different destinations across South Africa to rekindle the memories and create new ones.

Media coverage in revered publications, including an eight-page story in the Sunday Times Magazine, became a core feature and valuable exposure for the tours.

We experienced pub cultures and found wonderful people from across Europe who were captivated by our presence, wrestling with the notion that we were 'the South African Beer Drinking Team'.

Each pub we visited received a Castle Lager Tavern Tour plaque that future tours would find in later years.

The tales that unfolded, the stories created, the songs that were sung, the cheer, the fun, friendship and laughter, were beyond measure.

Each year the concept grew in stature and exposure and liquor traders even asked us to bring the promotion forward so that they could increase their turnover from the excitement created.

Needless to say, there was never a 'successful' Castle Lager Tavern Tour of Europe in the sense that we never found a beer to match the taste of Castle Lager in Europe, a continent steeped in beer heritage.

I believe that Castle Lager to this day remains one of the world's finest lager beers created for the thirst of the hot continent of Africa. It was no surprise that Castle Lager was voted the Best Bottled Lager at the International Brewing Awards at Burton-Upon-Trent in 2000.

Tour stories are a book on their own. I guess the personal sacrifice to lead a tour of this nature three years in a row was to blame for one of my not-so-good finishes in the Comrades Marathon, thus sadly my final Comrades.

I will always reflect on these memories, the unforgettable people I met, and the sadness at losing some of them in tragic circumstances, given that they lived lives larger than most and were always going to be more vulnerable.

I attended a reunion two years back … they were really the same people with the same passion with the same youthful heart, just 30 years on.

'A long time ago, way back in history, when all there was to drink was nothing but cups of tea, along came a man by the name of Charlie Glass, he invented a wonderful beer that tasted truly class.'

John

What a legendary promotion. The thoroughness of it; you entered as a team, had to get up on stage, compose an ode to Charles Glass, sing your song and make an absolute fool of yourself. After the rigour of the selection process from the performance to just spending time with the guys and observing, I would like to think we got it 90 percent right. We did ten tours and stopped and then Ally brought one back in 2011.

I was fortunate. I went on two tours, one as a trade host and one as a consumer host. There was the consumer group and the trade group. Let's be honest, the trade group was like the B-Team and the consumer group was the A-Team, and never the twain shall meet (although it did happen). What a wonderful trip.

The consumer group lugged ten thirsty fellows around Europe. We had been to the UK, had done Ireland, and arrived in Holland. There we were, miraculously finding ourselves in De Walletjes, fired up on local Heineken and possibly something to smoke from the local 'coffee shop'.

Oh, we had a couple of chuckles there… then we were off to Austria and Kitsbühel.

Half of us couldn't ski. We had three days there and really wanted to ski. We got kitted out on day one, and were given our instructor, who looked at this motley bunch, took us off to the nursery slope and taught us how to snowplough.

'Put your knees together for braking purpose,' he told us.

We explained to this poor, young, unsuspecting instructor that we had another two days and that he should stop buggering around with this snowplough stuff. We were from South Africa, and we wanted something more severe. So up we went, totally unprepared, inappropriately dressed in jeans and red Castle Tavern Tour tops that weren't that warm.

The eleven of us set off. Up the slope we went, bloody steep ... within ten minutes we had more than 50 people watching us with a mixture of gasps of horror and enthusiastic applause; it was like a freestyle skiing exhibition. It was unbelievable, some of the positions we got into, skis attached. It remains a mystery to me how we survived.

We would ski in the morning, if you could call it that, then stop somewhere for lunch – we had built up a bit of a thirst – enjoy a hearty Austrian meal washed down with copious volumes of Austrian beer, and then we were obviously bulletproof.

The afternoon session was always a good one. Again, the crowds returned, clapping and cheering, some in absolute horror. How there were no injuries remains a miracle. We all looked the same: like football louts from Liverpool or Manchester.

We arrived in Munich for the Oktoberfest, 1995. South Africa had just won the Rugby World Cup, and we were fired up with much South African passion and pride, having beaten the Australians and the New Zealanders. Sitting in the Hofbräuhaus, we decided we weren't going to be outdone by any Australians sitting there ... we began with numerous hearty mugs of good German beer and started to sing.

There was much standing on tables and subsequent requests to get off.

As the tour leader I carried this moon bag with my passport and all the travellers' cheques for the next ten days. At some point these Australians were also getting a bit rowdy so we gave them a hearty browneye, proudly South African ones I might add, and at some point, I pulled my jeans over the moon bag. I didn't notice this, and I had a few more beers. After an hour, I needed some cash to buy another round and alas, the moon bag was gone.

We reported it stolen. And we had no cash. Temba, one of two

Tembas from Soweto, said: 'Johnny, we'll sing.' They were from a local choir and these boys could sing.

We went outside into the street, all eleven of us, placed a beanie on the sidewalk and started singing at the tops of our voices. People donated cash, probably to encourage us to stop, and 20 minutes later we went back in with enough for another round.

The moonie was still missing, with my passport in it, and reported stolen. I was now making plans … but we weren't going to let that dampen our spirits. Miraculously, at some point when there was a call of nature, I made an adjustment to the block and tackle … and discovered the missing moon bag in my jeans.

A call for celebration. We gave the Australians another good South African moonie and carried on. That was some of the shit we got up to. It was magnificent.

Then the reunions. Every year these buggers got together under their own steam, by and large. What a band of bandits, a brotherhood of wonderful people. My goodness … if you put out a call that you were in trouble and needed help, I promise you, you would have ten guys at your house in no time. That's the kind of fellows they were … doctors, pilots, lawyers, a cross-section of society, but just good, honest wonderful people with a passion for the good old amber. That fun, friendship and laughter, that camaraderie, that's what our brand was about, what our company was about.

STUART SCOTT

If you take the heavy hitters like the Castles and Black Labels, and Hansa in its time, it was phenomenal how every year the game was lifted and played to the emotions of consumers. The brands resonated with consumers. There was always excitement.

I think of all the Castle campaigns over the years. The big above-the-line campaigns pulled the heartstrings, and then the tactical stuff, whether cricket or rugby or soccer, was what it was all about. That's what got the people going. You don't see that anymore.

I know things change with time but there isn't that same emotion that we had with the brands then.

I'll never forget the Durban MS&D conference when Hunters began taking the market by storm, and Peter Savory stood up and said: 'Just remember one thing: this business will never produce a cider.' Meyer alluded to that maybe a year or two later. It wasn't long after that we were forced to go into those categories. You've got to be where the consumer's mindset is.

People still talk about the adverts and the emotions. They were brilliant.

GERALDINE SCOTT

Look at that New York advert and the guy with the trolley. That was one of the greatest ads ever.

And you talk about in-trade execution; we used to stress ourselves because it wasn't 100 percent right or this was wrong or that was wrong. At least we had something to criticise. With the exposure that I have now, the in-trade execution is at about 20 percent. We didn't know how good we were.

Stuart

You can have all these fantastic campaigns, but you have to bring them to life at consumer level. That's what the business managed to do. It was a complete through-the-line strategy, executed with passion, and the longer you were in the business, you just got better as you innovated.

It just went from the next level to the next level. There was never a doubt that when you went into the trade, no matter where it was, who would stand out. It would always be SAB.

John

In Africa Mosi was a great brand. Ally and I had worked on it before there were any marketing competencies in a lot of African countries. We were the marketing team based in South Africa. We would fly in like seagulls, consult and develop, fly out and work on stuff in Johannesburg and then implement it. It was like picking up a lot of the old work we had established and passing on the baton.

For many of my 14 expat years, we carried the baton that Ally and I had created. I remember those days when I think back to Tanzania, launching Ndovu. All the work that went into it, the clandestine stuff we got up to, was wonderful.

In those days, when a poster was unheard of, radio commercials and a suite of marketing support materials built the Castle brand across Africa.

I remember Castle's market share at about 68 percent in South Africa. It was an absolute powerhouse, a machine. We sponsored the South African cricket team, the football team, darts, lifesaving and the Premier Soccer League, and then started developing the COSAFA Castle Cup.

We took that into Africa as a wonderful football communication vehicle and brand-building opportunity to engage with the passions of consumers in Africa. Those years of work were unforgettable.

BARRY SMITH

Our advertising was very good, I think, but we lacked the competition that could expose our weaknesses. We were great advertisers, but I am not sure we were great marketers. That was exposed when we got into competitive countries like America.

We had success with Redd's and Black Label, which won the best beer in the world award, and we relaunched Castle Milk Stout. Hansa Pilsener became refreshingly different, a very clear positioning. Castle had much momentum behind it already and ran like a train.

Then there was the embarrassing thing: through very poor management, Lion Lager declined throughout my term of office. I struggled with it. We had various positionings and because we were trying to take the brand to places that were perhaps not going to work at the time, we battled to find and underpin a core proposition.

At one stage we had this thing where they would go into shebeens with a big fat guy. I said that couldn't be right. They said no, no, in their culture fatness was a good thing. But there comes a time when your gut-feel says that's wrong. Our positioning was all over the place.

I had to present to the board, and they could see this line relating to Lion sales going down.

I was too slow in making changes to packaging, specifically the non-returnable bottle. We needed to do something about that old dumpy bottle. Norman Adami was on my case, and I said I had other things to do. We should have done that much earlier.

I was in Poland when we launched Lion Lager with a blue label. I don't know how that ever, ever, went through. It was shocking. We went from around 1 million hectolitres (which was low, because Lion was at one time about two million hl) and it was down to 60,000 hectolitres in about three or four months.

That must go down as one of the worst marketing gaffes. Anywhere else in the world, guys would have been fired.

Ally

Lion Lager had been a brand as majestic as its namesake and an icon of the South African beer landscape.

'Golden Good, Rich with Flavour. Down a Lion, Feel Satisfied' … it was one of a kind, a sweet beer with a distinct flavour made with caramel and other rich ingredients. Its golden label bore a proud red and black Lion that signified strength and leadership.

Yet the brand story is one of a magnificent franchise losing its way and eventually going to sleep – to be re-awakened as a name but never the same regal male.

Lion Lager was a classic case of messing with the crown jewels. The SAB leadership allowed tampering and experimentation with something sacrosanct.

When Castle Lager changed its label in 1989, consumers believed we had changed the beer itself. The exodus by beer drinkers was mostly to Lion Lager, which doubled its market share in six short months The uncertainty would have given global brewers a perspective that beer brand loyalty in South African was shallow and even then, worth a punt.

In Butterworth Brewery in 1989, the brewer had to change the complete brewing cycle to switch to Lion Lager from Castle Lager. It was a direct switch that took place overnight, based on a marketing blunder that shook the market to the core.

In the early nineties, Lion Lager became the country's favourite beer. Its logo was worn with pride on the Springbok rugby jersey in 1995 as South Africa won the first international title as world champions. Lion Lager was truly leading the jungle as it had done in its history many times before.

Through a series of leadership changes, ad agency experiments and the influence of personal egos, the brand became schizophrenic. It moved its strapline from 'Down a Lion' to 'Full Flavour' to 'Go all the Way' to 'Braskap' to 'Under 21', and its colours from gold, red and black to silver and blue, from five percent alcohol by volume to four percent and from leadership to zero. In fact, the Lion went to sleep and became a case study of how not to manage a leading brand.

If SAB had been the Lion Lager Beer Company, it would have been bankrupt. Because SAB had a 98 percent share of the market at this time and for most of the '90s, beer consumers could only really move to an SAB alternative and the likes of Castle Lager, Carling Black Label and Hansa Pilsener became power players, while Castle Lite also emerged from the wreckage later on.

When ABInBev took over SAB, a value-for-money offering was launched using the same bold red and black lion head, naming convention and gold can and label. The intrinsic was, however, fundamentally different, as was the alcohol level. The price was at a minimal ten percent below mainstream Castle Lager.

In an extremely price-sensitive market, the-value-for-money offering, combined with the powerful colour palette and naming convention, enjoyed an immediate uptake that has continued to grow to this day with no marketing support outside of price management and awareness.

What a pity that such a great brand had been nearly destroyed by messing with what it stood for in the first place. How sad that the real Lion no longer roams the beer plains of Africa. Don't mess with the Rolls Royce. Rather polish it!

TONY VAN KRALINGEN

One of our most challenging times in South Africa was the loss of Amstel, which we had brewed under licence for decades and built into a formidable premium franchise.

Our loss of the brand was regrettable. It was a long time in coming. One must wind the clock back to the early '90s, when we agreed to bring in Heineken as an import brand in '91. It was a successful launch.

However, we had to revisit the contract we signed with Amstel in 1966 which said we could never place a brand at a higher price point than Amstel. Heineken was going to do so.

Graham wanted a closer relationship and we had lots of discussions about Heineken being produced in South Africa. In retrospect Heineken were smarter than we were (meaning me) because I was marketing director at the time.

Heineken's position was that they couldn't have Heineken as a brand that we would manage on their behalf while we had a clause in the Amstel contract that was forever. They wanted us to bring in Heineken but to give up on the clause that allowed us indefinite rights to Amstel.

Graham, Norman and I consulted with some high-level silks including David Unterhalter. He said, ultimately: 'You can't protect that sort of contract because the brand is owned by the brand owner, not you, and for you to have indefinite rights to that brand is unsustainable in the modern world. If it came to a court case, you would lose. It's probably a good thing to give that up, but make sure you protect your rights'. As a result, that's the road we took.

The mistake we made in the contract was that it said that if SAB did something that might damage the Amstel brand anywhere, we would lose it. That was what ultimately caused the loss. We should have stipulated 'damage the Amstel brand in South Africa or Africa'. We missed a trick, and they were smarter than we were.

When we brought in Heineken, I think that they thought we would never become the competitor that we did become. The relationship became one in which we managed their brand's competitors. That dynamic changed their attitude towards us as being against them.

In a way that talks, I think, to the arrogance of Heineken's leadership when they were not buying businesses but negotiating people's right to produce their best brand for them.

They did create a significant brand, but we usurped them in size, profitability and market capitalisation because we realised that the bulk of beer was mainstream. That's where you could make money if you were efficient, and I think we were better operators.

In 2002, they wanted to remove the Heineken and Amstel brands because of some infringement; I can't remember what. The advice Norman received was that they had the rights to remove both.

Norman made big offers about doubling their royalties. I then had a meeting with Heineken in Amsterdam. It was a game of bluff, I guess. Pod McLoughlin and Garth Saunders were with me.

Heineken wanted to do something, and we would tell them why they couldn't. I said: 'You must decide whether you want to remove it. I am not convinced you have the rights or the authority to do so, but if that's what you want to do you must make that decision and bear the consequences. And the consequences might be big.'

They wanted me to tell them why. I refused. I said: 'These are negotiations in which you told us you want to take it, so take it.' They blinked. They took Heineken but left Amstel.

It was great but it was a stay of execution because now they wanted to take Amstel. We were now their competitors and they wanted to set up against us.

(Interestingly, at that time they were negotiating to buy a 22 percent share in South West Breweries from Interbrew, who were no longer interested in Africa. I intervened and tried to buy that 22 percent share. The List family wouldn't sell it to us. They felt that we treated the South West Breweries with disdain and impudence and they didn't want the relationship.

If we had maybe managed it better, we would probably have bought it and it would have closed off that opportunity for Heineken. Not forever, but it would have delayed it. We offered 30 percent more. Then Heineken bought it.)

As was written in the contract, we had arbitration in London, a two-week hearing before three judges. At the end of the first week, they thought they had lost. We thought we had won.

Then the crucial issue arose. The question to Graham was: 'Did you mean, when you made that (a previous) statement, that you and the Santo Domingos were going to expand beyond the businesses you bought in South America?'

It was that statement that triggered the Amstel clause. And Graham had to say: 'Yes, I did.'

So they won the arbitration and were able to take Amstel away.

It was a big loss to SAB. Amstel at the time was 25 percent of our profit and 12 percent of our turnover, at 2.4 million hectolitres, but I think SAB managed that loss incredibly well. We launched Hansa Marzen Gold. They tried to stop us, realising that it was a smart move.

They were naïve operationally because they thought we would be so desperate to keep Amstel that they would be able to build a brewery and we'd want to manage Amstel. We had anticipated the loss and ran down Amstel stocks.

In the year that followed, we held profits level. Marzen came close to a million hl. It wasn't sustainable, of course, because the brand wasn't founded on any real truth. It was positioned as a stop-gap, which it proved to be. It was difficult to follow through with anything because we didn't have the armoury or the depth of that tiering of brand pricing.

SIMON HARVEY

I was General Manager of Egoli at the time and was 'polishing the Rolls' effectively, but we had that slap in the face when we lost Amstel. I was general manager of the region and 24 percent of my volume was Amstel. I remember receiving a phone call from Tony, saying that we'd lost the case. I said: 'That's a bit of a problem.' He said: 'Yes, we're going to have to find a way.'

We had done some work, but all the lawyers were telling us we had nothing to worry about. There was no way we could lose the court case. I remember saying to Tony: 'I'm going to pull all my team in.

Is it possible that you as MD and CEO could come and have a chat to the team?'

He said they had a board meeting and if we could make a plan to do it close to head office he would arrange to be there at least to talk to the staff. I said I'd do it at the Wanderers Club.

Tony's office phoned and said he would be there with a couple of additional people. We set up the presentation of what we were going to do and how we were going to deal with it, with a 5.00 p.m. start. At 4.55 p.m., I looked up and there was Tony walking down the stairs. With him were Meyer, Graham and the board.

I stopped him and asked: 'What's the protocol? Are you going to say anything?' He said no, he'd had a chat to Meyer and Graham, and both would like to address the team.

'Ok, what's the order?'

'You go first, then Graham, then Meyer and if need be, I'll go last.'

So I did my little speech, and I think I talked about Herschelle Gibbs hitting the Dutch in the World Cup for six sixes. I used that to show what we could do.

Then Graham got up. Graham was always very eloquent. He didn't become cross about anything whatsoever. That was the only I time I ever saw him show emotion in a speech. You could see in his eyes and in his voice that he was pissed off.

He wasn't even informed by Jean-Francois van Boxmeer or Heineken. He found out via the web. Van Boxmeer told him he was trying to phone and couldn't get hold of him.

Graham said: 'I understand Simon is emotional and you guys want to make things right, but don't forget about the consumer.' He used the words: 'Make love to the consumer.' He was emotional and cross.

Then it was Meyer. And Meyer is a beaut. There are hundreds of stories of what he has said at conferences. He said: 'Guys you've heard Simon say you need to f... up the Dutch. You've heard Graham say you need to make love to the consumer. Just understand which of them comes first.'

He carried on: 'Simon, you are not going to lose a single hectolitre. I'm expecting you to do six million in the next year and my team has made that commitment.' And it became more like an awards party than a commiseration at losing 24 percent of our volume. That's where I saw passion inside a person second to none.

Ally

Meyer warned: *Hulle gryp aan die leeu se ballas* (They are grabbing the lion by the balls. See how angry he's going to become).

Simon

Heineken did not expect us to turn the taps off straight away. They expected us to take the year and to milk the brand as much as we could. We made the decision that we were not going to sell even one more case of Amstel from the day we were told that we had lost it, and we would take the financial write-off in the bottles.

A year later, we sold six million hectolitres of our brands. We did not drop a single hekkie (hectolitre). And we sold about 600,000 hectolitres of Marzen Gold.

It didn't make up for all of the Amstel we'd lost, but Black Label accounted for some and Castle Lite accounted for some. It was the one thing I disagreed with the marketing department. They said that Hansa Marzen Gold would do everything. We said every gun in the shop is going to take that bullet. We'll take whatever we can, however we can.

We talk about passionate people. In that year, I think I did six nights a week in the trade. It was a portfolio strategy as opposed to a one-horse trick. When Dreher was launched, we had Carling Black Label, Hansa Marzen Gold, and Castle Lite … everything was just pulling a couple of hekkies here, a couple there.

Ally

I worked with Ian Penhale three times in my career. First on the Castle brand group, then when I came back to Castle in 2009 to run the 2010 FIFA World Cup, and to our final chapter of SABMiller, and finally across Africa as custodian of our regional brands.

Then Norman Adami came back from the US – asked to return because of his competitor experience in Miller Brewing – and Tony van Kralingen moved to SABMiller group headquarters in London. Norman's mandate was very different from Tony's. It was really about winning mostly on costs. Another era.

SAB's loss of Amstel was tough, but Norman poured money into marketing and sales and resourcing was flowing. It was a 'virtuous cycle', a lovely articulation of the strategy. Bring expenses down wherever you can in the organisation and put it up front.

We relaunched Carling Black Label and moved Castle Lite onto the 'extra cold' platform. Castle Lager had the 2010 World Cup and Hansa Pilsener was rejuvenated through the character of Vuyo.

In 2009, Norman Adami asked me to return to Castle Lager to tackle the flagship brand. It was in trouble. The previous incumbent handed me a ring binder with four pages of requests as part of the handover relating to the 2010 FIFA World Cup. It was March 2009. The World Cup was 14 months off.

André Lombard, a previous account service director at Ogilvy and I met to scheme how best to tackle the ginormous task of welcoming the world to Africa with the iconic beer brand that had made us famous.

Frank Zappa once said: 'Every country needs a beer and an airline. A fairly skilled soccer team is a good thing. However, the very least you need is a beer.'

We worked with a creative team for 29 days on the trot to develop a 14-month programme that would be episodic and take Castle Lager back to where it belonged: at the top.

A month later, we presented a comprehensive and creative approach to Norman and his leadership team and were given the thumbs up to commence with one of the biggest campaigns in the history of any of our brands.

Budweiser was the official beer of the World Cup. We needed to be very careful not to contravene their strict legal rights around the event, but there were ways to leverage our 20-year standing with our national soccer team Bafana Bafana, who were the hosts and had automatic entry to the event.

Our story began with the introduction of 'The Superfan'. We went about physically selecting the number one superfan of each premier soccer league team and bringing them together.

Although the meeting of Superfans, particularly from Kaiser Chiefs and Orlando Pirates, was a little strained at first, the conflict disappeared as they became the 'unofficial/official Superfans of South Africa', who would rally the nation behind the national team and welcome the world.

The campaign broke a year in advance of the World Cup and began to excite all South Africans and unite them for the country's one big opportunity to show the world our mettle.

The Superfans traversed the length and breadth of the country, at one stage spending three months on the road and visiting some three hundred taverns to create hype and excitement around the flagship brew. 'It all comes together with a Castle'.

Closer to the spectacle, we embarked on another campaign that flowed from the Superfans to welcome the world to South Africa ... 'Welcome to our Home, Bru'. It captured the imagination of the nation and began to return the brand to its former leadership role. Growth was like a brushfire.

When the world came to Africa, we had a slogan: we told ourselves 'Budweiser may have 48 square kilometres, we have three million. Let's get busy'.

Fans from around the world drank Budweiser from PET bottles inside the stadia but the moment they left the stadium, it was Castle Lager. FIFA even approached us to run ten 'fan parks' around the country, where local and overseas fans gathered in ten key cities to watch the games on big screen TVs and be treated to a South African Lager – which was essentially Castle Lager – and they all knew it. In restaurants and taverns across the country, overseas guests asked for Castle Lager.

CNN and Sky News featured our Superfans as the channels took the global spectacle around the world and profiled our beautiful country. It was a world-class event from every perspective. The country was proud to be the host. So was Castle Lager.

Research after the event showed that South Africans saw Castle Lager as the number two sponsor of the World Cup after Coca-Cola, which spent a billion rand, although Budweiser was the official beer sponsor.

CLIFFORD RAPHIRI

The FIFA World Cup was a catalyst for innovation. When I became technical director, the amount of innovation we did was enormous and complex.

We did the 2010 can, where you could pull off the entire lid and drink out of it like a glass. We tried to upscale Miller Genuine Draft to move it out of Chamdor into Alrode. We launched Peroni. We were doing 30,000 hectolitres of PU, but invested ahead of time at Rosslyn and Newlands breweries at the same time. We did Hansa Marzen Gold, and when Norman came we started all those packaging upgrades. We introduced probably 10 different public offerings of 12-packs and six-packs. We were basically running breweries with innovations as though we were a supermarket.

Ally

The Superfans followed the Proteas cricket team to India the following year and the Springboks to Australia after that. A concept that recognised the fan as the hero became an integral part of the brand story over the next four years and Castle Lager regained its prime position.

This case study went on to win the company's in-house Grand Prix Mercatus Award in 2011 and eventually, when SAB celebrated its final chapter of Mercatus in 2016, Castle Lager achieved the ultimate accolade for the campaign that had globally stood out as the best.

The irony of the story was that in 2017, as the global brand custodian of ABInBev, I was to launch Budweiser officially in South Africa and take a hundred fans to the World Cup in Russia.

The trip brought back great memories and made me realise why Budweiser also had such a great global equity. What a privilege it was to work on two phenomenal big hitters.

Norman Adami's return to South Africa from the US saw a marked change in strategic focus across the business and more especially in the brands.

NORMAN ADAMI

I came back to South Africa and found us in trouble. All our core brands were waning. We were spending more on Pilsner Urquell than we were on Castle Lager.

People were in denial. They were chasing niche brands and relegating our core brands to the back room.

I used to go into all our big retail outlets and there was not one of our power brands visible on the floor. They were all in the back room. I saw only Peroni and the new products we had.

More than 90 percent of our profits came from our five power brands. Yet they were the brands that had no effective marketing behind them, no airtime.

One of the key lessons was always that you could not grow unless your core brands were growing. And you couldn't grow as a company unless your local premiums were growing. This holy grail of chasing green with green captured the attention of the business. It was obsessed with Heineken having taken Amstel.

We fell well below 90 percent market share of the beer market; we were sitting in the low 80s. Castle was nowhere; Black Label, Hansa, Milk Stout and Castle Lite were on the skids. Again, we had to develop a new strategy. It was a big part of the problem but not the only one we had.

Our route to market had neglected independent redistributors (IRDs) completely. We dropped the IRDs and the urban redistributors (URDs) who were a big portion of our market share. They were irritated with SAB.

We had to make our key brands resonate, stabilise our foundation, and expand our productivity. We had lost our operational excellence in many parts of the business. Even in the declining market, we also had out-of-stocks. The breweries couldn't supply. We had to regain our productivity edge and our efficiencies. We had to shape superior routes to market. That meant re-engaging the IRDs and URDs.

A one percent drop in Black Label equated to about a 600 percent growth in Peroni. But Black Label was our biggest brand, and it was tanking. We had to reposition Black Label, Hansa and Castle Lite.

We premiumised Castle Lite. It had been in decline, and we set it on fire again. We repositioned our brands correctly and beefed up our brand teams. We invested in our people, our brands and our routes to market. We put more sales feet on the street. We invested in our distribution service. We invested in the marketplace. And we achieved a lot of savings to reinvest in the market. We turned the business around and got it growing again.

We managed to keep Heineken at bay, and they won just a minimal market share. They couldn't reach break even.

Clifford

When Norman came back with an American contingent, he began a rebuilding phase to bring back confidence of people. We didn't have Amstel. Competition was very different. And the economy was struggling a little at the time. But everybody rose to the challenge.

The biggest change that made a difference to me was that the IRDs were elevated again. The 'go direct' flow was undermining the role the IRDs had played in the growth of SAB for decades. Not having IRDs as partners was a recipe for disaster. You were basically giving away route to market.

The second biggest was rebuilding brands. Castle wasn't top, even amongst staff. A lot of work had to be done around rebuilding the quality of Castle, and the confidence in it, among brewers themselves.

Rebuilding the brewery tours was part of rebuilding the Castle franchise and it took a lot of work, but there was great passion for it.

Trade brewers like Ben Lamaletie, Denis da Silva and Ken Russell did a lot of work to get the brewers' confidence back and restore consumer confidence in Castle quality. We used to go into pubs as well and give talks and into companies to educate them. And that helped. We became transparent in a very aggressive fashion, getting people to come into a brewery and see how we brewed the beer.

Ally

I sincerely believe that Norman's strategy to make 'key brands resonate' was profound. It was something which we'd lost along our way. We were spending lots of money on Pilsner Urquell and Miller and Peroni, while the bread-and-butter brands were floundering.

ANDREA QUAYE

I became VP Marketing at ABInBev after a career in SAB marketing, and remember Norman saying that people who gave up on their major brands were lazy marketers. It was a huge lesson.

Tony was the MD when news came that Norman was coming back – that guy with the cigarette, I was dreading it – and when he came, he did so with his three henchmen, Charlie Frenette, Paul Pendergrass and Jeff Jacobs from McKinsey.

We went to this senior executive workshop in George, and we were given a one pager that talked about five strategic thrusts to make key brands resonate, obviously written for Norman by Charlie Frenette (ex-CEO of Coca-Cola Africa) but we thought it was a brief and we had to come up with our own ideas.

We took that thing and muddled it all up. We figured we've got to do this and do that, and we presented it back. It went down like a lead balloon. Norman said: 'What part of 'key brands resonate' don't you understand?'

For the next two months we kept going backwards and forwards and the structures changed. Black Label was one brand. I lost the others. I remember feeling demoted. I remember Charlie saying: 'Don't worry, you're going to have to go deep on Carling.'

Black Label had not immediately received any money, while Castle had, with the FIFA World Cup coming. Castle Lite was given money because it was a premium brand and highly profitable.

I'm not sure if they decided that Black Label was going to be a power brand. But our structures moved from two people on Black Label to ten. I had three marketing managers. At that time, I was pregnant with my second daughter, and we had to do these brand plans. I will never forget the amount of analysis we did.

Charlie sent us an Excel spreadsheet, which I still have, with the different questions you had to ask yourself. Two hundred questions that went from consumer, to packaging, to liquid, to in-trade, to TV, to radio, and we spent months and months and months analysing. It questioned everything. It was epic and painful.

And we had to fill in that spreadsheet and extend it for miles. The consumer insights managers had to do all that work, and we just ratified what they did.

You would have to present to Norman. Six months before that you started brand planning. I had sessions with Charlie where he'd give me feedback. In the beginning I enjoyed it because I kept learning. But at one meeting, I just cried, thinking: 'Clearly I'm not made for this.' I packed my stuff and I left.

Charlie came and apologised afterwards saying: 'Sorry, I didn't realise I was pushing you that hard.' And then I made my first presentation to Norman. I didn't go as far as I'd like to, because I had dared once to put up a slide about price elasticity and how sensitive Black Label was, and he grilled me about: 'What do you mean price elasticity? How do you calculate it?'

I didn't really know. I knew at a conceptual level, but he wanted it at a much more granular level. 'What level of statistic relevance is there in this elasticity?' and blah, blah, blah.

Presenting brand plans used to take six hours at least, sometimes eight. Norman would be eating chocolates and smoking cigarettes. The room would be full of people, the whole board. He would grill you and grill you. My greatest growth came from there. My greatest leadership lessons, too, because you had to believe in what you were saying.

With all the pre-work and analysis, we had done for six months, you knew that behind every slide you needed another five slides. You had to back every statement you made and then unhide some slides and show him 'that's how I got to that statement.

The challenge was how, by fixing it, you could make sure that you grew the pie. There's that whole thing that says when Black Label grows, Castle Lager declines. There was an interchange between brands. I suppose that is why the category strategy evolved.

You would present your brand plans to Norman at least three times before they were approved. The second time I presented to him, I reached the point where we were talking about activities and about some event in the taverns, where the DJ would be playing music. Norman even wanted to know who was going to choose the DJ. That was the level of granularity that he dug into.

You had to know your stuff to the nth degree. How many scratch cards were there? What was the redemption ratio? It was ludicrous. But it just brought us so much closer to the sales guys. It made us think and made our work a lot more credible.

When I started at SAB, Castle was in decline, Black Label was in decline, only Hansa and Castle Lite were growing. Then we both started growing and Hansa began declining.

We had a very healthy portfolio as Castle Milk Stout also started growing. Four of the five key brands were resonating with consumers. It wasn't that Hansa was not resonating with them, it was just that the other four were resonating more. That's very healthy because suddenly we were protecting our temporary sole supplier status.

Clifford

When you are in SAB, you don't know only your own brands, you know the competitor's brands as well. At times you met with competitors at industry conferences. We knew Heineken was a good beer. There are some older SAB brands that were far superior to those that ABInBev had, but you think they should be given a chance. Now Castle is a better beer than most in their stable.

Technically, and in its marketing, Heineken is a truly global beer. No other beer has achieved that.

IAN PENHALE

We achieved a lot and turned back the Heineken and Amstel tides. When Heineken took Amstel back from us it was at 2.4 million hectolitres, growing at 30 percent a year. A few years later, it was less than 1 million hectolitres. Heineken admittedly was getting traction and Windhoek was not doing badly. Hansa Marzen Gold was a stop-gap strategy that got Heineken very excited. We had a head-butt with them and changed the colour of the foil. They had been very aggressive legally, but we got the job done and Marzen Gold reached 750,000 hectolitres.

We tried to launch Dreher, but that didn't work. You can't make a silk purse from a sow's ear. That's what we tried to do.

Then we launched Flying Fish. I remember Andrew Wolff saying 'You must be f...ing joking – you can't call an alcoholic brand that.' I told him: 'You stick to what you do, and I'll do the marketing.'

Sherwood Light Cape Lager was another flop on my watch. It was ahead of its time. Low alcohol failed dismally. Dooleys was a failure. Solantis Spice was another where new product development created it and then marketing cocked it up – they took the *gemmer* (ginger) out.

Dakota Ice tasted a bit like Miller, but we couldn't get any scale. Ohlsson's went on my watch, too … we learnt from all these things. You were allowed to make mistakes. We took risks and we were adventurous.

At this time, countries where SAB operated were fiercely independent and the hub in London was subservient to them. We set about a different strategy – to drive a central best practice agenda across the regions and to hold them accountable. To push back quite hard and to show them what good looked like.

Initially there was some conflict, and there were difficult discussions at the start, but I think we won them over by sheer force of proof of concept – 'we can help you do it better'. I think we were engaging. I don't think we used a big stick although they felt threatened. They were right to feel that way as we were a powerful team. I think the standard improved dramatically and showed in the work.

There was a transformation … not to be negative about the past, but to bring to bear what we were trying out in other regions that was pulling people up.

We raised the ceiling as opposed to raising the floor.

The standout was the people, a wonderful set of human beings, still my friends today. I can phone them and they are there for me. I don't think anyone else in other companies could have that bonding type of culture. Look at the reunions, the example of the guys getting together to this day and from all around the world...

One could argue that one of our shortcomings at SAB is that we were a beer company taking on the world without a global brand that had a universal truth and appeal across the world: the Coca-Cola of beers. My sense is that Heineken is the only beer brand that has cracked this mantra and, having been the marketing director for Heineken in South Africa in the '90s, I can attest to this.

Corona has global brand equity that I believe has tapped into a universal approach and language that augurs well for the future. It resonates with the youth in its articulation of enjoying the great outdoors and escaping to beautiful places. The ritual of the lime in the neck of the bottle is on another level.

Our global brands had provenance cues and aspects of equity that related to their home markets, like Pilsner Urquell in Czechoslovakia and parts of Europe, Miller in the US, and Peroni in Italy and perhaps the United Kingdom. Our brands sadly did not achieve global status. But this was not a drawback given our choice to make local country brands the focus and heroes of our marketing endeavours.

Our approach in SAB, as explained earlier, was to work in our new countries to elevate and position the local brands, uplifting the quality of the liquid, substantially improving the packaging, including bottles, cans, graphic integrity, labels, crowns, shrink film and every imaginable consumer-facing aspect.

Later we would go on to positioning the local hero brands credibly and dial into execution at retail level. In addition, we would adopt an experiential approach and tap into local events and sponsorship opportunities for the brand to resonate even further.

In some regions, we had begun the journey to develop regional franchises like Castle Lite across Africa, where the cold proposition, green bottle and premium cues became virtues that stood the brand in good stead from Cape Town to Cairo.

We failed dismally at a global brand level. We started too late, we bought what was available, but we weren't good enough at marketing in general and certainly not at global marketing.

The organisation was competing at a regional global level and that created issues. Globally you had the same internal competition that you had in South Africa. The things that made us phenomenal in some areas, especially operations, sales and manufacturing, were never shining stars on the global stage, and we never invested enough in them. We never won sufficient buy-in from the organisation.

Maybe they were the wrong assets. The barons – the Bowmans, Lipperts, Smiths, Adamis – were all very good at working out what worked. If something didn't seem right, they could smell it out. We tried our best but that was an enormous failure because we paid a lot of money to buy those global brands and then never put any money behind them.

Group marketing was basically a small island among all these regional continents, and its people were doing their best to row from their island to the continents to enforce their will, but it really was a complete failure.

The Mercatus Awards was a great initiative as it rebranded us as a marketing organisation. It was recognition of brand excellence around our SAB world, across 84 countries, and again, similar to the principle of recognition that started in South Africa, was a way to recognise extraordinary insight and application around our brands.

I still think we struggled to live up to that, mainly because all our brands were local and we didn't have that thread, the Heineken thread. Heineken is global because of Heineken, it's not an accomplished marketer of local brands. Look what a shit job they did on Amstel in South Africa. It was messy, hideous.

18 On the Shoulders
of Giants

Amid the motivation, encouragement, entertainment, inspiration and camaraderie engendered by the MS&D conferences, every year there was a timeslot dedicated to the acknowledgement, recognition and genuine admiration for the SAB masters. It was a celebration of SAB Masters who had retired or were still working for the company, and for the induction of new masters.

In October 1992, from a third-floor office at our Sandton headquarters, sales services manager Kevin Hedderwick circulated a memo to the company general managers.

It said: 'Going around the country recently, rolling out our very successful one-day beer-selling training programme, I got the impression, again – and there are obviously exceptions – that some of our 'old bulls' are beginning to feel somewhat threatened by the increasing number of 'young Turks' being brought into the business.

'Of course, there's no need for them to feel insecure. The so-called 'old bulls' who are still in the business are salt-of-the-earth salesmen of whom we make exceptionally good use, both now and as we begin to swing the focus back to a selling culture; and even more so when hopefully, in the not-too-distant future, we will be faced with a direct competitor.

'While I am aware that in many cases you and your marketing district manager go out of your way to make these guys feel loved, I thought it might be a good idea to organise some kind of old boys' reunion for them as another way of elevating and recognising them.

'The plan is that I would put together a dinner for them at a venue in Johannesburg, sometime in November, which incidentally would work well as it was in November 1979 that we saw the demise of Intercontinental Breweries.

'We would make a real fuss of this small group of survivors and ask, say, Graham Mackay to address them, reinforcing the message that we need the old bulls.

'The qualification for cracking an invite to this event – which I would appreciate if you could keep confidential as we would like to surprise them – would be that they should be 50+ years of age and have been with SAB since 1979.'

And so it was. At a surprise function at the Dainfern Golf Club in Johannesburg in December 1992, in the guise of a confidential sales briefing and old boy's reunion, the managing director at the time, Graham Mackay, inducted the first 31 SAB masters:

Robbie Barnard, Malcolm Butlin, Ross Clements, Sandy Colquhoun, Hugh Collier, Roy Coverly, Mannetjies Gericke, Peter Heine, Justus Hill, Doug Hopwood, Vernon Keys, Fanie Kuhn, Gene la Cock, Tiger Lance, Stan Maduo, Noel Magadla, Solly Mahasoa, Iggy Makwea, Mick Marriott, Lofty Nel, Ivan Randall, Peter Savory, Colin Schmidt, Gavin Scott, Peter Spolander, Bruce Starke, Cliff Thomas, Albert Tshabalala, Corrie van Vuuren, Reg Vorster and Harvey Wannenburg.

Barnard, Gericke, Hopwood, Kuhn and Nel were all rugby Springboks; Lance and Heine were legendary Springbok cricketers; and Gavin Scott and Roy Coverly were premier league footballers.

Each was presented with the now-coveted master's blazer, a set of cufflinks, and a commemorative beer mug.

Many of them were veterans who had encouraged South Africans not just to drink beer but, more specifically, to persuade South Africans to drink certain brands of beer. They were veterans of the 'beer wars' in the 1970s that enabled SAB to secure its leadership of the South African beer market, against competition initially from fertiliser magnate Louis Luyt and ultimately from business icon, Anton Rupert.

For years, some still called on the pubs, clubs and bottle stores they knew so well. Others reached retirement age. Many passed to the great beer market in the heavens. The survivors were revered as an elite band of employees, esteemed for their lifelong dedication to fostering a beer culture in South Africa and for the responsible enjoyment of the golden beverage.

To be a master was to be recognised for having made a career-long contribution of professionalism in the disciplines of marketing, selling and distributing beer at SAB. The badge they wore with pride was a symbol of the company's gratitude for the inspiration they offered young employees who were in the beginning of their careers.

Selection criteria were amended slightly from time to time to maintain momentum of the cadre and, without diluting its exclusivity, acknowledge younger but still key frontline players in the business.

The 50-year age limit was abolished, and eligibility widened to employees outside of sales and distribution whose work nevertheless brought them close to the sales community.

In an era that often looked down on people who dedicated their lives to one company, where corporate progress was defined by 'moving in and moving out', the masters continued to invest in the company, indeed the beer industry, with the passion and intellectual capital to spur future generations and sustain SABMiller's world class status.

As I look back, I think corporate business really underestimates the value of service, endurance, commitment and leadership.

Norman Adami recognised that surrounding a company with a combination of experience and youth was a winning formula to ensure that mistakes were never made twice and that employees with tenure were to be revered rather than scoffed at.

In most people's careers at SAB, I know for a fact, the master's recognition was the pinnacle and the most revered accolade they received in their lifetime.

It was inspiring for me to hear recruits who set their sights and ambition on becoming a master at a time when the youth were all about gaining as much experience across numerous corporates as was possible to champion their own career paths.

In later years, masters donned a blazer embroidered with the coveted badge and accepted their embossed beer mug at an emotional, often tearful, ceremony that would be remembered in perpetuity. At the MS&D conference, the masters were invited onto the stage to welcome the new masters to the fraternity amid a standing ovation of 1,700 delegates.

It was usually accompanied by a rendition of a Josh Grobin song:
You raise me up, so I can stand on mountains.
you raise me up, to walk on stormy seas.
I am strong, when I am on your shoulders
you raise me up to more than I can be.

What was particularly special about the masters, was the fact that each year, all retired masters were invited back to the conference, a tradition upheld until SAB was taken over by ABInBev in 2016.

The continued association with the retired masters, some of whom continued to mentor individuals working in the company, embodied a heartfelt appreciation and sense of purpose.

For me personally, receiving my master's blazer and beer mug was a milestone and confirmation of achievement on my journey in this venerable company.

I went on to celebrate another 14 such functions as part of the welcoming party to new members. At every one of them, I was in awe at that look of sentiment and pride in the eyes of each new master as they donned the blazer and turned to face the audience for acknowledgement of dedication and excellence during two decades with more to come.

For many years, the masters fraternity remained in touch through the leadership of Frank Johnson, a master who epitomised the passion and leadership of the SAB greats who live on to reminisce about the greatness of their company.

Tony van Kralingen told me that one of his favourite parts of every conference was the masters' song and how those 'old buggers with the crock knees' would make every effort to be at the conference, put on their blazers and cherish their moment of recognition.

It wasn't just the people of today; it was the people of yesterday. It was the company saying: 'We won't ever forget you.'

In later years, the brewing fraternity did a similar thing. At first it was 'SAB Brewing Legends', then it became more broadly technical.

Wayne McCauley wondered: 'What other companies would do this for their employees? For many years before I became a master myself, I watched those people and saw how proud they were to come to the sales conference, to walk onto that stage and experience the acknowledgement they received.

'They were the people who built the company in the days before we arrived. To have them on a stage in front of a whole bunch of the next generation, and to see the way the newer people acknowledged them with a standing ovation, was what made the company so special.

'When you became a master yourself, the pride you felt to be standing on the stage and be awarded that jacket left nobody in doubt about how much SAB your valued service and dedication.'

The masters' award was acknowledgement of the whole person, to the extent of inviting people, flying them to the conference, and making all their arrangements. The treatment shown to the masters was exceptional. It was the DNA of the company. That's what we did.

CLIFFORD RAPHIRI

The 'masters' and 'legends' concepts were unique to SAB. I didn't know of any other company with something like that. In essence, they recognised people who rose through the ranks, had demonstrated hard work, passion for our brands, embraced the SAB ethos and spirit, and were more than just ambassadors, both internally and externally.

Ally

In all the times we selected people, I can't remember one occasion when anyone questioned the integrity of our choices. Everyone who was chosen was absolutely deserving. The beauty of it was that none of the people who were selected actually considered themselves legends. They were all surprised. The honour was announced at their table.

The careers of people who were selected as legends were generally very rich careers. Seniority didn't necessarily make you a legend.

Those things were some of the X-Factors of the business. I had youngsters who came to me and said their dream was to become a master in the company. You don't often get tenure in any business of that length of time. These days people move around companies much more freely.

For Stuart Scott, it was an inspiration to many people to want to stay on in the company because they realised there was a longer journey on their career path, and it kept people engaged.

Every year there was great anticipation about who was going to walk onto the stage. There were always surprises. You thought you knew everybody, but you didn't, or how long some people had been there, and how someone had done 20 years. It was a great institution.

NORMAN ADAMI

Reward and recognition through things like the masters and legends became part of the culture. People took them seriously. They had a lot of respect within the business. The honours were highly sought after.

Recipients were people who, no matter at what level they operated – they could have been at the most junior position in the company – were recognised for their contribution to the success of the company.

That made a big difference. It brought our people-oriented culture to life.

Everyone in the company put their energy and passion behind the objectives of the company, believed in the company, and wanted it to succeed. They wanted to play their role and they did.

19 **The New Hero**
in Town

Nigeria, with more than 182 million people, is a country on the move. One can feel the vibe and the entrepreneurship and the 'make a plan' mentality of all its people – it's a hustle from early morning to late at night, with bustling streets and a persistent hum of activity.

Initially I flew into Port Harcourt, Onitsha and Elisha, where we had developed a brewery footprint. Our strategy was to develop value for money brands below mainstream in the form of Hero and Trophy. It was a strategic approach to upset the market with highly credible and great-tasting brands at a much lower price point. We clearly upset Heineken and Diageo, who had ruled the roost for decades, and gained unprecedented market share that made a massive impact on our African business.

Our ex-pat community was a bunch of pioneers who worked hard and played even harder. People were living in communities, mostly under the protection of armed escorts and armoured vehicles, given the risks of kidnapping and Boko Haram, who were active where we worked.

A cycle ride or a game of golf entailed a rigmarole of security and escorts, and the limited trip to the shops for groceries needed rifle-wielding gunman to protect staff and their partners.

Local restaurants in Onitsha offered 'point and kill' on the menu. It involved essentially a one-metre deep tank of murky water inhabited by barbel-like fish. As a patron, you could point at the fish you desired for dinner, and it was speared and placed live on the fire for later consumption.

Nigeria was the second biggest beer market in Africa after South Africa, with low per capita consumption and incredible potential and upside.

Lagos, a city of 21 million people, was the headquarters. Our office and ex-pats were resident on Banana Island. The Ikoyi

Southern Sun Hotel was our residence around the corner from the office and housed a Castle Lite tap around which most residents gathered to quaff large quantities of the delectable draught.

Lagos was the cutting edge and new frontier of our African business and I visited it monthly for just on three years. We had huge hopes pinned on our ability to make it happen in this thriving and bustling economy.

I always sensed excitement when I visited Nigeria. One felt a little on edge, as anything could happen at any time. It was always an adrenalin rush from the airport, an absolute shambles; it took up to three hours to exit and make the trip through the city across the longest bridge in Africa to Banana Island.

South African Airways landed around 8 p.m. and by the time you exited the airport building, it was well after 10 p.m. Most would head for the Ikoyi Southern Sun about 45 minutes' drive away. I was usually whisked to a restaurant downtown to meet the management team.

Usually, my welcome would be a tray of Jägermeister with a Castle Lite chaser to get me up to speed and able to converse in some way with the leadership team who at this stage were leaderless.

Three a.m. was usually the return to check-in to Ikoyi for a three-hour nap before the first meeting at the office around the corner. Somehow everyone always attended on time and the intellectual prowess was surprising.

A new brewery built just outside Lagos became our fourth brewery in Nigeria and spoke volumes for our performance, and to how brand nuggets can drive a business and build a special relationship with consumers.

We launched Castle Lite in the premium sector of the market and later Budweiser, which was a winner with its 'American Dream' connotation. With tactics that were often surprising we developed spiritual homes in Lagos that rattled the competitors.

I will always revere the spirit, passion and energy of the SAB team in Nigeria. They took on the most challenging country in Africa and won.

MARK BOWMAN

When I took responsibility for Africa, André Parker told me that, after many years of trying, SAB had bought a brewery in Nigeria. The corporate finance folks said the deal was done but after about six months it turned out that it wasn't. We had been dealing with a Nigerian opportunist who owned a brewery and was playing us for more money.

Eventually I felt this didn't look as though it was going to happen. I saw the problem as SAB trying to be briefcase salesmen: sending someone in with a briefcase to do a deal and then leave.

Nigeria, like the rest of Africa, was a complicated place. We decided we would appoint someone there to get us going and sent a single expat, Peter Studdard. Seemingly within a blink, he had bought a brewery. In hindsight it was a huge mistake but at least we were in the country.

The brewery was in Pabod in Port Harcourt, not the best place in Nigeria for a comfortable lifestyle but not a bad place to start a brewery.

Senior managers weren't allowed to go to Port Harcourt because it was considered too dangerous, which we hadn't told the four South Africans we sent there. The brewery was selling 400 cases of beer a month, 50 of which were donated to the local chief as some sort of tithe, and we started to build a little momentum. But the brewery was a bit of a dog.

With time, it seemed to start coming together, mainly because we had these pioneering South Africans, and we slowly built up a team of excellent Nigerians. They had worked in the industry and saw us as the underdogs, but as they began to work with us, we started to grow. Johan de Kock, Andrè Lubbe, Craig McDougall, and Boyce Lloyd all climbed in to help.

It was tough. They were living at the brewery without the armed escorts who guarded everyone else. There were kidnappings but we were too poor, so nobody was going to kidnap our people. So there was no risk really.

At some point we decided we needed to build a brewery. By sheer coincidence, our distributor, Peter Obi, was elected as the governor of one of the states and he wanted an investment so that he could show the populace what value he could add. He kept trying to persuade us to build.

Some of our executives went to Onitsha and drove around in a cavalcade to view a few sites he showed us: like a marsh, another marsh and then another marsh, before we settled on an old mill at a former clothing manufacturing facility.

Of course, the minute we showed interest nobody wanted to sell at a price that was reasonable. So Obi effectively just confiscated the mill and sold it to us. It was all legally done to clean up the deal, as the state was also a part owner.

Before we could get approval, though, we compiled a complete business case and presented it to Graham and Malcolm. About halfway through the presentation, Malcolm asked some awkward questions about our plan for actual growth. Were we going to take share from competitors or was there natural growth? John Kirby kicked me under the table.

'We don't have all the answers to that right now, Malcolm, but we'll get back to you,' I said.

SIMON HARVEY

The big deal was always Nigeria. Three or four times we presented to the board saying we needed to get into Nigeria and put a lot of work into looking at whether we needed to buy a brewery or build one. Mark and I agreed that rather than involvement in another disaster brewery like Port Harcourt's, why don't we just build a brewery?

Nowhere in the world had a beer company gone into a country as a number three player, but we really believed the opportunity lay not in taking Heineken and Diageo head on, but in homing in on the local beer – usually three or four months old before it was consumed – in this huge market.

We went to London for a day to talk to the board, looking for $150 million. We presented to the entire board. The business was a bit flush at that stage and needed another big opportunity. At the end, they said we could leave and they would debate it.

As Mark and I walked outside, he said he felt it had gone quite well compared to other presentations. We had really packaged the case well. I'd said we wanted to build the local brand into something special and talked about the history of the Igbo people living there. We were going in not on a wing and a prayer but because we thought it was an opportunity.

We went back in, and Graham said the board knew this was high risk but were prepared to give it a go.

'You guys seem very passionate, but understand that if this goes tits up, it's on you two.' As we were about to leave, he added another caveat: 'If you want this thing to succeed, one of you will need to go and live in Nigeria to make sure this thing happens.'

Driving back to the airport, Mark said: 'You do understand that between the two of us, I'm not going to Nigeria?' In my mind I was wondering how the hell I was going to go home and tell my wife that we had to go to Nigeria. I did not have much sleep on that flight back.

When I got home my wife asked how the presentation had gone. I said it had been all right, but we would have to live in Nigeria.

She said: 'You are off your trolley if you think I'm going to Nigeria. You can go and live there by yourself.' With two little children, that wasn't really an option.

The next day in the office, Mark asked: 'How did your wife take it?' I said: 'She's thinking about it.' About a week later I eventually persuaded my wife at least to get on a plane and go to see what it was like. So we flew to Lagos and landed at what must be one of the worst airports in the world, at around 9.00 p.m. After an absolute mess of getting through formalities we reached the hotel around 11.00 p.m. Walking up to the room, my wife said: 'You have absolutely no f... ing chance of me bringing my kids to this shithole,' and then went to bed.

The next day, in a better mood, she said: 'Let's go out and have a look.' Johan de Kock had already found a house for us, and we went to the local shops. 'This is an absolute shithole,' she confirmed.

In an African context, Nigeria was probably better only than South Sudan. We spent three days there and it was not looking promising. From a career perspective I had really no choice. It was a choice of going away and leaving your family or leaving the company. After about two weeks at home and lots of conversations, my wife and I agreed to give it a go. And she did. We spent some two and a half years there. It was tough but when we left Nigeria and went to London my wife said she would rather stay in Lagos.

For family life, it was the best we ever had, because there was nothing else to do. You could give dedicated time to your kids. Even in South Africa, most weekends you'd be working, at a function or the cricket or the rugby, entertaining customers. In Nigeria, your job was to run the business and the weekend was your own.

Mark

In truth, we didn't really have any idea where we were going, but we knew that if we had a brewery there, we would get growth. Graham and Malcolm never said no, but they also didn't always say yes. I always felt if they didn't say no, that meant yes, and we would tell all the other people that Graham and Malcolm had approved. They never said no, we don't approve.

So we bought half of the mill land and established a brewery with semi-approval for a $150 million business. John and I decided we had better take Graham up there to have a look.

Graham was happy to travel in Africa, again without escort, and Obi agreed to meet us there. He took us on a tour through the city. After about 20 minutes, we couldn't move anymore; the crowds were heaving and screaming: 'Obi! Obi!' He was that popular. Graham turned to me and said he wished people would shout his name like that when he travelled.

In Nigeria, Onitsha is called a town, but it's a city of five million people. It could justify its own brewery. It had only one defunct operation but so many people that we felt if you couldn't sell beer there, you couldn't sell it anywhere.

Almost from the day we built a brewery we struggled to keep up with demand. We told local shareholders how it was working. They said: 'Well, we told you so.'

We flew up to the brewery opening. Nigerian President Goodluck Jonathan was coming to do the honours and all the dignitaries – local chiefs in full regalia, shareholders – were among the 700 guests at the ceremony. The temperature was about 34°C with 100 percent humidity. The opening was scheduled for 1.00 p.m. We were all there at 11.00 a.m. One o'clock came and went and there was no action. I was the only SABMiller person in that whole audience.

I was sitting, still waiting and becoming a little frustrated. I was sweating profusely. I was like a wet towel. I asked one of the local kings what the story might be.

'What do you mean?' he says.

'When is he coming?' I ask.

He explains: 'If he came at 1.00 p.m., it would mean he didn't have anything better to do. He's an important man. Of course, he will not come at 1.00 p.m. He's got lots of other things to do.' Eventually he arrived at about 4.00 p.m.

I realised then how dangerous it was to be a president in Africa. He came with an entire militia, all with AK47s pointed in a hundred directions. I thought the risk of him getting shot by accident was considerable. He made a short speech, stayed for about eight minutes, and left. Everyone else partied like crazy.

Initially, we sold a brand called Pabod, which we didn't think was right. We decided to develop a brand for the new brewery. We did a lot of research and came up with three brands. As management we settled on *Akikanju*, a local word for hero.

One of the local marketing guys came to us and made an appeal: 'Don't call it that,' he pleaded,' because the local vernacular was not as powerful as using the English name Hero, and he gave us this whole construct of why Hero is such a powerful English word. To our credit we listened to him.

Simon

The new brewery was in the home of the Igbo people. In the past, Nigeria had always been served by regional breweries, with Trophy in the south west. We asked ourselves: what could we do to build a brand that would be good for the Igbos? We did some research and eventually came up with a brand that we thought we could deliver.

There were two names: Hero and Enyi, the Igbo word for elephant.

I had learnt from my time spent in marketing that no matter what you think is not important, what matters is what consumers think. We learnt from the consumers that if you wanted to have a successful beer, it had to have an English name. If you gave it a vernacular name it was seen to be a traditional beer, like sorghum.

So we put a plan together. Our marketing buddies thought we should be marketing Castle Lager and bit of this and a bit of that, but Nigerians didn't like anything that wasn't local. If we went down our route, and it didn't work, and the brewery was a cock-up, it was on my head.

We took the patronising view of something that would suit the locals in the vernacular, so we created this Hero brand that appealed to the Igbo people. Their symbol was the rising sun, which we built into the logo, so everyone recognised all these cues in the brand. And Hero had a very powerful connotation in Nigeria.

The background was: In May 1967, seven years after Nigeria's independence from Britain, military officer Chukwuemeka Odumegwu Ojukwu declared the eastern region's secession from the rest of the country.

A series of military coups had fuelled ethnic rivalries that killed tens of thousands of Igbos. Ojukwu's breakaway region was renamed the Republic of Biafra.

Ojukwu's act led to a bloody civil war that lasted until January 1970. More than a million people in the eastern region died from starvation, fighting and disease.

Nonetheless, Ojukwu was seen as a regional hero for daring to challenge the federal government. Throughout his life, in much of southeast Nigeria, Ojukwu was celebrated for standing up for the country's southeastern region and its predominantly Igbo population.

(Ojukwu went into exile after the war ended but returned in 1982 when former president Shehu Shagari granted him an unconditional pardon.)

When Ojukwu died in November 2011 at the age of 78. His casket, covered in a Nigerian flag, was flown around the country and to his birthplace, Zungeru, in northern Nigeria. He was buried in March 2012 in his hometown of Nnewi with full military honours.

Former president Goodluck Jonathan and other dignitaries were among the crowd at his funeral, which was held about 20 km from Onitsha.

When the new brewery offered a beer branded Hero, Igbos readily believed that it referred to Ojukwu and almost immediately nicknamed the beer 'Oh Mpa', Igbo for 'Oh my father', in honour of the secessionist leader.

The beer sold for 150 naira (roughly $0.90 then), a price below that of the major mainstream brands dominating the market. It quickly became popular in local pubs, bars, restaurants, lounges, clubs, and inns throughout Igboland.

A local trade magazine later published consumer reactions. It declared: 'The beer was made in our region, by our people for our people. It gave us a sense of belonging; this is our own. Drinking it felt like you're playing a role in the Igbo struggle.

'The brewer localised the brand and it gave the people a sense of ownership. It has a common story with our history and struggle; we find ourselves and our cause in Hero Lager.'

In May 2018, Hero Lager was knighted with a new 'red cap' crown cork to mimic the red cap worn by respected chiefs and elders in Igboland, which served as a symbol of respect, achievement and social recognition.

The Obi of Onitsha, the city's traditional leader, bestowed the beer with the title *Mmanya ejiri mara Igbo*. Literally translated, it meant 'the beer that identifies Igbos'.

I remember a call from John Kirby shortly before the brewery opening. He said: 'Simon, I think I need you and Andries du Plessis to come down (to Johannesburg) for a cup of tea.' When you were called to head office for a cup of tea, it was never a good conversation. I said: 'John, let me have a look at the numbers again and I'll see what I can do.'

He said: 'Simon, you're not hearing me. You and Andries need to come and have a cup of tea. Don't worry, we'll give you some cake as well.'

We thought: 'Oh dear, *hier's kak in die land*.'

Andries and I put a presentation together about what we were doing and what we believed and headed south. We had dropped our forecast numbers by about 100,000 hl for the balance of the year, and we were launching Hero Lager in September. We were about two weeks away from the opening.

We flew down and gave the presentation. Andries gave all the statistics and trends. I gave the marketing schpiel, blah, blah blah. We presented for about an hour. The tea was there and there was cake on the side. John and Mark were there. We presented to just the two of them.

John finally said: 'Nice presentation, very good and very insightful. But ... tell us what help you need from Mark and me to get back to your budget.'

I turned to Andries and thought we where not going to get out of this alive.

They said: 'Look guys, you asked for $150 million, and we gave it to you. We gave it to you based on a business plan based on volumes, which were your budget volumes. Don't come with your cockamamie story now and say that after you've spent your money you can't meet your budget.'

We said: 'Point taken. We'll deliver our budget.' The success story with Hero enabled the brewery to pay for itself in two years. We delivered the budget, and then some. It was unbelievable.

Mark

At the brewery opening, I sat chatting to one of the distributors (we selected distributors by the degree to which they were disaffected by Heineken. We were small so we had to find people willing to take the risk of dealing with us).

He explained to me how Hero was this powerful brand. He spoke for about 10 minutes about what this brand meant to him. I realised that he had never tasted the beer. He had seen it that day for the first time. He had completely internalised the brand.

In the following months we would go to bars that had six or seven local name brands. Outlets that were exclusive to Heineken all carried the local brand under the shelf. You would just say the word and it would pop out. It developed a life of its own. It completely captured the imagination of the locals.

Heineken had apparently completed a report on the brand when they saw it launched and come to the conclusion that it would fail because it was an ethnic brand, because it was targeting the Igbo.

We thought that was fine, because there were something like 160 million people in Nigeria of whom about 30 million were Igbo, so we wanted only them. It didn't matter to us.

The interesting thing was that the Yoruba and the other tribes, when asked if they would drink Hero, confirmed they would do so, because they subscribed completely to the values, even though it was an Igbo beer. It was no problem at all for them to take the brand on board.

Similarly, Trophy was seen very much as a Yoruba beer but was acceptable for various reasons to the Igbo.

Simon

Nigeria was a challenge of note and incredibly rewarding. We went from being the number three brewer with a 1.1 percent share to become the number two player in just two years with just under 20 percent market share. That was Hero and Trophy.

At that stage, we were also doing a deal with the Castel family. As mentioned earlier, we had a problematic relationship with the family, generated by an issue in Angola where they had a business and we had a business, both big businesses fighting each other.

The patriarch, Pierre Castel, had always wanted to solve the problem but we had been unwilling to relinquish a business that was doing about three million hl. Eventually, however, we reached an agreement, through Project Royale, that they would take over Angola and we would take Nigeria.

The new brewery was doing about 700,000 hl to 800,000 hl and Port Harcourt about 200,000 hl, so together it was about a million, in a market that was about 20 million. Their brewery was at Ilesa. And our new brewery was at Onitsha.

Not many people get the chance to build their own brewery. I was lucky enough to build that brewery, to renovate the Port Harcourt brewery, and to put two new lines into Onitsha brewery that were double the size of Ilesa's brewery's.

As a normal SAB person, you're lucky to get one brewery. I spent $450 million in two and half years on one new brewery and three upgrades.

Within two years Hero became the biggest brand in Africa outside of South Africa, and it was purely around the Igbos and it being their beer. There was pride and passion around their brand. It was the right thing, in the right place, at the right time. The beer took off like a bullet. We had identified a brand truth and found a way to resonate in the market.

Most brands take seven years at least to build – if you persevere. This was an overnight sensation.

We also restricted independent redistributors' volumes. They wanted to buy truckloads. We said: 'You can have pallets. We'll deliver to you every day if we have to, but we do not want stale beer in the trade.'

Research had shown that the average beer from Star and Diageo was being consumed in six to seven weeks in Onitsha. So our unique proposition was a fresh beer.

We also had a unique price point. We said what would be the price point we could hold for two years. Inflation was running high. We said we've got to launch this at NGN1.50, which was $1 at that stage, and we believed a dollar was about the right price for a beer. Star was being sold at $2 and Gulder was also about $2. We said: 'Guys we have to stay at this, we can't change the price within the first 18 months to two years.' We squeezed economies of scale.

We went after a green bottle, which imparted more premium brand cues.

It was known as an economy beer, and we had come out with some brand guidelines that said that economy or lower mainstream beers could not use metallic ink. I said: 'I'm going with metallic. You can take the difference between the cost of a non-metallic label and a metallic label and put that against marketing.' I told the technical guys we needed a label to talk to consumers. So we allocated a portion of the cost of labels to marketing as one of the marketing drives, and it just flew.

It became a phenomenon. Nobody had come to Nigeria, because it was a shithole. Now they were eager to come and see how we had been able to take something from nothing and build this business.

We also updated Trophy. Throughout Africa, country by country, pride of origin had worked successfully. In other African countries Safari, Mosi, and Kilimanjaro were all success stories. But Nigeria was 190 million people, and the population of Igbos was about 30 million. We just rejuvenated the label and went with the same bottle for Hero and Trophy.

The people had a pioneering, can-do attitude, with no moaning.

Lagos was a shithole and if you went to places like Ilesa or Onitsha, there's not a hotel, no coffee shops, no restaurants. You have a compound where you live. You and your family stay there. There's nothing else. It's where you work, eat and sleep.

Those years in the breweries were hard work and hard play. People were rewarded for what they did. We used to give our guys three or four breaks a year, plus their annual leave, just to get them out. They didn't have to be in South Africa. They could go anywhere they liked for the price of a South African ticket. I told

HR: 'Guys, this is what it is. If you want people to live in this part of the world, doing what you want them to do, we have to be flexible.'

When I started there, the business was losing $4 million a year at EBIT level. When I left we were making $74 million EBITDA. We had the biggest volume growth in Africa. We were the second biggest business in volume terms outside South Africa. We had become bigger than Tanzania in volume. We became the number two player in the market. We were the number one in the two regions in which we operated, and we were planning to build the fourth brewery, which was later built between Lagos and Ilesha.

Mark

There were one or two occasions when I thought my career at SAB was completely exposed and Nigeria was one of them.

I said to John Kirby, after six months: 'I'm either here or I'm not.' We had spent $150 million on a brewery in Nigeria, with no track record other than a beer business selling a few dozen cases a month down the road and offered a new brand we had never tested in the market.

If it hadn't worked, I would have been bulleted. Even in SAB terms, that was too much money just to forgive. But it worked.

From a standing start, within two or three years, we were number two in the market (Guinness exited the lager beer market in this year). We exited making close to $80 million a year of EBIT. It was unprecedented. We took some bold bets. SAB was prepared to do so and had the resources, and we had incredible Nigerians and some fantastic South Africans.

Ally

We realised the personal sacrifices that our expat communities made. Every time we took the SAB jet, we packed twenty-kilogram polystyrene boxes for each expat with high quality frozen meat; mostly fillets, lamb chops, rump steaks and boerewors, which were seldom available and, if they were, required taking out a bond to afford them.

In all my time in Africa, I always thought of the expats and what small home comforts would help them. Even a copy of the Sunday Times was gratefully accepted. These guys were the true heroes of the story.

To the Home
of Pilsner Urquell

Pilsner Urquell was the first pale lager in the world, going back to 1842. The beer had a crisp clean finish and a good balance of bitter hops with pale malt.

GARTH SAUNDERS

I remember the small team who were initially sent to the home of the beer, the Czech Republic.

It was Tony van Kralingen, Ian Penhale, me, and a few others. Tony was smart. He just allowed the guys to work it out for themselves. He was a bit like Graham in some ways.

I remember some of the Czechs coming out for their first sales conference in South Africa. And they went off after the conference, to see our depots with their best practices, and said: 'You're very good and very impressive. But we've tried that, we've done the other.' They spoke of all the things they had already done.

Six months later, if that, it was more of: 'I think we should do this. It's a good idea.' It was exactly what they had found in South Africa, but it was now their idea. And then it flew. They were like machines when it came to implementing.

The Czech business was owned by a Japanese investment bank. It held all the shares. The bank lined up breweries and invited brewers to buy them. They were interested only in how much money they could make; they never really cared about the brewery.

Heineken had been there a week or two before us, as had the British brewer, Bass, before them. There was concern among the Czechs at first as to whether they could work with us, but they seemed to overcome that quite quickly.

So we bought Pilsner Urquell. Then they told us 'No, we have two more breweries.' The three breweries were in Pilsen, about 100 km from Prague; another one about 30 km from Prague; and a third about 300 km to the east in Moravia.

We went all the way back with a team split in two. They didn't want to know us. Uninterested, they hadn't arranged translators; the bankers were going to translate. That was a disaster for starters. We spent the whole first day going nowhere. They didn't answer any questions. They simply did not want to be bought, not by anybody, never mind South Africa.

That night we all went – them and us – on the same bus to a chateau for dinner. Now what could we do? We drank their beer, not just a couple, quite a few.

Then suddenly the owner stood up to propose a toast to us and the future. Prost! … and down goes the slivovitz. Then a second fellow – the second most important person on our visit – stood up. He also wanted to propose a toast. The second slivovitz went down. Then the bank representative had to stand up.

I don't know how many slivovitzes and beers we drank but everyone was rotten by the end of it. I remember one of the bankers fell asleep in the bus. Every time it hit a bump, he was thrown against something. I'm surprised he's still alive.

The next morning you couldn't believe the difference. We were suddenly people they could work with. We were just like them. The whole situation changed, just like that, overnight. I'm sure this happened time and time again. It was a culture thing.

The interesting question is how come so many of us had that culture? What was it that we managed to get into people? We didn't always get it right. But it said: work hard, play hard. The difference was that the Heineken buyers would not even have gone to dinner. That would have been the difference.

I had got there (Czech) in January. They said you've got to produce the numbers. I thought that was unfair, but they were adamant. I looked at this thing and thought I don't know what I'm going to find.

We provided for everything we could. I got hold of the guys in Europe and said what profit number did you have in your books for Czech. They said we had a loss of I don't know how many million. So we made up that loss for them by putting away provision. Pete Lloyd hated it because he could never work out how much that was. I think they released those things for about five years afterwards. All that stuff was written off against an acquisition account. But the business ran really well.

Then I had some drama with my kids, and I said look, I'm going back. If Breweries can find me a job that's fine, otherwise I'll find one. I can't stay here. Already they had given me extended leave. It just wasn't working.

Then Gavin Hattersley went off to America to Miller. He and I had been in the running for the CFO job. He got it and I didn't. That's when I got the Czech job. But Tony wanted me to go because he and I had worked on a retail project when we changed the credit conditions. He and I worked quite well together.

IAN PENHALE

My move to Czech in 2000 was an inspiring experience. We weren't in too many countries yet. We had just bought Czech.

Prior to that we bought Poland, where Barry Smith launched the SAB portfolio. He took the portfolio strategy map approach from South Africa to Tyskie and Lech and improved the quality of the beer dramatically, making it more affordable. Stealing with pride was something we did really well, particularly in the earlier days.

I don't think Hungary made any money for the company. It was school fees, but it was tough school fees and a tough market where we didn't have a big share. Hungarians are not very nice and it's not a beer drinking culture, so it was always going to be hard.

I remember the first meeting we had in Czech. We were very gentle and appreciative of what they had, of their beer, of their culture.

Tony was brilliant; he was hugely sensitive to the fact that we had bought this company that represented the national silver, and of course they invented the first clear beer in 1842, Pilsner Urquell. It had become a famous beer in the time of communism in Russia, producing beer for the communist bloc, and their people were very proud.

They worked on a different system, an eight-hour day which wasn't really well managed. You could start at 6.00 a.m. and end at 2.00 p.m. We had a bizarre flexitime on a clock card.

The Czech people loved us. I think we pioneered and exported our culture very well. We brought a Czech sales and marketing team to South Africa every year as part of an incentive reward programme, to share best practice and to give them cultural exposure. They loved that.

We were becoming more international, so we had the first global leadership conference held in the Czech Republic. Johan Nel phoned me six to eight weeks before and said: 'Ian, can I ask you a favour? Do you mind running the first global leadership conference for us in Prague? But don't be too quick, to answer, it's in just less than two months.' I said: 'Sure.'

Anyway, we hosted 120 people from around the world and we put on a professional experience. Czech, of course, is magic, a local company that did so well, and it fell into place. It was a wonderful group of people where around 115 out of a total of 120 were from SAB Limited, so it was a family affair. It was uplifting.

We went on a tour through the underground cellars, we went to Pilsen, and we had fireworks orchestrated to music. Pete Lloyd was muttering about the cost, which was only $1,000 dollars, as he was scratching his right goon.

Tony van Kralingen led from the front as he steered the Czech venture to become a sensational business taking key learnings from the journey we had travelled in South Africa.

TONY VAN KRALINGEN

The building blocks we had been taught for 20 years were all there. So, it was easy to fit in and plot the way forward. We bought three different businesses, with three different cultures.

They brewed Plzensky Prazdroj, which was the biggest brand at 5 million hl; Radegast and Pilsner Urquell, about 1.4 million hl, and Velkopopovicky Kozel, about 0.6 million hl.

For the first three weeks I just travelled with an interpreter to get the lay of the land.

We learnt there was a gap between the South Africans and the Czechs, no matter which company they were from, along with a level of mistrust, exacerbated by the president of the company, Pezina, who had been told he would be the president and I would be the managing director. He would look after the external issues, and I would handle internal affairs. But he didn't want me there. I didn't realise how serious that was, but I did know that if push came to shove, the business would back me. Fortunately, he saw the futility of his expectations and left before too long.

One of the big issues remained this sense of mistrust between the Czechs and us. The Czechs are a suspicious crowd, which is understandable in the light of a history of being run for 400 years by the Hapsburgs. They were very good at saying 'yes sir' and then carrying on the way they were.

The mistrust was never externalised but some of it you could see in their body language. I felt it, and it was difficult. At our first planning conference, with just the executive team, it was three guys from one side and five from the other, and they wouldn't talk to each other.

A young planning guy, later planning manager, named Vidsez Lachek, was a big help in talking me through the way they saw things, rather than just me trying to interpret them. He helped me to think about the challenges of the business through all their doubts and anxieties.

We hired McKinsey to work with us to determine what this business could look like. We did it functionally, not something you typically do, because I wanted each function to own its journey.

It then started engendering fights between the Czechs. The biggest fight was between Otto Binde (from Pilsen), who was in charge of sales and distribution, and a fellow named Stanislav, the head of manufacturing (who came from Radegast). They hated each other.

Theirs were the two biggest breweries in the land and for 40 years they had fought one another. They were enemies. When we were trying to find a solution, these little battles resurfaced.

Finally, Otto and I came to an agreement: we would take out everyone who came from Radegast because they could never work for someone who was from a different business. That's what we did. In the first six months we retrenched 600 people, 20 percent of the staff out of the three businesses.

That was a brave decision (McKinsey must take some of the credit for the process we put in place), but we made function owners own the answers. It wasn't a case of telling Otto what to do, it was, you tell me what you're going to do to get this business right, then we can have a conversation about whether we all agree that it's right.

Stanislav blew his top when we told him we were going to retrench 100 out of Radegast. He said how can you do that? They are Moravians. I said they will never support Pilsen.

So, what do we do?

We then went through the functions and narrowed them down. Going around and asking people questions, I learnt an astonishing thing: the HR director at the time told me that if you were paid 100 dollars a month, you received only 50. After three months, your boss would decide whether to give you the 150 taken over the three months, or a percentage of it.

I asked to see performance reviews and the targets set. He said, no, as the boss, you just decide. 'Are you happy with that?' I asked. He said that's the way it was. So, I fired him.

It sounds harsh but I didn't know how I was going to work with a guy who had no sense of what good looked like. Culturally I could understand where they came from, but it just didn't sit with who we were.

I said this method of payment was unacceptable and I told the team that I was going to write a rule that the 100 dollars they earned was what they earned. I was not bothering about this game they played. Everybody would get their full salary from day one.

It was one of the small things that worked. People said: 'Well they've retrenched 600 people, but they're really looking after the people who stayed.' It made them feel part of the organisation: 'They're thinking about us, not just worried about the top.' And we gave good salary increases.

The second thing was that the brewery really hadn't been looked after. We modernised the brewery, but the site was grubby and plastered together. Our offices were terrible. Gary Bull came to work for me as procurement officer and he wanted new offices. I said: 'That's the last thing I want. We'll work out of Pilsen until we start making money.'

What came before that was the 100th anniversary of building the brewery gate. The Czechs said: 'We have to restore this gate, it's in terrible condition.' I agreed. 'Let's put some money towards fixing the gate.'

Instead of builders, we hired craftsmen who were specialists at restoring these heritage sites, guided by a lady named Andreschka who could trace her family history back to the 1500s and was custodian of the history of the business.

I learnt that Pilsen had emerged from many breweries that had come together and founded this miraculous brew: 40 independent businesses invested in a 'citizens' brewery' that was a combination of Gambrinus and Pilsen. The people of Pilsen saw the brewery as theirs, not ours.

We won a lot of favour when the first thing they saw us do for this business was restore their gate. In doing so, we discovered buried artefacts about the history and the leaders of the business. We celebrated it as a discovery and kept the finds in our museum.

We wanted a celebration of opening the gate with all the people of Pilsen.

The mistake I made is that I didn't close the brewery and let all the shift workers attend. I didn't realise how important this was. We made amends later, but it made me realise you're really dealing with someone else's property. In their minds, it's not your property, it's theirs. You're just temporary owners. Someone else will own it one day, which is what happened.

So we inherited a business that in today's currency made $40 million. Three years later it made $240 million. It was a very successful time.

The other thing for me was to realise that whoever ran the business needed to talk about the business, particularly in a foreign country. The community wants to see you. You are the person they want to look at, to decide if they trust you.

A journalist phoned wanting an interview and asked to talk to me. She was told she had to talk to Pezina, our corporate affairs manager. She said no, she wanted to talk to me, as I ran the business. And she said: 'If he doesn't talk to me, I will write what I want to write.'

I went to meet her at a restaurant and sat down. She was very polite at first. She asked: 'You come from South Africa?'

I said: 'Yes.'

She said what she knew about South Africa was that it produced gold and diamonds, and the third thing, violence. 'And you've got no education and you have no claim to run a business with the heritage of ours.'

'You want me to respond?'

'Yes.'

'You are caught in a mindset that is not fully informed. Let me give you a perspective of the Czech Republic that you won't like.' I could see her becoming a bit bristly.

I said: 'I had a farewell in South Africa, from my team and from the brewery. At the farewell, someone came to me and said: 'Why are you going to Chechnya?'

She said: 'F... Chechnya. Chechnya is Russia. We are not Chechnya.'

I said: 'So they were wrong, weren't they?'

She said: 'Can we start again?'

She eventually became a big supporter of ours. It reinforced that you must be very thoughtful about the mindsets you come across.

In 2001, we had the worst floods in 50 years in Poland, Czech and East Germany. Parts of Prague were flooded as were large parts of Pilsen. A section of the brewery was under water. People had to leave work to look after their homes. We closed the brewery for a couple of days.

In Pilsen we had the biggest restaurant in Central Europe at the time, Na Spilce. It had 600 seats. I sat with the team, and they said there was really no place in Pilsen for people to work and get fed, other than at the brewery. I said we'll open a soup kitchen and everyone who is working and trying to salvage their homes and shops can come to eat, morning noon and night, at Na Spilce, free.

The Czechs said: 'Are you mad? This is going to cost a fortune.'

Garth did some numbers and we worked out the cost at $100,000. We went ahead and did it. I think none of those people would probably ever drink any other beer after that. We weren't wanting to buy loyalty, but it seemed like a no-brainer.

Czech had almost an obsession with heritage. In 1942 they had a big ceremony when they switched from oak barrels to stainless steel cylindro conical tanks. The brewers tasted every beer they produced to ensure that the beers from each tank tasted the same to overcome the scepticism of people who might say the new technology was getting in the way of the old traditional beer. It was obvious to even the most insensitive person that this was a really important issue.

In the first year, every day, a horse and cart would emerge from the brewery loaded with barrels to be delivered to pubs near the brewery.

I spoke a lot to Andreschka, the lady who could trace her family back to 1500, and she said the nine copper kettles were the heart of the brewery.

McKinsey had suggested getting rid of the coopers who made the [oak] barrels, because they were a waste of money. I said: 'No, they're our history.'

What's the cost of nine coopers and running a barrel-making operation? What we did was to eulogise them; we reinvested in this knocked-down brewery and built a cooper's museum situated on the way to the brewhouse. What Andreschka did was very clever. She made wax models of the coopers who were working at the brewery at the time. The head cooper was the biggest of them and the model of him was the most prominent. It was as though he was there.

I was told the lovely story of one of the brewers who might have overdone his tasting while on shift. He saw this guy working on a barrel, and he thought it was his mate Waslav.

'Waslav,' he shouts. But it's a model, so of course there's no response. 'I see; now that you have this prime spot, you're no longer talking to me.' People talked about it and came to see it.

When we took over, I think 50,000 tourists a year used to go to Pilsen; this was a brewery that was truly a tourist attraction. We never even took people around the bottling hall. The tour ended at the end of the brewery.

It was all about the beer. You could see a bottling hall anywhere in the world. You could never see that brewery. It was all about the people and the beer. I think that now there must be 350,000 people a year who visit Pilsen, because we gave them an experience and kept true to what it was. I think successive GMs have built on that.

Another matter we had in Czech was that when we took over, we had 42 percent market share. When I left three years later, we had 48 percent. It's doesn't seem like much but it's quite a lot of volume. There was no decrease in volume.

The Czechs love beer, but they never abuse it. It is just part of the fabric of life. I never saw a Czech staggering around out of control. The per capita consumption was then around 160 litres, which is a lot (about 45 percent more than the next biggest beer-drinking country, Austria) and everybody drinks it. In other parts of the world, there's a core that drinks too much and some that drink very little.

I was proud to be awarded the keys to the city of Pilsen. The keys relate to the time when cities in Europe had walls and only people the city trusted were allowed keys to enter. I think it was really a tribute to the way SAB treated Plzensky Prazdroj as a company and its people. I just happened to be the leader at the time.

To me, one of the great successes of SAB was that in promoting and moving our people, who came out of this deep culture where intellectual integrity was highly valued, we managed people and respected their sense of dignity, and we showed a humility that allowed the people in the businesses we bought to flourish and thrive. It happened in the Czech Republic and in Poland.

Most of the businesses we went into at that time were a success. We didn't look down on the businesses we bought. We used their brands, identity and people, and they made them work. We just gave them better structures, processes, disciplines and principles, rather than telling them we were clever, and we would do it all.

Right
-Sizing

SA Breweries' global expansion beyond Africa, starting in the 1990s, took it to Russia in 1998. It was very different from anything South Africans were used to in climate, geographic scale and culture.

SAB went there very much as a premium business and built a brewery in Kaluga, a city on the Oka River 150 kilometres southwest of Moscow. It was a strong premium business but probably a bit schizophrenic as it expanded more into mainstream beer. It was also a very profitable business for one that was quite small.

GRANT HARRIES

Russia was at first a great place to do business. Beer was treated as a soft drink and distribution was pervasive, sold through kiosks much like South African spaza shops, at bus stops, railway stations, subways, anywhere. You could just buy beer. You would see people in parks drinking beer as they would a soft drink.

It was a very competitive market. The trade was all these little kiosks everywhere. Living there is like living in a time warp.

Russia did, however, have an alcohol problem, driven mainly by spirits. When the current president, Vladimir Putin, came back from his stints as prime minister (from 1999 to 2000, and again from 2008 to 2012), there was a lot of societal pressure around alcohol. In 2010 the beer excise was about two roubles per litre. By 2014 it was about 18 roubles per litre, and the government closed all 250,000 kiosks and restricted distribution enormously.

My call to Russia came as a shock. There was this view that if you were not European and had no European experience, you wouldn't make it. Even SABMiller guys were not really wanted there. So I was surprised.

Graham employed a different strategy there. The focus was on the premium portfolio. We had 10 percent volume share and 11 percent value share. It worked very well. My predecessors there had done a fantastic job. They had taken a brand like Zolotaya Bochka – Golden Barrel in English and based on a Castle Lager recipe with three strength variants – and made it the biggest selling premium beer in Moscow. It came from nothing. The name had not even existed.

I had been there for two months when the government slapped a 200 percent excise tax on beer. All the big players were there: ABInBev, Heineken, Carlsberg, Efes and us. The entire industry took a beating.

We went into restructuring. I couldn't sit back and wait for things to change. I had to retrench some people. There was resistance from the local Russian HR team. They said have faith, this is a volatile country. Things will come back. I said we can't wait three years for that to happen.

I'm glad we did what we did, because we managed to maintain our EBITDA contribution when everybody else's fell off the bus. The other four players didn't react.

I lived in Moscow but travelled a lot. It's seven time zones from Moscow to Vladivostok. The place we had bought off-strategy was cheap, a real Stalin-era type of building with broken windows. It was grey and hadn't been painted. It was butt ugly. I felt nervous to even drink a beer out of that place.

They were making all this economy brand stuff. It was totally off-strategy. The plan had been that we would brew Zolotaya Bochka and the likes in the far east of Russia and distribute it there without all the transport costs. But all the bottles in Russia were non-returnable. The business plan had not been done properly. We had to move all the empty bottles there to fill them.

But we worked within the strategy and the portfolio of brands there, cleaned them up, and fixed the brewery and the quality department.

The sales director, a Russian named Vladimir, said he had not realised that the business was not profitable in the bigger scheme of things, because it had been subsumed in the numbers. I told him the business was making a loss. He said he didn't understand why, so let's go and fix it.

Much later, we went to a convention in the US and Graham told me it was fantastic that we had turned it around into a positive performer. I treated it as a separate entity and just tried to make it profitable.

Russia was a real experience. I was there for three years. We lived in a compound in Pokrovsky Hills about 13 km from Red Square. All the expats lived there. The US and Canadian Embassies were there, and the MD of Heineken lived there. Pick a company, the boss lived there. Right next door, on the other side of the fence, was the school. The kids could walk the 200 m there through a side gate.

My daughter, Katie, loved it, because 90 percent of her school friends lived where we lived. I had little girls running in and out of our place every weekend, all weekend. It was among the top three international schools in the world.

The sheer vastness of the place was astonishing. In SA, we used to think twice about building a brewery 600 km away. In Russia, 2,000 km or 3,000 km was nothing.

We used to put beer in containers going to the east but in December had to budget for write-offs because they froze. We had to load them into sealed temperature-controlled containers to keep the cold out.

Moscow for me is one of the most vibrant cities in Europe, and St Petersburg is the most beautiful, even more so than Prague. But in the rural areas it's like a time warp, from the cars to everything else.

I often say to people I wish they could have seen life through my eyes because it was just sheer amazement and contrast. I remember looking at a beach on the east coast. The whole beach was just snow.

Travelling was something else. We would travel on one of those Suhoi aircraft, with the steps coming up the back. We all had these little yellow boarding slips and waited in a holding pen, much like a prison cell. It would be snowing hard so everyone would sprint to the plane. There were no allocated seats and you wanted to get one because the airline always overbooked. Guys would stand in the aisle when we took off, holding onto seats, and then went and sat in the stewardesses' seats – if they were working.

Flying in Russia was downright dangerous. It has the highest accident rate in the world if I'm not mistaken, but the news just gets buried in the press there. It was scary.

Russians are understandably nervous of flying. That's why the biggest sales of liquor are via duty free shops in Russia. Air travellers smack it hard before they board the aircraft, so they don't have to worry.

The Russians were good people. Everybody sees them as cold and dry, but they're not. Their levels of trust are not like yours and mine. If you read Stalin's books, you'll understand why. They would take a year to understand what we were trying to do and that we were working for them. Only then would they open up.

It wasn't that they didn't want to work, it was just that they were a closed book. In the beginning it was tough. When I left, I had grown men crying in my office; hard Russians, some of whom I didn't even know that well. They're people just as good as people anywhere else. In fact, they're wonderful people.

At one time, we had a convention in Turkey. There wasn't a local centre large enough to accommodate the 700 people we took to these gatherings, so it was cheaper to charter planes and have the convention on the Turkish coast.

Our executive team included Russians, but they could all speak English. At the first convention, I hadn't learnt enough Russian and had a translator on stage with me. The second year, after a lot of lessons, I had written my speech in English and my PA translated it. By then I knew a few words and how to pronounce them. I changed the spelling of the words in the speech to the phonetic spelling. She then retyped the speech for me. It was about 25 minutes long.

After I spoke, everyone stood up and the place rocked. I still get goose bumps thinking about it. Unfortunately, it all backfired at the tea break. People came up to me to chat – in Russian.

ROBIN GOETZSCHE

I followed Grant to Russia later when the Russian beer business had shrunk from about 110 million hl to about 70 million hl, in a population of 140 million people, with a big impact on the profitability of businesses. It was losing around $100 million.

As a result, SABMiller and Efes, the Turkish brewing company operating in Russia, decided to merge their businesses.

The Turks then ran the business. When they merged the businesses, SAB was making about $150 million EBIT and Efes about $50 million. The business plan was to be at $300 million EBIT in three years. When I arrived in 2014, they were minus $100 million.

Shareholding was about 50:50, and SABMiller had another 25 percent of the Efes group business as well as the Coca-Cola business. SABMiller had a seat on the Efes board, but the Turks were running it. I was asked to run the Russian business.

It was tough. We had about 8,000 employees and had to retrench half of them. We had to close a lot of breweries and restructure the whole operation. By 2016, we got to break even and stopped the bleeding.

We had about a 15 percent market share. Fortunately, we were more premium, although 80 percent of the market is in two-litre PET packaging. But we had some great brands like Velkopopovicky Kozel from Czech, and over time we developed and strengthened a lot of the local brands. It became a very nice portfolio.

We had breweries across the country, from Kaluga across central Russia to Vladivostok in the east, seven time zones away. That made it interesting to manage the business. We had conference calls with the guys in Vladivostok, but it was eight in the morning in Moscow and four in the afternoon in Vladivostok.

It's a huge country with a fascinating history but a tough environment in which to operate. We were a small player, which was an advantage because we were below the radar when ABInBev bought SABMiller. ABInBev were very keen to continue the relationship with Efes.

We started very quickly to merge the ABInBev business with our business in Russia. Efes were about the same size as us, so it was a great opportunity. It got us to about a 30 percent market share, about the same as Baltika, who owned Carlsberg.

It became a great business because of the opportunity for leveraging scale by joining the two businesses together.

I was then offered the chance to run the Efes beer business out of Turkey with SABMiller as the joint venture partner. I had gained a lot of exposure to the European business and worked closely with Sue Clark, who had done a brilliant job in corporate affairs. But I spoke to Alan Clark, Johan Nel and Mark Bowman to say I didn't really want to go there.

I had completed my two-year contract in Russia and was still an SABMiller employee. I always had my sights on returning to SAB and after Mark had merged the South Africa and Africa operations, I was keen to go home again after a run offshore of over a decade.

I would have loved that. Then the deal in Russia happened, and Alan said, why not take the Efes role?

The problem with Efes was that it was what I call a 'founders trap'; it had a bureaucracy of middle management who were very arrogant but had none of our processes. They knew everything.

At the same time, Turkey was a totally dark market with probably the highest excise tax in the world, driven predominantly by President Tayyip Erdogan, who was very anti-alcohol. As a result, the business declined both in volume and profitability.

I was seconded to Efes but remained an SAB employee. My agreement was always that it was an assignment, and I would return to somewhere else in the company. At that time, I had a dotted line reporting into Sue Clark who headed SABMiller Europe. I spent about 14 months there.

SABMiller helped me fantastically with best practices. I was always invited to their conferences and meetings. They would also provide us with resources and help. It was the best of both worlds.

I was offered the role of president of Efes, running the Turkish business and the Russian business in Moldova, Ukraine, Georgia and Kazakhstan, and a seat on the board of the Coke business. At that time SABMiller was being bought by ABInBev.

It was tough in Turkey. The Turkish business was in trouble, losing share and profits and moving from SABMiller's meritocracy approach with a lot of team play, sharing and camaraderie, to a family business where the founders had been very entrepreneurial and built a great business.

By the time I arrived, the third generation of founders was in control. I had family members who were multi-millionaires reporting to me. I knew, however, that they were there because they had to do the hard yards in the business. It was very difficult to manage them.

At the time, we also had a level of professional management stuck in the middle because they had about 80 different businesses, from cars to McDonald's to property development, and so on. And there was a head office crowd who constantly enforced their policies.

The board included 22 non-executive directors. Board meetings were held monthly, and members were expected to report back. Every one of them had an opinion about the business. Many of them were family members or friends of the family who had been given board membership. It was a political environment that was very difficult to manage.

The Turkish elite are very well educated, however, and there was a balance of competencies amongst management. Some were good, others not so good.

Turkey is a wonderful country with enormous history, but it's also polarised as you travel from west to east, from the European side of Turkey west of Istanbul to the far east and the border of Syria. As you move further east it becomes more religiously conservative where the president pushed heavy conservative values and anti-alcohol ideology.

The liquor business was not permitted even a branded cooler or fridge. All you could have, were the brand colours. You couldn't do any advertising or outdoor billboards or things like that. Excise tax made the product expensive.

A big problem was also that they had never embraced a culture where everyone understood a performance management system and a meritocracy, where if you did well you were recognised and if you didn't do well, you were managed accordingly. In Turkey, there was a lot of patronage: family members, lack of accountability, people making excuses for non-performance.

I felt I was quite restricted in trying to inculcate SAB learnings, because there was always a group approach. Their management objective system was a group system that you had to adopt. You couldn't have your own system that worked in SABMiller.

Russia had been a tough country. When we went through downsizing, it was fortunately low key, although a number of managers were assaulted and some of the senior managers needed bodyguards. In Turkey it was more external.

We lived there in the time of the terrorist attack on Ataturk airport. We were flying in from Moscow but were delayed for about half an hour and fortunately missed the attack that killed 42 people.

In June 2016, gunmen armed with automatic weapons and explosive belts staged an attack on the international terminal. Three attackers and 45 other people were killed and more than 230 people injured. Media reports indicated that Turkish officials believed the three attackers came from Russia and Central Asia. No one claimed responsibility for the attack.

We also had several terrorist attacks in the Istanbul area including an attempted coup, where a lot of civilians were killed on the bridge that our apartment overlooked.

The coup attempt was aimed at state institutions, including the government and President Recep Tayyip Erdogan by a faction within the Turkish Armed Forces who organised themselves as the Peace at Home Council, and whose members have never been identified. They attempted to seize control of several places in Ankara, Istanbul, Marmaris and elsewhere, such as the Asian side entrance of the Bosphorus Bridge, but failed to do so after forces loyal to the state defeated them.

During the coup attempt, more than 300 people were killed and more than 2,000 injured. Many government buildings, including the Turkish Parliament and the Presidential Palace, were bombed from the air. Mass arrests followed, with at least 40,000 detained, including at least 10,000 soldiers and, for reasons that remain unclear, 2,745 judges.

At a personal level we didn't feel that threatened, but at a broader level it was quite worrying that they had this terrorist stuff going on.

22 **Supporting**
Team South Africa

SAB had long ago recognised the country's passion for sport and the way that sport could bring the nation together in support of a common vision – to win.

From the fifties, we were involved in the sponsorship of the Premier Soccer League, Currie Cup Cricket, and inter-provincial rugby – even darts, our longest standing sponsorship.

As we re-entered the global stage in the early '90s, we were the pioneers of our national teams' sponsorships when we hosted the Cameroon tour to South Africa; when our cricket team walked onto the field at Eden Gardens; and when we stood behind the Bokke as we prepared to host our first Rugby World Cup in 1995.

Our Castle Lager and Lion Lager brands were emblazoned on the chests of our players and around our sports fields. Many stories that we told in our advertising spoke to our sponsorships of our national sporting codes and the passion point of sport. It was always emotionally driven and won our consumers over to love our brands.

For decades we remained loyal to these sporting codes and built long term sustainable associations with sporting bodies and players ... standing the test of time.

My sense is that we contributed immensely to uniting our country at a time when there was little hope for reconciliation. The socio-political miracle that ensued was driven largely by sport.

BARRY SMITH

They were fun days when we sponsored sports. I remember the first game Bafana Bafana played, when Ally and Norman Minnaar went to Durban for the match against Cameroon.

Our guys did everything. They even had to take the players to Mike's Kitchen for supper while the soccer executives went for dinner with their wives. Somebody left his kit behind and Ally had to go back to find it.

We must have been one of the first companies who had those fundraiser dinners where you could buy a table and sit with one of the footballers. The SAFA guys and Stix Morewa set up one of them. With about two days to go, Norman Minnaar came to me and said we had a problem.

Neil Tovey and the players said they were not going to attend. They said they had no gear to wear. I said Morewa must sort it out. Norman said: 'Barry, we're supporting the side, we've got to help somehow.'

Tovey confirmed: 'We haven't got any clothing.' I remember tracking down a guy at Edgars and telling him these guys needed clothing by the following night. Edgars sent out someone who measured everybody, and by the following evening all the team had jackets, trousers, the lot. So, in those early days we did actually 'manage' those teams.

Rugby was a bit different. Louis Luyt was a good manager, and he took no nonsense. He did a fantastic job at the Rugby World Cup. I remember him saying to us – I was always with Norman and sometimes Tobin Prior – in his guttural accent: 'Manne, you must understand, I used to be in business. I know the importance of sponsorship. You guys pay the money and I'll deliver what you want.' And he did.

We once went to see him about a Lion Cup in Witbank where the guys were being uncooperative about erecting signage and such like. He was on the phone in a flash, and he shat all over the people. The signs were up the next day. He was controversial but we got a lot out of him. They were fun days.

Ally

A real privilege of working in sponsorship was meeting the players in our national teams. Some of them remain personal friends to this day. In addition, attending national team fixtures in South Africa and around the world was the realisation of a dream.

The journey began in 1992 when Norman Minnaar, Sports Sponsorship Manager, and I worked together to tie up a team sponsorship with Bafana Bafana, as the new boys on the block in Africa and the world.

It was before democracy came to South Africa that we brought the Cameroon team to South Africa to play three fixtures in Durban, Cape Town and Johannesburg. The visitors were captained by Roger Milla who, by spearheading Cameroons' success in reaching the World Cup quarter final in 1990 – the first African team to do so – was an African hero.

Bafana Bafana were led by Neil Tovey, an unsung hero in bringing together South Africans at a time when the nation truly needed unity.

We chartered a plane to fetch the Cameroonian team and flew them into Durban. The fixtures were brilliant. South Africa showed their skill and talent and won with a penalty by Theophilus 'Doctor' Khumalo. Headlines read: 'Bafana Bafana ('the boys') become men.'

At the second encounter in Goodwood, Cape Town, Bafana were defeated 1-2 and the decider in Johannesburg was a 2-2 draw.

From out of the wilderness, the team had shown up and performed. The nation was euphoric and united not just behind the team but behind Castle Lager, growing at the time by one percentage share point each month.

In 1991, the late Clive Rice led the first South African cricket team on an epoch-making tour of India only a few weeks after the country was readmitted as a full member of the International Cricket Council.

The series of three one-day internationals in India was also the first international sporting event in which South Africa participated after 22 years of isolation because of global opposition to apartheid.

At Eden Gardens in Kolkata, more than 100,000 fans squeezed into the stadium. Even more gathered outside. Such was the noise that the South Africans had to use sign language to indicate strategic moves on the field.

We arranged a pallet of Castle Lager for the charter flight of players and journalists and cleared customs in Mumbai telling officials that the team could not travel without Castle Lager. The team wore the Castle Lager logo on their shirts from the outset and the brand became synonymous with the Proteas team.

Many years later, in 2011, we took a hundred South Africans to India to watch the Proteas take on India in Nagpur. The stadium was packed to capacity and, as the only non-Indian supporters in Nagpur that day outside of the team and a few journalists, we sat together in a block battered by the jeers of ninety thousand Indians around us. But we laughed last.

India scored 296, which in those days was a formidable score. South Africa replied with 300 with two balls to spare. The stadium emptied in less than five minutes and a hundred South Africans went to celebrate with the team on the field and later in the hotel.

When the Springboks won their first Rugby World Cup in 1995, etched forever in rugby lore by the picture of President Nelson Mandela presenting the Webb Ellis Cup to Francois Pienaar, Lion Lager was there as the team's sponsor.

It was a moment in time that demonstrated our ability, our hunger, our passion, and our unity. We won: never before had we experienced this elation ... the streets came alive, the parade unified every city, the power of sport to unify a nation was brought to the fore, and Lion Lager was in front.

The final was a special moment savoured by all South Africans. I hosted customers at all the Springboks' fixtures around the country. I ended up on the final night on a corner in Hillbrow drinking beer with fans and residents late into the night.

In 1996, Castle Lager and Bafana Bafana under the leadership of Neil Tovey won the Africa Cup of Nations. He was a powerful leader, humble and respected, with incredible skill, and the team had an ethic under Clive Barker that this was a once in a lifetime opportunity ... work hard, play hard, not dissimilar to SAB and a connection that showed Africa what we were made of. This time Madiba handed the trophy to Neil Tovey and I joined the team in the changeroom to celebrate late into the night.

In 1998, however, I experienced the sporting week of a lifetime.

Tony van Kralingen and I, searching for a new UK distribution partner for Castle Lager, started our week in Toulouse. Yes, it was hardly the place to find a UK partner, but Bafana Bafana were playing Denmark in an encounter for the FIFA World Cup. We drew the game 1-1; the team acquitted themselves well and made us proud.

After crossing the channel to Scottish & Newcastle plc to explore any synergies for a partnership there, we went the following day to Lord's to watch the Proteas take on England. We won the test in four days of thrilling cricket and then had a day to spare before hosting the team at Langan's restaurant.

We went to Wimbledon, didn't we? We sipped champagne, ate strawberries and watched Steffi Graf in action before hosting the cricketers in celebration of a famous win at the home of cricket.

Back in England the following year, I attended a quarter-, semi-, and final of the Cricket World Cup.

The semi-final was that soul-destroying game in which Allan Donald forgot to run for the winner. The game was tied and Australia, with a higher average than South Africa's across the tournament, advanced to the final and a victory over Pakistan.

That Herschelle Gibbs had dropped a catch against Australia in an earlier round, where a defeat would have taken them out of the tournament, made it all the more a disappointing ending. Captain Hansie Cronje indicated later that the team needed meat and potatoes, and we took them to TGI Fridays. That side was the most likely to have won a World Cup, an honour which remains elusive to this day.

Irreplaceable memories of famous encounters, wonderful players, and celebrations, mostly.

NEIL HOBKIRK

SAB used sports sponsorships very intelligently. Leadership in the company knew that sport was a way to touch people and bring them together, and for them to get on. If they went to watch a game of rugby, cricket or soccer and had a beer together, you could manage to sort out any kind of conflict.

Sport sponsorship wasn't just for awareness, it was a strategic lever that provided a licence to trade that connected deeply with South Africans and linked with the idea of South African excellence.

Ally

It was an immense privilege for me to work in sponsorship when SAB was the pioneer of support, from national team level to development of unknown talent. Because of this alignment, I was given the opportunity to mix with the greatest, the heroes, the leaders and the teams who unified South Africa at a time of division, and we all came together to support a country that had been deprived of global competition for decades.

Personally, I got to meet some absolute characters during time spent in changerooms among cases of the amber beverages, listening to tactics, team talks, strategies and fines, and experiencing team spirit at the highest level.

Francois Pienaar was a household name and became a friend of Nelson Mandela. The outcome was a movie, Invictus, that tells the story of two leaders uniting a country. What I admire was Francois's post-heroic efforts in rugby to pioneer the MAD (Making A Difference) Foundation that went on to educate and elevate many global greats from dust to gold dust. He truly made a difference and showed what true leadership can do. This formidable organization continues to this day.

Hansie Cronje was possibly the best leader and character I ever met. He was inspirational, eloquent, strategic and comedic.

I once asked him to address our leadership forum at the Mount Grace Hotel. We agreed that the two of us would pretend to be the resident barmen when our executive came to the pub for a pre-dinner beer or seven. The executive was blown away to find Hansie behind the counter, less so by me as his assistant.

Hansie had called me late afternoon to ask me directions to the hotel. He told me he was entering Nelspruit and asked at which intersection he should swing a left. We were in the Magaliesberg outside Brits, nowhere near Nelspruit. I was showering in my room when he called, and I heard an echo – he was outside my room.

He was a prankster but would never let me down. He was always playing games and tricks with his teammates, even as a leader. Humour was a pillar of who he was. He was probably the biggest talent we ever had in sport and could have gone on to be an inspiration in South Africa.

One evening he called me to tell me that there was an announcement pending in the morning and that he had let me and SAB down. I think he knew my respect for him and that he felt accountable for what he had done. Ali Bacher announced the bribery and corruption case the following day and sadly Hansie became the fall guy for many bribery and corruption cases in global cricket around the world.

What materialised from here on in was what I admired. Hansie endured a commission of inquiry that was brutal to say the least and took the brunt for some atrocities happening in cricket at the time. Though he slowly faded from society, I continued to stay in touch with him as he began to rebuild himself and his credibility.

He was working for an earthmoving equipment company in Pretoria and doing charity work helping young cricketers in the Eastern Cape. I was running the Charles Glass Society with Derek Macaskill and we asked Hansie to appear as our guest speaker for the first time since his indictment and move underground.

He was anxious. We normally hosted our Charles Glass Society meetings at the Wanderers Rugby Club. We put the invitation out and received more than 2,000 responses whereas we usually had only 200 members attending monthly. We moved the function to the Rivonia Holiday Inn, recruited a top security company to assist us and, on one evening, raised record funds for cricket development: R250,000. Hansie received a standing ovation for nearly ten minutes before he could utter a word.

Our friendship continued and he came one evening to SAB in Park Lane for a few beverages and to catch up. We left the Brewhouse and I invited Hansie to join me in Rivonia's News Café for a *loopdop*. I was at the counter ordering when he called me.

'Hey Ally, look out the sliding doors, I am in my car outside but seem to have a problem with my central locking. If you don't mind, I'm heading back to Pretoria.' It was the last time I saw him. The aircraft taking him back to George crashed in the early hours of Saturday morning some 40 hours after I had seen him.

I was absolutely devastated and remain that way to this day. He was a special human.

Two months later, we hosted a Hansie Cronje benefit concert with the legendary Johnny Clegg. The proceeds were donated to building a Hansie Cronje wing in an Eastern Cape school where he had been actively involved.

John Smit, now a legend, attended the same school as I did, Pretoria Boys High, and had a skill and leadership that took South African rugby to its peak, the World Cup. John once took me back to Pretoria Boys High where he made an emotional speech that must have inspired pupils at the school to go above and beyond. Today he is still inspiring and leading and making a difference in South Africa.

Neil Tovey is an unsung hero of South Africa. He was an outstanding full back and skipper of Bafana Bafana and led our country to possibly the only true great football trophy thus far. He had style and charisma which, coupled with Clive Barker's coaching, made them unstoppable.

I will never forget the changeroom festivities in 1996 with buckets of Castle Lager as we celebrated something that was to become an achievement etched in history and another step in the country's unification.

There was, of course, Graeme Smith. He was another leader in the ilk of Francois Pienaar and has gone on to do so much more. He has leadership skill and, although a little unorthodox with a bat, an ability to win for South Africa in more ways than one.

Cricket fans will remember 2008/09. With the Test series secured, the Proteas and Australia headed to the Sydney Cricket Ground for the final match.

In the first innings, Graeme's hand was broken by a ball from paceman Mitchell Johnson, forcing him to retire hurt. The Proteas managed 327, batting with one man short, before Australia set them a target of 376 for victory.

The Proteas tried to salvage a draw on the final day. Tailenders Dale Steyn and Makhaya Ntini offered strong resistance with a 50-run stand but when Steyn departed many thought that might have been the end of the game.

The entire SCG crowd rose to their feet in applause as Graeme walked to the middle to try to see his team home.

He frustrated the Australian bowlers until Johnson knocked over his stumps with only 11 balls remaining, giving Australia a 103-run victory.

Despite losing the test match, Graeme was lauded not only for his bravery but for captaining the Proteas to a first series win in Australia.

Lucas Radebe was an inspiration to our nation. Bafana was his passion, but he went on to play in the English Premier League. I was running Castle Lager in the UK and Hilary Jamieson, our country lead, had called to ask how she could inspire the UBEVCO sales force to reach new levels.

I asked her where her next workshop with the sales team was taking place. It happened to be in Leeds. I called Glynn Binkham who was Lucas Radebe's agent, and asked him if Lucas could make an appearance and talk to the UK team about how Castle Lager had supported him and team Bafana Bafana over the years.

He stopped by on his way to a training session and made a 20-minute impromptu talk that turned the tables for Castle Lager in the UK. He remains a great friend of SAB.

I would say that Abraham Benjamin De Villiers, the celebrated 'A.B.', is the best batsman yet to grace the world cricket stage; the humblest of sportsman with a talent that was freakish. He always wore his Castle Lager and Protea kit with absolute pride and was an ambassador of Castle and South Africa at every level.

He once asked for beer for a golf day in Bela-Bela (formerly Warmbaths) to raise funds for his charity. I arranged an allocation and asked him to take a case of Chocolate Milk Stout. He was not that keen but said he would try it. After night one, he asked me to please send a replenishment vessel. What a special person to work with.

Schalk Burger was a character of the game of rugby who defied all the odds. Rugby's du Plessis brothers, Bismarck and Jannie, once lifted me up between them at a prizegiving. Bismarck tackled me at the Durban Country Club, and I was man down for several days. He once asked me if we could launch the 'Man of the Match' two litre glass bottle as a permanent fixture. Jean de Villiers was another great leader with a sense of humour who brought a new dimension to our Springboks.

Shaun Pollock preferred not to partake of the amber nectar but nonetheless supported Castle Lager as a sponsor. He always came to our Brewhouse evening and drank a chocolate milkshake as a forfeit, which I think is more difficult to consume at speed and endure the brain freeze.

He once joined our Charles Glass Society meeting at short notice after a withdrawal by a celebrity sportsman at the last moment. He asked me if we could help him to auction a Brian Lara jersey that the West Indian cricketer maestro had hoped would raise funding for a cerebral palsy victim he had met that day in Soweto. We asked Shaun how much was needed for an operation for the lady. One of our members purchased the jersey for the full amount of R40,000.

The next day, The Star newspaper led with a picture of Brian Lara, Shaun Pollock and our Charles Glass Society team handing over the cheque to the lady in Soweto. Shaun was remarkable. So were the Fellows of the Charles Glass Society who operated in every city across the country and did purposeful projects to help less fortunate people and communities.

Then there was Jacques Kallis, in his time, cricket's best player. I used to send ten cases of Castle Lager to Morgan's Bay for him and friends to enjoy on their annual holiday. I realised Jacques preferred Redd's Premium Cold so that became the favourite for him. He was a humble person with a wonderful disposition and a rare talent.

My favourite story is about him batting at Centurion and reaching 150 not out at tea. Arriving at the changeroom, he took a call from business billionaire Johan Rupert, who told him to concentrate, because he had never gone on to make two hundred despite his talent. He offered Jacques life membership at Leopard Creek Country Club if reached the double ton.

Mark Boucher quickly saw the opportunity to play golf with his best mate at Leopard Creek in the future and told Jacques to take a shower, change and concentrate. J.K. went on to his richly deserved maiden 200. In celebration he swung his cricket bat like a golf club to signify his illustrious nomination. He is now an honorary member of Leopard Creek.

As a sequel to this story, Mark Boucher asked Johan Rupert how he could have been given honorary life membership to Leopard

Creek, to which Johan replied that he would have bestowed this honour should Mark have achieved 1,000 wickets whereas he had sadly achieved only 999 wickets. Mark then asked a statistician friend to pull up his personal statistics and it turns out that he did achieve 999 wickets behind the stumps, however he had also turned his arm in a dead rubber fixture against India and had achieved one wicket as a bowler, which shows on the record books as 1,000 wickets in total. Johan awarded him life membership at Leopard Creek with glee and has been a top fan of both Kallis and Boucher to this day.

Another memorable tale was that of Protea teammates Pat Symcox and Fanie De Villiers sharing a room as senior players in the team while Jacques and Mark roomed together. On arrival in Antigua in the Caribbean, Jacques and Mark sprinted up the fire escape ahead of Pat and Fanie to secure a room with a view over the swimming pool.

This disregard of protocol was not taken lying down by the two stalwarts. They visited the market the next day, bought a large fish and persuaded housekeeping to open the room. There they removed the grid from the air conditioner and placed the fish over the unit behind the grid. A day or two later, the odour of the rotten fish was rounding the corner before Boucher and Kallis. Can you imagine what went on ...?

I deliberately leave Mark Boucher until last. A close friend, he is truly a legend of the story of South African cricket and so much more. Australia's fast bowler, Brett Lee, once told me that Australia could never be sure of victory until Mark Boucher was out. He is still not out, having endured incredible challenges including the loss of sight in one eye after being hit by a bail, an unfortunate incident just before his final three tests in England.

Mark has gone on to make a huge contribution to conservation through the Boucher Legacy, where we share our passion to make a difference to endangered mammals in Africa.

As the coach for the Proteas, he made a fundamental contribution in turning our fortunes as we begin to regain status in global rankings across all formats of the game.

Not unlike all the celebs I have mentioned, 'Bouch' is making a big and meaningful difference to South Africa and is giving back in so many ways.

Many of these sportsmen and others remain valued friends on my journey.

All are special in my life yet genuine and less overtly famous when in my company.

Sponsorship gave SAB an opportunity to work with and learn from the best. Yet if you ask them, they learnt from us, too. It was a mutual respect that endured. We still share that bond.

The Beer Guy
from Africa

In December 2002, Norman Adami received a call from Graham. He told Norman the company wanted him to go to America. He had ten minutes to make the decision. We had bought the Miller Brewing Company. What we paid for it was more than half the market cap of SAB at the time. It was a huge move.

NORMAN ADAMI

To buy, in a first world market that was the most competitive in the world, a company that had been in decline for 18 years, that was losing market share, and that was under the whip in the most complex and competitive environment in the world, was really bold.

I remember sitting at the board meeting. I didn't vote for the acquisition of Miller. But we bought it anyway.

The plan was that the MD of the company, John Bolun, would stay there and run the company. We would send in a few South Africans.

I didn't have a particular affinity for Miller. Nor did I have any in-depth knowledge of the detail of what Miller was about. I had not been on the mergers and acquisitions team.

The call came out of the blue that Bolun wasn't cutting it. We had to send someone and the only guy who could go was me. There was no one else.

I had just got divorced. My children were in South Africa. It wasn't something I relished, because I wanted to be close to my family. I knew that I couldn't take them with me. I had to leave them behind.

Graham also told me I was not allowed to tell anyone. Not even my family. I could tell them only on New Year's Day.

Nobody knew about it. The MD didn't know about it. They couldn't disrupt Miller. It was a sudden, short, sharp takeover. That was another bold move.

He cajoled me into going. I went more out of a sense of loyalty to the company than anything else. Because of my personal circumstances, there was no real excitement in it for me.

I had been very privileged in my time in SAB. The company had been very good to me. I was fortunate that I was always at the right place at the right time, and I felt privileged to be given the opportunities I had, long before I ever expected them.

I never chased promotion. None of my promotions was something I was expecting or hoping for. Before I could even think about it, I was being promoted. It wasn't as though I was ever in one job for a long time.

I knew nothing about how bad Miller was. My thoughts about Miller weren't half as bad as it turned out to be. It was much worse.

I had no time for due diligence or to understand what was going on. I couldn't go for a recce. Graham said I had to be ready to go on 1 February 2003.

What stressed me the most was being unable to tell my children. When I did tell them they just cried and cried. It was the most heartrending thing for me.

I got a helluva send off. My departure spawned several farewell celebrations. At one of them Meyer said: 'Norman, please go now. I'm tired of making speeches.'

Ally

When Norman left South Africa for Miller Brewing, we arranged several send-off parties to pay tribute to the legend. Pod McLoughlin and I wrote 'The Book of Norman' which captured the classic metaphors that Norman had used liberally across South Africa and for which he became known across the globe: 'You can take poison on it.' 'The pots are on the stove, but no one's eating.' 'Do you think you're Mother The f...ing Resa?' 'I can sell more beer out of the boot of my car at Makro on a Saturday.' 'Whichever way you turn, your arse is still behind you.' ... And so the stories went on, eventually gathering abound 50 expressions that were all hilarious.

We also produced a limited-edition beer can bearing Norman's face for all the farewell functions for him. By mistake, a pallet of them reached Soweto. I heard a consumer ask: 'Was Charles Glass Lebanese?'

Norman

The guys were good to me and so gracious. I was grateful and privileged. It's in those moments that one sits back and reflects and realises people do appreciate what you've done. It's a good feeling. I felt humbled by that. One didn't expect it.

I loved South Africa and I loved the company I was running. There were still more things I wanted to do. We had just started on the marketing front, trying to lift our game. But the company was running well.

It was more the personal circumstances that were holding me back and making me concerned. It was so far away. You couldn't just fly overnight to be back. It wasn't London or Eastern Europe.

I arrived in Milwaukee and got the shock of my life to discover the precarious position Miller was in. It was being battered on all fronts. People were demoralised, distributors were disillusioned, and the brands were in decline – all of them. Miller Lite, the flagship brand, had been in decline for more than 12 years. The entire portfolio had been in decline for more than 18 years.

Anheuser-Busch, with strong momentum and a growing market share every year, had reached more than 50 percent of the market and had more than 70 percent of the profit pool of the beer market in America. They were powering ahead.

Everywhere you looked in Miller there was a problem. There was no straw to clutch, nothing to say here's a strong foundation we can build on. There was a negative sentiment in the business.

I encountered two attitudes. One was denial. People didn't even know that their company had been in degeneration for more than 18 years. People were scoring fours and fives on their performance ratings, yet the company was tanking.

Or they were in despair. Their feeling was there was nothing they could do. The juggernaut was coming after them.

Milwaukee was the home of the beer world. Schlitz and Pabst, the oldest brewing companies in the world, had their headquarters there. On my way to Miller, I would drive past them. These were relics of the past. They were closed, old buildings. Miller was heading the same way.

Everybody believed that once a brand was regressing, it couldn't be recovered. Nor could a brewery that was failing. There was no belief that Miller could come back.

My appointment was also not met with a lot of fanfare or celebration from the staff or the distributors. The distributors threw up their hands in exasperation. 'How can you bring in this South African with the funny voice, who knows nothing about America, nothing about the competition, nothing about the regulations? How is he going to come here and turn this company around?'

The staff were demoralised, knowing that change was going to come and that they could be in the firing line. They had been through seven turnaround strategies by seven different MDs in the previous 12 or 15 years before that. They were used to this churn.

Miller was owned by Altria, a holding company created in 1985 that included Philip Morris. It was a successful enterprise. But Miller itself was something of a stepchild, a stepchild that was a pain in the arse.

At the time, the pundits and the analysts said that SAB had bet the farm. We were a well-functioning business but if Miller failed the whole of SAB would crash.

There was a lot of pressure on me because the stakes were so high, and because the situation was so much gloomier than I had ever imagined.

Ally

When I was plying my trade in international marketing, we were investigating the opportunity to launch Castle Lager in the US. The market was competitive with craft brewing as a new fad and premium imports on the rise.

We targeted Washington DC as a transient city where consumers come and go and could possibly pick up a trend and take it home with them, so spreading a viral lager pandemic that might take the entire US by storm.

We developed positioning statements and mood boards, including a pack and price, and set about some research amongst transient consumers in DC.

The takeout was encouraging, and we were excited to take these to the global EXCO to share our progress. They too seemed very excited by the response and opportunity of bringing an African brand to America.

I was called by Graham Mackay in early 2003 to inform me that we were buying the Miller Brewing Company and that the knowledge shared by the Castle Lager case study had been very informative and had played a role in the purchase.

I was very disappointed. I was convinced that this brand had potential beyond Africa. I still have that belief.

Be that as it may, I was offered a choice of an executive development programme globally and I chose to attend Kellogg's University in Chicago, a programme focused on value chain alignment.

I had always thought that it was fundamental to get everyone in an FMCG business aligned to focusing on delivering the best intrinsic product, beer in our case, to the end consumer and this took great understanding of the role that everyone played along the way.

I arrived for my three-week programme on day one, suffering severe jet lag after an exhausting flight via Atlanta to Chicago, and attended the first lecture. We were asked to introduce ourselves, where we were from, why we had chosen to attend the programme and what success may look like for us at the end of it.

There were 49 attendees, 46 from the North American continent, two from the UK, another continent, and one delegate from Africa, a 'country'. Not 54 countries, just one!

Answers came from around the room. When it came to my turn, I gave it my all even though I was exhausted. 'Hi everyone, my name is Ally Hewitt from South African Breweries. I come from South Africa, a country at the southern tip of Africa, one of 54 countries on the continent of Africa. You may have seen in the press yesterday that our company, the South African Breweries, took over the Miller Brewing Company down the road here in Milwaukee. I'm here to learn about the connections and alignment required in the value chain with the end consumer in mind.'

The last sentence fell on deaf ears. Shock and horror that an American company could have any association with something from Africa. They found out more at tea when they went online to verify if I was a bullshitter or not.

The rest is history. SAB became SABMiller and from then on, we continued to grow to become the number two brewer in the world.

I was later to have a much deeper relationship with America when I worked on the global brands portfolio of ABInBev.

I attended a global brands conference in New York in 2017. Africa was held up as a benchmark for launching global brands. A case study won an award for excellence in the way we had approached launching Corona and Stella Artois in South Africa.

Later Budweiser was launched in South Africa and Nigeria and was again heralded as a world class example of best practice. I realised in 2003 and again in 2017 that Africa is underrated. We have talent and can show the world many lessons. Africa is not for sissies! Do not mess with us ...

Norman

I stepped off the plane the morning I arrived and had to give a talk to introduce myself to the business, to tell them in broad terms where I was going and what I wanted to do, although I didn't know that much.

Later, the distributors summoned me to a meeting. There were two dozen of them from around the country. They presented me with a list of complaints about Miller.

I had a spiral-bound notebook and filled it with grievances ranging from lack of supply to inefficiencies, ineffectiveness and lackadaisical responses. They just laid it on thick; how bad we were and how bad Miller was. They didn't hold back because they were *gatvol* (fed up). They were also disillusioned by my appointment. I just listened.

Marketing was totally ineffective. We were trying to emulate Bud Lite, the dominant brand in the market. It was forging ahead while we were losing ground. And all we had was an ad with an imagery that tried to emulate Bud's. I always said sameness kills a brand. You must differentiate.

There was no strategy. It was not as though I walked in with an SAB blueprint of what we now had to do. I had to start all over again and remember that SAB had already owned the business for at least 18 months. It was not as though they knew what they wanted to do and how to go about it. I had to make a new plan on all fronts.

We had to focus on stabilising the foundation and improving our operational efficiencies. We were out of stock, notwithstanding our decline. The business just didn't supply distributors. It couldn't order and what they did order never came on time and not in the right quantities. We were out of stock all the time.

Our brands were nowhere. All of them were shrinking. No brand was growing. There might have been a little niche product that had shown small growth, but it was the square root of nothing.

Part of the DNA of the SAB people was a competitive growth mindset. That belief did not exist in Miller. One of the key lessons that South Africa had proved was that if your core brands were not growing, you couldn't grow your business. There was no culture I could grab and build from.

I believed the next moves had to be huge and bold. We had to restore Miller Lite to growth, build our portfolio and get our core brands growing. Three imperatives were distributors, brands, and local market execution. We had to revamp the organisation, build capabilities, and foster a culture in the business.

We had to re-establish and re-engage the distributors, who were totally switched off by us. And we needed exclusivity with the distribution, as Anheuser-Busch had.

AB had a three-tier system and had choices among their distributors; we didn't have that. The distributors could choose which brand they wanted to play with and build. Miller wasn't on their list of choices. They had already written it off. They were chasing Heineken and all the brands in their portfolio, rather than Miller Lite.

Secondly, we needed local market planning and execution, which didn't exist.

Thirdly, we needed productivity, without waste in the system, and correct the supply chain to rebuild the organization.

The key focus areas posed huge challenges on all fronts.

We started by trying to get the brand positioning of Miller Lite right. We had to correct our marketing, starting from a zero base.

I recruited people. Gavin Hattersley was already there. I looked to South Africa and brought Maurice Egan into operations, Barry Smith to run strategy, as well as Johan Nel and a few other HR people. I also hired Americans: Tom Long into marketing and Tom Gardella, into sales execution. Wayne McCauley and Roy Bagattini came over. I brought in other people from South Africa and we redeployed.

A priority was to differentiate Miller Lite if we were to have any hope of turning the business around. It needed a proper positioning with some effective marketing behind it. The previous work was absolutely useless. It did more harm than good to the brand.

Another bold move was to take on Anheuser-Busch. It's one thing to challenge. It's another thing to be able to do so. We adopted an 'able challenger' mindset for the brand and its positioning. Repositioning it was no easy job. We looked at what we had, and the beer itself, and how they had gone about it in the past.

We went back to the physical attributes of the brand. It was really that this brand had more taste with half the carbs and half the calories of Bud. We positioned the brand around that. We came to 'more taste, half the carbs and less calories'.

The guys were scared of Bud, but we took it on directly. They were scared to 'tickle the lion's balls' and never thought about going there. They went there with trepidation. But we got the brand going in the US for the first time in 12 years.

We built great marketing around it. We had taste challenges around the country. We had the distributors engaged. We ran our conferences with the help of South African people.

The other thing then was to get the distributor network going. We decided to establish a new relationship, so we arranged this whole institutional, ceremonial event where we said we were going to build a new relationship based on three principles: we would deliver great marketing and they would have to provide great support for it at the local level.

The traditional model Miller had followed was that they created the push above the line and the distributors created the pull. That wasn't working. The market had moved on. You had to market through the line and do it through the distributor.

The second principle was that we would deliver local marketing and they would go and execute it.

The third principle was about collective strength. We all needed to contribute to the collective strength of the Miller system so that they could help each other as well as the Miller Brewing Company.

We said we would take the lead. That worked. As Miller itself latched on to the challenger mentality, and the willingness and passion to pull together, the distributors started pulling with us.

We also did things like building a pub. There had been no camaraderie, engagement or conversation between functions. Everyone worked in a silo, came to work and went home, and knew nobody else in the business. No one felt part of a team. It wasn't like anything we were used to in SA.

Ironically, the last to come to the party were the people at Miller. Although we were working on that all the time, bringing in new people, redeploying, restructuring, retrenching, re-orienting, making this a market facing business, there was internal conflict. We tried to reposition the business, to focus externally on the competitor, not to fight with each other within the business.

Eventually it all proved a success. Miller turned around. For the first time, it began to grow. It was delivering 12.5 percent growth, which was unbelievable. The system was re-energised.

I was on the SABMiller plc board at the time. I sat at a meeting of the main board at SABMiller, with Graham, Meyer, all the English directors, the Altria Director and the Santo Domingo family members. I remember Meyer saying: 'Graham, you know, Norman and his team have saved your bacon.'

For the first time in decades, AB had lost market share. We were gaining. AB's market cap dropped by more than $12 billion. Our market cap climbed 190 percent. This was showing that SAB could compete globally, in a First World country, and succeed. That meant a lot to shareholders, analysts and investors. Our shares started to fly.

Meyer, as only Meyer can do, told all these guys on the board, that Norman had saved their bacon.

It was one of my proudest moments. Both Graham and Meyer acknowledged and appreciated what we had done. That was 2.5 years on, in early 2006.

BARRY SMITH

In the US, I was appointed Vice President for Market Strategy and Development, but this period was not my finest hour. Marketing did not report to me and the incumbent from Philip Morris was very weak.

London office was briefed to oversee the marketing to take Miller to an international brand. I didn't always subscribe to the central marketing approach around global brands and the credit that was often taken for the great work done in the hubs and in country.

We had Miller Lite, the flagship, which was losing ground, and Miller Genuine Draft. The central marketing team were adamant that we had to create a family, merging the extrinsics of the two.

When I arrived there, they were changing Miller Lite to a blue label. I asked why. They said the guys liked blue. I asked them what it conveyed to the consumer.

'No', they said, 'the guys just like the colour.'

They also dropped the slogan that had made the brand famous: 'Great taste, less filling'. I asked one of the guys at one time what the alcohol content of Miller Lite was. He couldn't tell me. I told Mark Sherrington they were crazy: that the word Miller was happenstance, they were two different brands with their own extrinsics and brand promises.

They said no, we're going to put them together.

They launched a campaign to market the 'Miller family'. It was a disaster. Eventually they dropped it and let the brands continue down their separate paths.

Distributor/wholesale development supposedly fell under me, but Norman brought in Charlie Frenette, who essentially took it over. I spent most of my time investigating acquisition targets for our London office, like Molsons, Bavaria and a small brewery in Belize. We did well, we learnt a lot and there is no doubt that Norman was very good.

The wholesalers loved him. We had 450 of them who distributed Miller. They had never come to previous conferences because Miller wasn't doing well, and they saw no point to attending. But now SAB had taken over and they wanted to see what was going on. All 450 came.

It had been costing $8 million to run the conference. Norman said: 'Bullshit.' He contacted Val Carter in South Africa and she ran the whole thing from South Africa with South African performers etc. and the whole thing cost $2 million. It blew their minds.

Previously they would show the wholesalers the ads they would use to launch new brands, and then never flight them. The conference was always to market to the wholesalers, and they just wasted money.

Meyer came to Norman's conference to be the guest speaker on the first day.

Three weeks before, Budweiser had held their conference. At that time August Busch IV was running the business. It was his father who had really built the business and he went on stage at some part of the proceedings, whereupon his son genuflected in front of him. Why he did so was unclear, but he came across as a silly little wimp. Word spread through the whole industry how the son had taken the knee in front of his father.

At our conference, Meyer was due to speak after the tea break. I looked around and couldn't see him. The MC, a TV personality, then announced the introduction of Meyer Kahn (pronounced 'Mayer'), chairman of SABMiller.

When the lights came up, Meyer appeared at the back of the auditorium. The audience and MC were applauding, but Meyer just ambled towards the stage. By the time he reached the podium, there was a silence.

Finally, he said: 'Ladies and gentlemen, I'm led to believe that here in the US of America, there is a custom that people pay homage to seniority (and sniggers). Norman Adami, do not come up to this stage and kiss my arse.' The audience collapsed.

He then gave a 45-minute classic Meyer Kahn speech. They hung on every word. When he was finished, he was given a standing ovation that went on for five to ten minutes.

WAYNE McCAULEY

Once Norman had a degree of confidence that he knew what you were talking about, you got him on side and won the game. Then he asked me – and it came out of left field – to go to the US. I wouldn't say he was floundering, but I think it was a bit overwhelming. He had gone to the US and right away was on the back foot because people were asking: what can an MD of a company with a 99 percent share of their home market come and tell us, with 20 percent or 25 percent of the market of the most competitive beer market in the world? How can you send this guy over?

I think he had to overcome that. He did a wonderful job of winning over the distributors.

When he went there, he stopped over, before even reaching his office in Milwaukee, at a distributor in Houston I think, and spent a day engaging with them. Just that little act quickly spread the word that here was a guy they could talk to. To this day they still speak his name. In fact, he was featured as Man of the Year in a financial magazine and appeared on the front cover.

When I went there, he was looking for a person to put in the field to help him get the message across on KPIs, performance management, how we operate, and so forth. He wanted ears on the ground.

We had several conversations on what was getting through and what was not. He was using me as a dipstick to confirm what was going well and what wasn't. And he trusted me to be direct with him where sometimes in the tendency in the US is to talk around the issue.

I was running the Midwest: Ohio, Kentucky and Indiana. There were about 12 of us as general managers across the states. It was tough at the beginning to get used to a completely different market, but I built up a lot of capabilities that I never had before, with key accounts, group stores, and the like. What an invaluable learning. Like everything, it became easier as I went along but it was tough. It took you completely out of your comfort zone to a foreign place where you had to settle the family and get on your feet, to understand a market and earn the respect of the people.

That's what SAB did for a lot of the guys around the world.

I was there for just under four years. There were four vice presidents of sales. I looked at them and realised they weren't going anywhere. I had done my three and a bit years and I was looking for a new challenge.

Norman

From being seen as a pariah among the distributors, I could then do nothing wrong. Because of the success we had, whatever I asked them to do, they would do, because they were growing and making money. I was a hero to them.

A magazine article said, 'Norman Adami has taken over from August Busch IV as the most loved beer man in North America'.

I was in the spotlight there because there were newspapers published weekly about the beer industry and the insiders. AB reacted badly to our success because they had now taken a back seat. They began discounting their brands in an emotional reaction. It was the worst decision they could make.

It marked the start of the takeover of Anheuser-Busch. InBev then got a foot in the door with AB because AB's market cap got nailed. Their profitability dropped. They were doing irrational things to stop the bleeding and the turnaround of Miller.

August Busch III was going ballistic. He threatened to 'unleash the dawgs'. They had a conference all about Miller and flighted a video showing the Anheuser-Busch Clydesdales running all over me. It was a tough environment to deal with, but we survived that as well.

It was an uplifting experience, and I learnt a lot. In all my roles in SAB, wherever I was from day one, I had been on a learning path until I retired.

That was part of the people attribute in SAB. We were all learners, and we learnt every day. We learnt from our mistakes. We were open to learning. That was the nice part about our culture.

When Graham first asked me to go there, it was to be a three-year stint. I was into 5.5 years. I told Graham my family was still in South Africa; my ex-wife was ill with cancer and my children were stressed.

I figured I had turned the company around, I had recruited a successor, Tom Long, and was grooming him, and the business was on an even keel. I felt I could return to South Africa. That's when I moved back and retired.

Graham didn't want me to leave Miller. He understood the family scenario but wanted me to stay. I told him I had done my bit and I now had a personal commitment to my family. I couldn't desert them now when their mother was dying. She passed away just before I returned.

I stayed in Kenton-on-Sea for a while because the kids were at boarding school in Grahamstown. I had a short break, obtained a helicopter licence, and returned to SAB after the Heineken defection and the loss of Amstel.

America is a very different market and we learnt a lot there. It's a different situation. You couldn't cut and paste and do what you did in South Africa. You can take some of the principles, but you can't apply the actions. You need to apply them to the situation you're in.

24 Doing
the Hard Yards

SAB was a very generous company in so many ways. Generous in the way staff were nurtured, generous in training and education throughout the business, generous with company perks (including 56 dozen beers a year), medical aid, provident fund and other benefits. The company taught generosity; we worked in hospitality and with a social lubricant that was an integral part of the way of life in the countries where we operated.

That said, the people of SAB would run through a brick wall for the company and those who succeeded were prepared to go to great lengths to give their all, sometimes at huge personal sacrifice.

The hours were long in the workplace and if you were on the frontline in sales and marketing, the commitments at night and at weekends were also immense. The work/private life balance was mostly out of kilter and families sometimes took the brunt of the hard yards travelled.

I personally put in those hard yards. Though we worked smart, the hours were long and so were the social engagements. My stints on Castle Lager were rewarding but came at huge personal sacrifice. Travel, sponsorship commitments across national teams, premier soccer league, promotional properties like Castle Tavern Tour, were hectic to say the least.

In my international marketing role and later in Africa, my travel schedule was frenetic. I would travel up to three weeks of every month, returning for weekends and then fly out Sunday evening or Monday morning at sunrise. The travel logistics and accommodation were not always plain sailing and conditions in some markets were tough.

The other challenge with travelling to markets was the social interaction with expats who were so excited to see us that they laid on a social programme and schedule to see the trade that were tiring at times but always enjoyable.

We often took a few provisions to colleagues in Africa. Meat was often scarce. A Sunday Times newspaper was always a hit. I once took, a critical component of a brewing line required to set our Kenya brewery in motion. The technical piece weighed around twenty kilograms and fitted into a long canvas duffel bag. The part was valued at around R200,000 and would have attracted some import duties. They were of little concern to us but the paperwork side of bringing the part into Kenya would have been enormous and the timing to clear the part would have had huge ramifications on the start-up of our brewery.

I took the personal risk of taking the part in my own luggage. I remember going through the airport in Nairobi. The entire technical team were waiting outside in anticipation of me making it through customs.

I sent my clothing luggage through final check point security scanner, and walked with my trolley to the other side, having left the bag with the technical component on my trolley. I made it through, collected my clothing luggage and walked to the waiting team outside.

They were cheering and shouting by the time I got out the airport. People around must have thought I was a celebrity of note. The brewery fired up that night for the first time. We were in business.

Security was sometimes an issue particularly in markets like Nigeria and Colombia, but I have to say I always felt safe in the company of my colleagues on the ground. They were streetwise and knew the turf.

In striving to do my best and going beyond expectations, I never felt alone. All around me, the people I worked with and those who supported us through the value chain had the same drive and mindset and worked incredibly hard.

I remember the likes of Graham Mackay, Malcolm Wyman and Meyer Kahn travelling the world and the nights they must have spent on aeroplanes.

They were everywhere, leading from the front and acquiring new businesses along the way. Incredible commitment.

The people of SAB were truly remarkable. SAB at work was something to behold.

BARRY SMITH

From the time I left South Africa to the time I retired, which was after 16 years of service, 75 percent of the time including Saturday and Sunday I was away from my family while the kids were growing up. When we first went to Poland I was flying backwards and forwards looking after Tychy, while my kids were finishing school. We went across there and lived in Warsaw and every Monday morning I'd get up at 4 a.m. to catch a train to Lech and catch it back on Friday at 4 p.m.

When I was in Milwaukee, I'd leave home in Morristown, fly up to Milwaukee, get there at 10 a.m. and fly back every Friday afternoon.

When we bought in Latin America, besides during the due diligence when I was never at home, I was flying down for about nine months while my kids finished school again. I was sitting in a hotel in Bogota, and when we bought those companies, I was flying to all those countries that reported to me, plus I had to go to London, which was 24 hours door to door, to sit in meetings. And there was a seven hour time difference. Graham was similar. He was travelling all over the world.

GAVIN HUDSON

SAB offered many people the opportunity to move. If they were prepared to work, they would be well rewarded. It was all about pushing people to make the best of the opportunities.

In my career at SAB, I had 19 different bespoke jobs, my wife Wendy and I moved house 18 times. We've lived in 16 different provinces or countries.

My daughter Jamie attended seven schools by the time she matriculated in Russia and my younger daughter matriculated in Turkey after attending five different schools. On average we moved every 18 months.

In 2011, I was in Cape Town when Norman Adami told me there was an opportunity open and asked if I was prepared to move to Colombia in South America. Evidently it was the third time someone had asked for me and Norman had turned it down. I said it would be great.

I was told that if I agreed to move, I had to be committed, and the family had to be committed. I couldn't arrive and a little later say my wife was unhappy, the kids did not like the culture and everyone wanted to go home.

With my wife and daughters, aged 11 and 9, I had a family meeting. I told the girls how tough it would be. I warned them they would be saying goodbye to all their friends, have no family there, would go to different schools, and would have to learn Spanish. Without batting an eyelid, they said: 'We're in.'

Wendy and I went to see the place. At the Bogota airport, everything was in Spanish. We couldn't even work out where to go. A driver was there to meet us, and he took us to our hotel.

We were meeting Richard Rushton the next day, so we had a night to orientate ourselves and went out for dinner. I couldn't even order a beer. I knew the word was cerveja, but I wasn't sure how to pronounce it properly. There were no pictures on the menu. The food we received was not what we thought we had ordered.

But we accepted the move, and I went ahead a month before the family. It's difficult to learn a language from scratch. We don't have an ear for it, as we might have done had we lived in the US, for example, where Spanish is often spoken.

By the time the family arrived I think I had learnt how to order a beer and about 100 other words. Pronunciation was always difficult. It remained a challenge to order food because you can't understand what you're reading on the menu. You learn just the basic please and thank you.

On day one in the office, my secretary came to meet me. She spoke not a word of English. She led me through an open plan environment to my office. Everyone knew I had arrived. I had a laptop with a landing page in Spanish. The filing cabinet had various files in Spanish.

There were board minutes I had to read, all in Spanish. My management team was Spanish. I had to employ an interpreter.

To arrive as a sales director in a company that would become the largest contributor to EBITDA with 2,500 people working for you when you couldn't speak a word of Spanish was daunting to say the least. The people were very forgiving, but the first few months were very stressful.

Richard Rushton and Karl Lippert could speak Spanish so there was little empathy for the new guy who couldn't. There was pressure from all sides.

The company didn't have conferences. We arranged the first conference soon after I arrived. We did it in SAB style and had 1,600 attendees. The distribution director and I had to do presentations, a dog and pony act, and I cringe thinking about it. I had written it in English, they had translated it and I really tried hard to learn my words, but I had no idea what I was saying.

What I was saying was pretty good for the conference, but I couldn't pronounce the words properly.

GRANT HARRIES

When I was offered the role of MD in Honduras, I had to look at a map to see where Honduras was. At the time it was the eighth biggest profit contributor to SAB, which I found hard to believe, because it was such a small environment. But it was before the Bavaria acquisition, then it slipped to number 11.

What an experience it was. Never mind all the training and experience I got through SAB and all the support from Central Office, you arrive at a place like Honduras and you're on your own. As a GM you are more of an operational type of guy, you don't make any decision on pricing or brands. Now you're dumped in overnight and you've got to go through those experiences on your own.

I took Spanish lessons, lived on site and walked five minutes to the office. I never took my laptop home. If I needed to work on weekends, I would just walk across the paddock.

At first living there felt strange but it was in a beautiful big house, and it was safe – San Pedro is still rated the most dangerous city in the world – so from that perspective it was a plus, although I never experienced any serious threats, and I went into the market a lot.

We had bulletproof cars and we travelled with escorts carrying 9 mm weapons. When we went into hotspots, there would be more vehicles and more automatic weapons. I often saw guys I recognised standing on street corners watching everything, but I never experienced any issues.

It was all a big change for us, coming from South Africa. But those guards become part of your family. They are with you wherever you go. If you went to a restaurant, they would be sitting at a table nearby, with one outside. You had to get used to it, because it's quite awkward. But across all my times in Honduras, Peru and Colombia, what a great bunch of people they were.

Our Reputation
is Indivisible

SAB took its reputation seriously. It was 1986 and apartheid was sadly still the order of the day.

Lucky Michael of Soweto had become the first shebeener to receive a licence to run a tavern.

Mamelodi, a township to the east of Pretoria, had been selling booze illegally for too long. It was their chance to shine and Mississippi Bogoshi and Solly Madraai were among the first shebeens in line to qualify for a tavern licence.

I helped them to lodge their applications and the licences were granted after much red tape.

In February 1986 I enlisted the assistance of a ratel, an army infantry vehicle, to take me into the township. I had completed my senseless military service five years back and knew how the system worked. While I was anxious, as a white man entering a township, I was escorted by the army to meet two gentlemen who had come to know me during our legal process to qualify them for their tavern licences. The neighbourhoods turned out in their droves as I disembarked from the ratel in my blazer, tie and flannels and embraced Solly at his gate. I imagine most kids in the township at that time had never laid eyes on a white man and were fascinated by my presence and my features.

To this day, Mamelodi is my second home and I always feel welcome and safe in the company of the tavern owners and friends who were so welcoming and generous of spirit.

I began with training them on basic bookkeeping and stock management. Income less expenses, mark-ups, gross profit, tax, model stock, stock rotation and saving ... Mississippi and Solly became model students of our Partners for Profit programme, and their journey as official licensed retailers began to take shape.

We celebrated their official openings with much joy with white SAB guests, again under escort by the defence force. The soldiers were beside themselves with fear but calmed down after a few quarts of Castle Lager as they began to feel the warmth and spirit of a township deprived of so much for so long.

The celebrations went on into the night and we exited the township after 11 p.m. to continue the festivities in Pretoria in more familiar settings.

Solly and Mississippi paved the way for many more shebeens to become licensed in townships across the country. I can remember the look on Mississippi's face the day that the SAB truck drew up outside his home. It was a proud moment for him when an SAB truck could deliver directly to his premises rather than him illegally running liquor on his bakkie and bribing the police to let him do so.

In 1998, Mississippi was invited as a guest to Sun City to tell his story at an MS&D conference. Twelve years on, he had built a thriving business and accumulated enough wealth to lead a wonderful life with his family. He drove a top of the range Mercedes Benz, which had been his dream since his youth.

He asked the lighting specialist to focus his strobe on a member of the audience whom he wished to acknowledge and thank for the mentorship and guidance he had received for more than a decade and for the friendship we had built.

Our corporate affairs teams around the world had a seat on the executive and played a major role in protecting our licence to trade. Societal leadership was a pillar of our strategy in South Africa and beyond, and our governance at every level was indisputable.

We dealt in a category that needed to be managed sensitively. Although beer is a beautiful thing, we recognised that there could sometimes be an ugly side to it if it was abused, and that needed our constant attention. We vigorously tackled alcohol abuse and untoward behaviour like gender-based violence that alcohol might exacerbate.

A focused, enlightening and multi-pronged approach kept our reputation, both as a corporate and across our brands, credible and responsible.

Our sincere belief was that a country should be better off by having SABMiller around than it might if we were not there. We made a real difference to our countries and to the communities in which we operated.

Meyer Kahn once told us that we were empowered, even in our small business units around the country, to respond to, and support, communities and people in need.

'You can apologise later for the expenditure,' he said, 'but if a community faces a disaster, a fire, floods, accidents, and the like, I want SAB to be first in line to help.'

This became standard in every operation, from breweries to depots to offices across the country. SAB people were generous in every way to peers, families and communities. It was an ingrained culture and something about beer people was unique and enviable.

We had relationships with key stakeholders at all levels, from government to local government, from national bodies to small communities to stakeholder groups.

We were proactive in driving the responsible use of alcohol and supported campaigns to drive that responsibility; we subsidised foetal alcohol syndrome centres; we reinforced education on the negative impact of alcohol on mothers; and we backed rehabilitation initiatives.

We aligned our advertising campaigns to ensure that we carried the responsible use of alcohol messaging and 'not for sale to persons under 18 years'. We helped local government to ensure that taverns were not located near schools and churches and worked with SAPS to ensure that underage drinking was not permitted.

We worked on drives to protect our roads from carnage at peak times with the setup of roadblocks to test motorists' blood alcohol levels.

Meyer was even loaned to the South African Police Services for two years and worked on a strategic plan to enhance security and the running of police services in South Africa. His contribution to the police force became evident over time and the processes and systems that were introduced were not dissimilar to what we used in SAB.

We used our nationwide distribution capabilities to deliver condoms to rural communities in the fight against HIV and AIDS.

We built schools, we developed community centres, we built clinics, we built sporting facilities.

We sponsored Team South Africa at the highest levels in sport in football, rugby, cricket and basketball.

Carling Black Label ran an annual campaign to highlight the extent of gender-based violence and stress its unacceptability in modern society.

We sponsored sports development, and through Castle Lager, helped to find Tomorrow's Bafana Bafana, a programme that used previous soccer legends to go talent-spotting in rural areas to unearth talent that may not ever have had the opportunity to be seen, and to bring it to a soccer academy to be developed for the future of premiership teams and possibly even Bafana Bafana.

We sponsored environmental programmes, supported many of the Kruger National Park's conservation efforts, and worked on rhino protection through the Castle Lager Boucher Legacy programme.

As the democratic South Africa developed, we supported at grassroots level many local community programmes to uplift society.

We launched the KickStart project which not only unearthed worthy entrepreneurs but backed their start-up enterprises financially and mentored them in their progress in the business world.

Our Zenzele share scheme created wealth for staff and traders.

We were pioneering, at the forefront of corporate social responsibility and social investment, and always ensured that we had secured our 'licence to trade' in South Africa.

We took these learnings and ingrained beliefs about driving purpose to every country in which we operated globally and made a real difference.

TONY VAN KRALINGEN

I was impressed by the company's sense of justice, fairness and awareness of its position in society. That never left me. I think it's another thread that went through SAB. Society of the '80s was very troubled and unjust but SAB was always conscious of the environment and the society we lived in.

CLIFFORD RAPHIRI

The role of SAB in South African society is like a chapter on its own. The outside-in view of communities, politicians, and so on: we probably don't have a full grasp of what the impact was. We can tell stories about the internal impact, but the external stories are another book.

NEIL HOBKIRK

SAB played a massive role in bringing people together in friendship in a positive way during a very difficult time in South Africa. It brought people together at sports fixtures; we always had mixed race customer and consumer trips; and every promotion we ran was for all races.

I think there's a whole theme around SAB and society and the very constructive role we played in developing young talent. You can look at a number of blue-chip companies around the country and there are ex-SAB people running them with confidence at senior levels.

There was a talent for uplifting society; there was integration with society; there was communication with society.

Our relationship with the government was particularly solid. I went to a Castle Lager function when the Springboks were on the point of going overseas. There was a bit of conflict because at that time we didn't have enough transformation or enough equity in the team and there was a lot of pressure. It was quite tense.

The team was there, and everyone was wondering: how is this thing going to be managed and not end up in slander or ill feeling?

Nelson Mandela walked up to the dais and received the usual standing ovation. Everyone settled down. The team was sitting there. And he raised the issue of this conflict.

His words said a lot about SAB's relationship with the government at the time and people's relationships with each other. He said every family has its squabbles. But we were done squabbling and it was now about South Africa playing against the rest of the world. We were now all on one team. We wanted to win together.

That summarised a lot for me of what SAB was about: a group of people who, though they had a place in history, were going out to play against the rest of the world and, as South Africans, to be as good as, even beat, the rest of the world.

VINCE MAPHAI

Richard Davies had called me. 'Hey Vincent, can we have tea?' he asked. 'As long as you pay,' I said. He said they wanted me closer to the company. I thought he meant they wanted to keep in touch. I agreed.

Then he arranged a meeting with Norman. I think Norman thought I had agreed to come and work for him. I sensed we were talking Greek to each other. I told Norman I was not about to change careers.

I should have known that Norman does not take 'no' from anyone. I received around three calls a day. But I was not happy at the Human Sciences Research Council (HSRC) at the time, and I was ready to walk away. It was the best decision I ever made.

I joined SAB reluctantly. Deep down I was an educationist. I was happy as an academic. SAB was a marketer; I was an educationist. At SAB I was kind of an appendage. My job was to be what they called, 'a remarkable person' whose job was to keep quiet in a meeting and pick up whatever I could.

I drank the product. I had no principle issues with alcohol.

I remember a meeting where everyone was talking loudly. The organiser asked me to speak. I spoke very softly. They all said they couldn't hear me.

I said: 'Of course you can't hear when you are making a noise.'

It's a trick I often used.

At a meeting in the early nineties, I said: 'Guys, I've listened to you the whole day. You spoke of 'their' government. None of you has said 'our' government. You worry about being alienated but you have already alienated yourself from government. It's somebody else's government, not yours. Why are you surprised?'

The first years were quite difficult. An MDC (managing director's committee) meeting was like a graduate ceremony. The brainpower in that forum was immense. Nobody was talking crap, nobody was floundering. I had to adjust.

I began to appreciate the value of Norman. I get credit for the foundations laid by Norman. I discovered where the issues were and realised that a business could not look just at commercial issues, it had to see public issues as a priority. The two go together.

Corporate Affairs in many companies tends to be what you do when you have nothing better to do. Norman made corporate affairs very central. There were five pillars to the strategy, of which reputation management was central.

We were very good with our customers and our communities, but not sure about the new environment in South Africa. My big advantage was that I knew all the ANC's new leadership. I had direct access to Nelson Mandela, Thabo Mbeki and later to Jacob Zuma. There was a time that I knew every member of the cabinet. I was never a member of, or affiliated to, any political party. I have never been a member of the ANC even though I served the party more than many of its members did.

My academic affiliation had given me exposure to all of them.

I understood that alcohol abuse was becoming a big issue. Norman had already picked this up. My brief then (in the mid- '90s) was to manage the company's reputation.

We had to understand what drove it. Firstly, it was financial performance. You can have the holiest of people but if you weren't making a profit, it meant nothing.

Treatment of staff was critical. They needed to understand reputation, how to treat communities, how to treat customers.

Shareholders were very important. They put their money in there. It struck me that shareholders are the last people to be paid. You pay your employees, suppliers, government taxes and communities with Corporate Social Investment. The shareholders get the balance. I began to study all these stakeholders to understand who was who.

I also had to make sure that I had the right team to handle the difficult task of retrenchment.

In 2003, Norman left to go to Miller. I left shortly after that. After time at BHP Billiton, I was at Discovery. Norman returned from America and heard about it. He told his people: 'Let's grab that bastard and bring him back. He should be at Park Lane, not one street up at Discovery.'

I got the call. 'Hey Vince, it's time.'

The Minister of Health at the time, Aaron Motsoaledi, wanted to ban alcohol advertising. The anti-alcohol lobby had consolidated and was vicious, but we had a good strategy and I set about implementing it. We began to own the space.

SAB controlled three major sports – soccer, rugby and cricket. We had many supporters in government who saw the incredible value that we added to sport, communities and the wellbeing of the country. We had established great friends in sports administration at all levels, and they also brought pressure to bear.

It was also key for us to go beyond our three historic national sponsorship codes and invest in women's netball.

Development sports were also critical in our endeavours to support sporting codes. One in particular was third division football. Ministers would come to games. Families would be involved. It all added up to protecting our reputation and our commercial future.

Powerful stakeholders were aware of the role we played. Their survival often depended on SAB's continuing support.

SAB became a port of call for government departments when some form of social intervention was required. We were seen as a social partner. Our relationships with government enabled us to have a dialogue around core issues and find solutions that were responsible and commercially sound.

Our support for the Boucher Legacy not only helped to protect the county's rhino but became a key framework for us to host government and other key stakeholders to show them what we were doing and convince them of its importance.

It was also a creative way of offering excursions that encouraged creating a dialogue in a relaxed environment.

In the past SAB had been too much of a 'boys' club'. It paid very little attention to wives, or women in general. When we hosted director generals and others with their wives, we were able to get the women emotionally on side. It was a winner from the outset.

Guests would arrive on a Friday afternoon, have a nice meal and drinks and then on Saturday morning, see our work with a rhino. Women tend to get much more emotional about such things.

By Saturday night, it was a celebration in an atmosphere where relationships flourished, and deals were discussed. We never visited the DG in an office. It was in these surroundings that we had the greatest discussions.

We took alcohol abuse very seriously. We introduced stringent rules first for our own staff. We supported the police on alcohol abuse, and we mobilised taverns. We put big resources behind these initiatives. People realised we meant what we said, and we were genuine in the work we did. Our leadership was there. The likes of Norman led from the front and showed true commitment to what we were doing to promote responsible use of alcohol. Our credibility as a social partner was unquestionable.

We were responsible in our advertising. We assigned space on all of our collateral to promote responsible use of alcohol and warnings that it was 'Not for sale to persons under the age of 18'. We advertised responsible messaging in outlets. We were part of the solution.

Ally

In today's world, the new generations are asking what purpose a brand serves in the marketplace, beyond making money.

The Castle Lager solution lay in two purpose driven campaigns in 2013 known as Tomorrow's Bafana and the Boucher Legacy.

Tomorrow's Bafana was a talent search for players living in remote communities where, without funds or proximity to big clubs, they would never enjoy an opportunity to try out for a top league team.

The programme was headed by Neil Tovey, who skippered South Africa's Bafana Bafana to the famous 1996 Africa Cup of Nations victory and the late Phil Masinga, one of the best strikers the country had ever seen.

Neil, Phil and other previous Bafana Bafana heroes spent six weeks scouting, discovered 30 young talents and took them to Johannesburg for a two-week training camp. That, in turn, culminated in an invitation to coaches from the Premier Soccer League to an exhibition game.

The outcome was that in 2013, five of those players were snapped up by the likes of Kaiser Chiefs and Mamelodi Sundowns, transforming their lives and catapulting them into eminence.

The programme continued to prosper, unearthing more than 20 recruits for the premier league over a period of three years. Some of these players eventually turned out for Bafana Bafana, hence the name of the programme.

Soccer-crazy fans relished the support of Castle Lager and that it was assisting the country to discover hidden talent for the sport of the people.

The programme spawned off-the-chart growth in reputation attributes like 'cares for the community', and the loyalty and conversion scores were tracking more strongly than ever.

At the same time, Castle Lager teamed up with Mark Boucher, who had come to the end of a venerable 15-year career behind the wickets in all formats of cricket.

The Castle Lager Boucher Legacy was established to raise funding for rhino protection and create awareness of the poaching threats posed to rhino who that are on the brink of extinction in our country.

High-tech equipment bought by the legacy hosted RhODIS, a system developed by Dr Cindy Harper at Onderstepoort, that uploaded the DNA of rhino onto a database that saved the identity of each living rhino.

When a rhino was killed, the DNA was used to link the horn to the specific carcass, allowing law enforcement to find and prosecute the perpetrators.

Thanks to the RhODIS programme, the DNA machine was, and still is, used as key testimony in court and many thugs are serving sentences behind bars today.

Much like Tomorrow's Bafana had done, the Boucher Legacy underscored Castle Lager's caring nature as a brand, and entrenched loyalty that resulted in immense sustained growth for our flagship brand.

Sadly, these programmes were relinquished as new blood took over the brands and sought to place their own stamp and forge new paths.

It has become clear to me that companies need to apply stricter custody rules to their core assets to protect them from 'new brooms' sweeping away the equity that had been decades in the making: to protect the 'crown jewels' of the company.

Brands with purpose are more likely to succeed than those without links to something that really matters for consumers or key stakeholders. As part of the fabric of South Africa, Castle Lager needs a purpose.

Vince

SAB was a company you were prepared to die for. I could never bear the thought of letting down a company that was more than

100 years old. I won many battles to protect it. From Meyer Kahn I learnt that business is like a wheelbarrow: if you stop pushing, it grinds to a standstill. You need double the energy to get it started again.

I apply that principle to everything I do. Keep on pushing. You never reach a point where you have arrived. It's like the horizon: when you think you've arrived, a new horizon looms. The MS&D conference was always a wonderful occasion. I didn't like slides and didn't really need any speaker support or autocue. I spoke from the heart. But the slides never really moved on in any case because I forgot to press the button to move them on. I loved speaking to people, and I guess my academic background was part of that passion.

Norman Adami was an extraordinary leader. He is a rare individual. The only other person I know like him is President Mbeki. Both have a combination of a very cosmic viewpoint and very good attention to detail, two skills that are seldom combined.

I met Meyer every month to tell him I was in the thick of things and he gave me perspective. He treated me like his son. He was very patient, very wise. Even after SAB, I could meet Meyer and spend three hours drawing from his wisdom.

I recall one minister giving us hell – he was on our case every day. Meyer told me: 'Vince, just issue this one-liner statement that says we take this in a serious light, and we welcome this matter being reported to the police.' I did and we never heard from that minister again. You won't get that from a business school textbook, you get that from someone who was in the trenches.

MAURICE EGAN

The finest memory I have of my whole career at SAB was back in those horrible 'civil war years'. Section 26 of Katlehong Township was where many of the Alrode brewery's employees lived.

Many had relocated there from the old Isando. Isando had been wound down and Alrode had been wound up. It was Phase 137, meaning 137,000hl a week, and many decided not to relocate from Tembisa, near Isando, but many did.

This was 1992, the year before CODESA, before the last referendum that brought post-apartheid democracy. Racial tensions were running high in the townships.

People were getting taken out left, right and centre. The 'comrades', essentially a self-formed militia, were running the townships. With the police presence, and to a lesser degree the army, it was a kind of no-go area. The only trucks, buses and vans that were not being burnt in the townships were SAB vehicles, because we had built such a rapport with the comrades in the townships.

People may facetiously say 'yes, that's because they were filled with beer', but every other food truck was burnt.

The ANC ensured there was no payment made for any services rendered by the apartheid state. No one paid for electricity, and the municipalities which were essentially National Party run, refused to supply electricity to the non-paying municipalities. Non-payers would steal electricity simply by running a crocodile clip and a wire over the roofs of their houses from the in feeder of the transformer which stood on the outskirts of the township.

And after maybe 400 crocodile clips had been attached, the transformer would blow up.

We cracked a deal. People like Phineas Mitita who was the chief shop steward representing FAWU at Alrode, and more particularly Alrode employees including myself, Deon van As, who at the time was our packaging engineer, and a number of electricians from SAB, great characters all of them, did a deal with GEC Altrop, Swedish transformer manufacturers, and the comrades.

We said we were prepared to repair this transformer and to go into this section of Katlehong and restore electricity to the homes, of which there were about 2,000. But only on one condition: that you start paying for electricity. They agreed to do that, because they were being hassled by many of the people who had been without electricity for three years. People were saying enough is enough.

On December 23, 1993, we and GEC Altrop installed a refurbished transformer. Now we had the trick of wiring it up, but we had no municipal drawings. We ran the risk of running in single phase when it needed three phase. Technically if you run in single phase you blow up all the electronics.

We ran in single phase and the comrades said 'don't worry about that, they'll all be replaced during the weekend. The lads will go grocery shopping'.

We managed to figure it out and the whole part of Katlehong lit up at about five that evening.

I'll never forget it. It was the most heart-warming thing that ever happened to me. This large breasted woman came running out of her shack, ululating. It was the first time she'd had electricity in three years, and what a wonderful Christmas present. She gave me the biggest hug ever.

The following day in Alrode the dynamic changed for the better and we produced quality and efficiencies never seen there before. It was the finest community gift ever seen on the planet, in my view.

Ally

SAB played a wonderful role in supporting local communities and organisations that meant well, across the length and breadth of South Africa. One such local organisation was the Kruger National Park.

Our Lowveld team supported not only conservation, but the Kruger Park cricket team stationed in the park village of Skukuza.

As part of our ongoing friendship and relationship with the Kruger, we safaried annually to Skukuza for a friendly cricket fixture, and occasionally to Newlands Brewery and even Centurion Park to host the annual get-together.

The cricketing events kindled friendships that last to this day. I remember one Saturday in the early years when we arrived at the Skukuza field, a pride of lions had brought down a kudu and were enjoying their breakfast out at deep midwicket.

While we waited for the pride to satisfy their hunger and move off, we sat down at the clubhouse – a fairly basic thatched rondavel – and sipped on a few cold Castles.

Around noon, play eventually began, reduced to 20 overs each. Not unexpectedly, the players were not the sharpest that day, and none was keen to field near the remains of the carcass.

The home side, who played together in the Lowveld's first league, won most games easily, but there were the odd exceptions, like when we brought imports along like Mark Boucher and Albie Morkel. In the main, though, the game was played in good spirit and the after party was always memorable.

The district manager of twenty years, Pine Pienaar, was a legend in our business and epitomised the character and passion of our company in everything that he did. His friendships and relationships across Mpumalanga and the Highveld were testimony to what made SAB great and showed what a difference we made in society, notwithstanding that we were selling alcohol.

Later we sponsored the Kruger Park Half Marathon, run from the Skukuza cricket field around a two lap course that took athletes deep into the bush. An armed ranger every 500 metres ensured the safety of the runners. The race is still fully subscribed annually with 1,500 athletes converging on Skukuza. The proceeds help to fund conservation programmes each year.

The park is, of course, an asset to our country and a major tourist destination for visitors from around the world, and SAB's contribution to it has been profound. The Boucher Legacy, and more recently The Legacy under South African-born England cricketer Kevin Pietersen, came about as a result of the relationships established over many years by SAB and the rangers of the Kruger.

SAB lived up to its 'Making Beer, Making Friends' mantra and most of all to 'Making a Difference'.

PINE PIENAAR

When Alan Clark was still our ops director, Hugh Page played for us and I bet the guys that if they won, I would streak. If we lose, someone else would streak. We did lose the game.

Everyone was sitting around the campfire, and I stripped and got this sombrero and ran naked to the pitch and back. That story was retold when I was awarded my master's blazer. My wife nearly divorced me, but I honoured my commitment.

An Expanding
Wasteline

In any business, you need to leverage your scale to develop and exploit synergies, reduce costs and avoid duplication. To do that, SAB established a hub in London.

It was saying we can't have this duplication of head offices, of pursuing goals and learnings and not sharing them. Initially, that was to a large extent correct. Over time, it became one of our biggest problems.

JOHAN NEL

When I went to London, I felt I should have a very small team. We have enormous talent in the countries and the regions. That's how we had grown. Why would we want to duplicate that?

Why would I think I could put a person in London, an expensive employment area, who would know everything better than everybody else?

Unfortunately, in some areas, the hub teams began to grow significantly with a desire to standardise.

Globalisation has two main axes: standardisation, and decentralisation. Standardisation doesn't necessarily seek to centralise. You can have zero centralisation and still standardise across the world. But people become confused and believe that to standardise, you must centralise. So, you end up with a lot of people looking after the people who were told what to do in the first place.

Unfortunately, that was underpinned globally by the belief that you now had to have systems that were integrated, like IT systems, and the same across the world.

The IT companies then set out to perpetrate the greatest fraud in business history. They promised companies the earth, and then proceeded to drag and drag and drag their implementation on ... for years.

In SABMiller, it was a 15-year journey, instead of four or five years. It started at a cost of hundreds of millions of dollars and became many, many billions.

Unfortunately, the hub was expanded and expanded again, in pursuit of higher levels of control by functional directors, who thought they knew better, who said we will do it instead of you doing it, or we'll tell you how to do it, and then you must do it the way we told you.

The hub grew to 1,000 people in Woking, and a few thousand in South Africa working on SAP. It was then copied by every country, which now also had much bigger head offices, enlarged from 50 people to 200 or 250, all of them high-cost employees who were all trying to do the countries' jobs.

I never knew why we employed such clever MDs in our countries if we wanted to do their work for them. As Norman used to comment: 'Why would you buy a dog and bark yourself?' That for me was sad.

The overall strategy was right; to say we would use this to leverage learning through the SABMiller Ways (which we spent an enormous time and energy creating in every function). The fundamental best practice would be updated by any country and then taught – in HR, for instance, it was about how we implement performance management and how we manage talent – and it added huge value to have a decentralised collaborative organisation.

The danger comes when you shift away from that to a circumstance where you now say: 'We will manage this on your behalf'. I will always say the level of energy put into SAP to pull change from the front, was wrong. Systems are supposed to support, not lead, strategy, and not be the strategy.

Initially SAP drove back-office integration, standardising finance and leveraging procurement from our supply chain. The belief was that if you standardised, systemised and computerised those things, you could be rid of 1,000 back-office people across a company of 75,000.

It ended up with a team of more than 1,000 SAP people because they tried to standardise the entire supply chain. It was simply unachievable. SAP couldn't do that.

Routes to market in Hungary are different from those in Poland or El Salvador. You end up reinventing SAP every day and trying to force-fit it into a market in which it serves no purpose. Hence companies said SAP came at a cost too high for their turnover, so they would have their own systems. The cost of all that was enormous.

It also became a huge source of frustration for the barons – the continental leads such as Norman Adami, Karl LIppert, Barry Smith and Ari Mervis. It was diverting energy. Hub costs climbed dramatically for years and diminished the barons' ability to be lean, mean, adaptable and empowered for their markets.

Years later, Graham – he and I were good friends – told me it was his single biggest managerial embarrassment that he had allowed this monster to grow. It wasn't his doing; it was other people's doing, but it happened on his watch.

When I arrived in London in my own capacity, the barons welcomed me. Visit us when you wish, they said, but don't tell us what to do.

I did not see the job as an HR task focusing on terms, procedures and labour relations, and I had no desire to force the same practices on the organisation. I felt we had the same values, with professional people in the countries; that countries' legislations were different; their circumstances were different at any given stage; and they were moving towards policies and procedures to align with our values, so why interfere?

My job was to help the places that needed help, to get the right people, which meant brokering the transfer of talent across the global organisation. That was difficult. Nobody wants to give up their talent. It was a process of encouraging all the organisations to accelerate their talent acquisition equally by investing in people whom they did not necessarily need themselves, but who we needed globally to grow the organisation.

That became a philosophy. People said; 'We will take on talent. We will bring people into the organisation as executive assistants, to create a bench for global expansion.'

And, of course, my mandate was to run change processes, which I did as a consultant. Where we had bought a business and needed to restructure it and bring in things like performance management, as we had to do in Miller, my job was to support Norman.

I never needed a big team. I thought I just needed a team to look after the people in Woking in London with policies and procedures. I thought that would be one person. But then Woking grew so that you had to have a big HR team just to look after the people in Woking. I disagreed with that, deeply. Every year at budget time I was distraught that the head office budget was skyrocketing while we sent the countries' hubs back to find more money.

Remember, we didn't sell any beer at head office. There was no revenue. You had to assume that those people who were necessitating this huge cost were going to provide some extraordinary future scale or knowledge benefits that the countries could not find by themselves.

DUANE BIRKHOLTZ

In the countries it seemed the people at the hub were just checking on you. There were more executive grades in London than in the countries. We were doing the work. In fact, though, 30 percent of the time you couldn't do your work because you were doing PowerPoint presentations for the guys in London, in a format that they changed every month.

One of the big projects I did in Botswana was with Gert Nel. We standardised Cispro, a system similar to SAP, across Africa. We looked at all the countries and said: 'Botswana has beer, wine and spirits, and Chibuku. It has everything. And if benchmarked, it's as good as anywhere else. So take Botswana as a template.'

For instance, we changed the travel form to cater for everyone and their different needs. They whinged a bit, but we said this is the way it must be done. The way it worked in Africa was that Gert Nel was empowered to do it. If the MDs didn't like it, they could go and talk to André Parker. That Cispro was put in for R20 million and it ran breweries all over Africa.

In a country like South Africa or Colombia, the head office doesn't need to come in and help you. You have the people with the skills. In Swaziland, where you are doing 200,000 hl, if you have a problem, you need one head office person who can come in to help. The head office staff should be maintaining standards, giving advice, that type of thing.

In Africa, everybody had worked in an African country before. I had worked in a country, so I had empathy for the people in Moçambique or a similar country. It's not as though I'm sitting in London and had never even been there. The people in London had never worked in a country. They had no credibility.

In Botswana, I received a call from the people in London. They wanted to come and see my treasury department. I said I could send them the spreadsheet I go through every Monday, which sets out the exact status of various key measures. I also have a 30-minute weekly meeting with two of my people. That's my treasury function.

If I wanted to negotiate something with the bank, I would talk to them. I'd ask for help if it was something complicated, but if it was a normal rollover thing, I'd do it myself.

Now three people fly from London to come and look at what I'm doing. I could have employed another person for the whole year for what it cost to bring these clowns to come and tell me what I'm doing. They didn't understand.

Heineken had a policy that you couldn't get your next job at head office if you had not been out and done your hard yards in the country.

Very few expats ever came back to South Africa. The hub should be saying things like: 'You've been in Lesotho for a few years, now go and run Newlands.' People learn immensely in the country. Instead, as soon as you crossed the Rubicon and went to work in Africa, you were not coming back.

If they needed a good finance person in Ecuador, why could I not go from Botswana to Ecuador? That never happened. They never said there are ten of these financial directors or marketing people ready to move. The barons protected their turf.

Looking back, I would have gone there in 2007; I would have worked for Jonno and Karl for four years, and my career would have been different, but I got tossed off into Vietnam.

London was a duplication of costs.

Take Grant Harries, who was running Colombia. When Karl was running it, he did so on his own. When Grant was running it, he had all these clowns from London asking him for things. He spent 30 percent of his time doing things for them, whereas for that 30 percent he could have been in the market, innovating and making money, coming up with ideas, bedding things down. Instead, he was doing things for someone who had never been out of head office, who had made a career of moving from one head office to another.

You could tell the people who had done time in other countries. We were able to interact with them. It was different. They had been in the trenches and come back. But many head office jockeys had never done anything else.

ANDREW WOLFF

When I arrived back in South Africa, a lot of the big procurement had been centralised, although it still needed to be managed at a local level. Negotiations were done from Zug in Switzerland, so we were effectively a hybrid of centralised and decentralised.

I think procurement should never have been centralised; the knowledge base should have been centralised. Regional supply chains are much more powerful because that's where relationships develop. You can have a knowledge base at a central level – how do you make a can, what's the cost of a can – but the relationship with a supplier is forged at a regional level.

Although we shipped 400 million bottles across an ocean, it's very difficult to maintain that long term, because you're shipping air. It doesn't mean the pricing has to be done locally, it's to keep the relationships going.

When, in Zug, they began populating the procurement process with people who did not necessarily know the supply chain in depth, we began to lose the plot a little. The procurement people still did a pretty good job, but on a lot of the scorecards in procurement you were marking yourself against yourself.

We ended up playing policemen, which became adversarial towards your global procurement team because they were overclaiming what they really saved. I think we were in a hybrid state of how best to manage the company then and I don't think we had applied performance management through the whole process.

Ally

It seemed we were becoming very heavy in Woking. We had the regional structure and the country structure, so it felt there was duplication and disempowerment, and a lot of contentious stuff was going on between those three different parts. The company was destined to go through some dramatic organisational change if it was going to come right. It was starting to go pear-shaped.

Andrew

It was already pear-shaped. We had four buildings. They duplicated the structure at a regional level, especially with the barons like Karl. He said: 'I'm not going to listen to Woking. They don't know what's going on in Latin America. I'm going to do my own thing.' He created his own structure.

I don't think our HR structures and the way we evolved kept up with the strategic intent of the company. It was allowed to evolve over time rather than for the strategic intent of running the company more effectively. At the same time, we had consultants trying to implement SAP at a million dollars a day.

Ally

Imagine what it was costing Woking for 1,000 heads, all paid in pounds sterling. I remember how it burnt Karl's arse to have to pay that fee to head office every year.

Andrew

The HR structures were also allowed to develop organically. Everybody was able to recruit whomever they wanted and create their own mini structures, which led to friction and contrasting ideas that set us up for conflict.

The same thing happened at Anglo American, but maybe at Anglo you could understand it. We had grown an organisation with a strong HR culture and were then not focused on how to maintain that momentum.

KEN HITCHCOCK

We were incredibly lucky to be part of SAB. There are many people who work very hard, but they don't come out where we did. The fact that many of us ended up in SABMiller and the way everything landed is unbelievable. How many of us would be retiring when we retired?

But in the SAB journey, my best time was in South Africa.

Once we started growing and moving offshore, I began feeling like a number. It was only friendships with guys in the company that still gave you a sense of being part of it. You made a couple of good friends internationally, but the enduring relationships were with the South African people.

I thought about it a lot. To me there was something else linked to that – Woking. I think Woking got too big and too strong.

The question of whether we sold in time or not, I don't know. At some stage they would have had to deal with Woking. I don't know if it was on the cards. There was a project being debated just before the buyout. The guys were starting to get a bit edgy. They knew they had to do something. I don't know if that involved Woking. I just think Woking became a monster and that, together with SAP, the business became paralysed.

Ally

The beauty of what we had beforehand was the empowerment and the ability to work and be trusted.

Ken

Yes. You were made accountable, and you were trusted to get on with it. Woking started to take that away, more and more.

What was surprising about Europe was that the people – Hungarians, Romanians, Czechs, Russians – all loved SABMiller and wanted to work with SABMiller.

They saw us as helping them make their businesses more successful. I didn't see that in ABInBev ever. The countries bought out by ABInBev went unwillingly. It was a very big difference.

When I got to Europe, Europe was already in trouble. They were losing margins and market share in nearly all the countries. The supply chain had a big, big contribution to make in getting costs down. I set up a task group system where I used Sue Clark and Ingmar Boesenberg to invite specialists into a team and to then measure and benchmark every brewery across Europe. All 25 breweries were measured in the same way by these five task groups. And then we just printed money. The way the whole thing came together was phenomenal. For some reason, the rest of SABMiller didn't pick it up and use it.

When we became
Lunch

We always knew that consolidation of the brewing industry was a reality. The big brewers were chasing acquisitions around the world as, not unlike the soft drinks industry, consolidation was the way to go, and critical mass allowed for scale and profitability while aligning with best practice.

SAB had been on a rapid journey in just over 20 years from our home base in South Africa to 84 countries to become the second largest brewer in the world. It was the darling of both the London Stock Exchange, where we had our primary listing, and the Johannesburg Stock Exchange, which had always been our home base and where we had our secondary listing.

We had heard the caution that in our industry, you needed either to eat lunch, or to be lunch. Given the journey we had travelled, we certainly never thought we could be the midday meal. Speculation had been around for some time that ABInBev was considering a takeover of SABMiller.

You always remember where you were on major historic occasions, like 9/11 or when Princess Diana died. For me the next one was when ABInBev bought us. I was in a workshop in Nigeria when the news came. Neil French said: 'Hey guys, sorry to interrupt, but we've just been bought.' That was the end of the workshop.

On 10 October 2016, ABInBev announced the 'successful completion of the business combination with SABMiller.'

The combined company would have operations in virtually every major beer market and an expanded portfolio that included global, multi-country and local brands, providing more choices for consumers around the world.

Customers would benefit from a broad distribution network and strong brand building expertise.

ABInBev would also continue to develop its business in partnership with its suppliers as it continued brewing the best beers using the best ingredients.

It would benefit from a geographically diversified platform, with a stronger presence in key emerging regions with attractive growth prospects, such as Africa and Latin America.

The growth opportunities in these developing markets, it said, complemented the stability and strength of the company's strong existing presence in developed markets.

The Financial Times said this was the third largest acquisition in history. The new company was expected to boast annual sales of $55 billion.

NORMAN ADAMI

For me the takeover was sad. I was no longer in the company, but it happened not long after I'd left. It was almost as though we gave up on ourselves, and that our investors had given up on us, not only Altria and Santo Domingo but also the other shareholders.

Some of them phoned me to tell me that while they had lots of faith in the management of the company, they now had this lucrative financial deal that they wanted to take. It was very sad.

I think most of the people felt that way because they had built this great success story, the second largest brewer in the world with an empire around the globe.

When I started at the company, we were selling 5 million hl a year. I can't remember quite where we ended off, but it was close to 200 million hl. We were in more than 84 countries. That all came to nought because there was a lot of unbundling that ABInBev had to do. Then to crown it all, they began making bad decisions on the way they ran the company.

South Africa was a classic example. The share price halved from the time they bought the company.

My 35 years at SAB was more than just a work life, it was my passion. It was heart-rending enough that SAB was taken over, but more so when ABInBev didn't do justice to the company.

They thought they could do what they had done with Anheuser-Busch. They thought they could strip the assets, take out the costs and the wastage and put that all into the bottom line without losing any market share.

That didn't happen. They couldn't do it. There was nothing to do. We had already done it. So, they had miscalculated, and they overpaid for the company.

There were moves we could have made before then that could have protected our vulnerability against a takeover. I was in favour of the FEMSA deal (the multinational beverage company in Mexico), but we never got that far. The due diligence team for some reason didn't recommend it. But I was a strong fan of the deal.

ABInBev, because of the competition law around the world, had to unbundle SAB. SAB as we knew it, isn't here today. A lot of the company has been sold off.

I wasn't close to the action when they took over, but there were some things they did that I didn't agree with. They were exactly the opposite of what I would have done.

They took their eye off the ball on the core brands. That's the first mistake they made. There were many others: the way they went to market, the route to market, the way they dealt with their retailers. They were bold as an organisation but not in the same way that we applied boldness to the way we did things.

They certainly didn't have the people attributes. I never saw evidence of passionate leaders.

I got the impression that they were short-term thinkers. I think in retrospect that they are listening now. I got the impression that they weren't listening at the start. They knew all the answers.

SAB showed boldness, it showed that it cared about people, not just its own people but all its stakeholders, and was able to build strong relationships. It had passionate leaders and that rubbed off on the organisation.

We had that depth of skill and talent, but ABInBev said let's get rid of all of this. That was our strength. They turned our strength into a weakness very quickly.

I look back at SAB and remember the Soweto riots in '76. The only trucks allowed into Soweto were the SAB trucks. That tells you something about local relevance, connection with the consumer, and societal leadership.

SAB – epitomised by Meyer – had heart and soul. That was ripped out of it with the takeover.

MEYER KHAN

When Graham died, and I was ill, shareholders were told that it was unlikely that I would get out of ICU. That's how sick and how long I was there. Malcolm Wyman had retired just two or three months before.

That's when Anheuser-Busch saw our vulnerability and struck. They would never have considered making a bid, and certainly not a hostile bid, had Graham still been alive. There is no doubt in my mind about that. I would never have agreed to the sale of the business.

I have no doubt that being forced out of our ownership of SAB was fatalistic because we couldn't have done much better than ABInBev have done over the last five years. With boycotts, COVID and unrest, our share price would in my view have been about R300, whereas we got close to R800.

I didn't know what the future held, but we had built SAB over so many years only to hand it over to somebody else ...? It was our baby.

The major shareholders had done a deal. I can tell you that if I had been in the saddle, I would have fought this with my whole being. I can't speak for Graham but, knowing him as I did as my partner for 35 years, I think he would have fought with me. We certainly didn't build SAB to see it chopped up and sold off.

The SAB they bought was not the SAB we built. SAB without Miller Coors, Snow (which I hardly anticipated), without Grolsch, Peroni and Pilsner Urquell (with the nuisance value of all they had to endure to get the South African business) is not the SAB we knew and the SAB we loved.

TONY VAN KRALINGEN

The final sale attracted much speculation. The best way I would describe the decision by ABInBev to buy us, and our major shareholders to sell, was 'not unexpected'. I think Graham expected that someone would come for us. He always argued honestly that if we created value for our shareholders, and people paid over the top for us, and our shareholders were better off, then in some respects we had done our job. Coldly and intellectually, he was right.

I think I speak for many, particularly South Africans, when I say we felt a loss of something we had built that was special: the name South African Breweries, SABMiller. Our home was in a land we were proud of, and for which we had enormous affinity, and we were robbed of the opportunity to continue to grow that story; to create a centre of excellence, if you like, that South Africans could be proud of, no matter where they were. It was the one great success story.

I felt, and there may be others who agree, that it was an opportunity lost. Intellectually you can see why it happened. Emotionally, it was very difficult.

A lot of people asked me what I thought. I said I found it intellectually very stimulating but emotionally very draining. It was hard to see the business where you had spent 35 years, knowing it's no longer going to be something you would be a part of, or identify with, because it would be so different in the future.

JOHAN NEL

When Graham became ill and Alan took over as CEO, it was a fundamental shift. Graham was supposed to have become chairman and that would have been a superb transition and continuity.

Before Graham's passing, some of the shareholders had been waiting to make certain moves, in particular Philip Morris, but couldn't do so while Graham was there. They decided they wanted to cash out.

We were left with a board determined to say that what had happened under the leadership of Meyer and Graham was not the way a British company should be run. They took very strong control and made it extremely difficult for the leadership of the EXCO. They became almost combative. It was mainly Philip Morris and a few board members who were angry about the amount of money that Graham and Malcolm had made. They were difficult times.

Alan Clark had known that ABInBev were out there. They had made an unsuccessful attempt at a takeover in 2012. When the second offer was made, Philip Morris was already wanting to sell and cash out. It was a massive amount of money. Perhaps they even colluded with ABInBev.

Alan was at the time looking at a global restructure to reduce the company's significant costs.

ABInBev had made a run at Heineken, which was a debacle. There were very few other acquisition opportunities. There was nothing left. But there was potential for ABInBev to look at our structures and say we will take out Woking and save billions. They saw the weakness we were unable to combat and were willing to go to a price that shareholders would welcome. We were a company better run than they thought, but that was the enticement.

My return to the company was to assist Alan with a global restructure. We had engaged a company of consultants to assist us with the restructure at global, regional and country levels. I was very excited but probably a bit naïve about it, because I would not have been a very popular person after that.

We would have taken many hundreds of senior people out. It would have been a culture shock for the organisation. We always said we loved talent and bringing people in, and now we had brought in too many. We kept working on it, but it never got off the ground. We were busy with the pre-integration after the ABInBev deal was signed and we ran the project on the side just in case.

At the end of the day, the board effectively said, how can you provide the shareholders with more value than the promise of more than £45? That was then 25 percent to 30 percent of the current trading price.

We would have had to cut costs dramatically. Europe's revenue growth was flat, as was that of the US, so South America and Africa would have had to provide it. All you could provide the board was a major realignment of costs and you would have to promise billions of dollars a year.

It was a fascinating time. Our project was not one you wanted to work on, but it was an interesting thing to do. We realigned everything. The whole of global HR really shifted to how, during negotiations, to create the best deal for employees globally, both for those who remained and those who left.

We took enormous amounts out of various marketing projects, experimentation projects etc. because they would become ABInBev's problem. And we reallocated that money to training so that people could go through programmes to prepare themselves, in or outside the company.

We did a lot of work to reposition our people in the best possible way.

I would have preferred to stay with this great company, but it became apparent that the new owners would take it apart.

I had the task of travelling around the world with their CEO, Carlos Brito. The difference between him and Graham was enormous. He was a man of integrity, and I didn't know anyone who worked harder, but I sat through him making the same speech, word for word, I don't know how many times.

I believe Graham would have spoken from the heart and with intelligence about specifics. Brito took a cookie-cutter approach. You could see that this was going to become a one-trick pony company and it was all about cost. They just didn't have the skills that we had in SAB ... the specific marketing, HR or technical talents, etc. It was sad to watch a great company being split apart and destroyed.

They told us that they would get rid of the entire executive committee. As far as I remember, just one member thought they would like to continue in the new organisation. They ended up taking John and me to help further with the transition for six months and then we left as well.

We were fortunate that it was all very lucrative for us. Many people had lost their jobs, but the severance package gave them a decent base to go forward. But it was sad to see all those memories being destroyed.

MARK BOWMAN

When the ABInBev deal came, it wasn't a complete shock. We had heard rumblings, and there had been a half attempt before, but it still left a bit of a hollow feeling. We had always been the aggressors in our expansion. Now to be the target was not a great feeling. The business was massively resilient in that year and incredibly professional in the way they handed it over.

I remember that the last few days was a sort of celebration in a nostalgic but positive way, to hand over the keys to what was going to be a completely different world. ABInBev were very different in their model but, to be fair, they were also very professional in their interactions and dealt with people equitably.

A lot of people were nostalgic about what could have been, but it couldn't have been better. One wants things to carry on the way they were before, but SAB wasn't shooting the lights out itself. There was a momentum around this kind of globalisation of beer that was going to end at some point.

Graham had always said we were either going to be very expensive or we're going to be the target, because we had a free shareholder base whereas others were protected by a dominant shareholder in some form. And we had had a transition after Graham's death that created a lot of points that made us more vulnerable.

The nostalgia people feel is more for the model as it existed and what was achieved, but from a financial perspective, for companies to live for a hundred years is incredible, and it's not as though SAB is dead. It has continued, it has a new livery in a way, and it will continue to thrive.

For some of the people there may be a bit of nostalgia for a different style of working. I don't think it's good or bad, it's just different.

Everybody was well rewarded. I think if anyone was done in, it was maybe the shareholders of ABInBev, because they paid such a high price. The board and the executive of SAB did a good job in getting the best possible price, which means ABInBev will have indigestion for many years to come from that, and anyone can continue to be a shareholder of the same beer business through a different ownership structure.

SAB was a South African company that made it big and there's a discomfort because it's gone. But we were an anomaly in a sense. I can think of only two or three companies that have done anything similar, and a South African managed company that got to number two in the world in such a big category from such a small base, is a rare and engaging story.

The fact that it's gone is not ideal, but I don't think it's something that one should fret about unnecessarily.

If you look at the listed South African companies run by ex-SAB people, there's no other company that has that track record. There are six, maybe more, JSE listed companies run by SAB alumni.

It would have been nice to be the number one in the world, but that was always a long shot and was never going to be. Being number one isn't always a smart objective. Heineken is looking like a smarter player than ABInBev in some respects. Carlsberg has chugged along and is doing fine.

We had a powerful ambition, but so did ABInBev, and those things collided in the end. We perhaps felt our project wasn't completely finished. The core problem for listed companies remains to find growth, and normally the best growth you find is through mergers and acquisitions. That's what ABInBev has wrestled with since. We were grappling with it ourselves. We bought Australia but that wasn't really a growth business. So you get a bit trapped because the market is expecting growth otherwise your share price starts drifting down.

At ABInBev there's been no merger or acquisition for five years and massive debt is still in place. With a 25 percent volume reduction in the US and people going, it's never going to grow.

ANDREW WOLFF
People often ask how we ended up becoming the hunted, not the hunter. Strategically, the ABInBev board was far more aggressive than our board would ever allow Graham to be. ABInBev was allowed to go to 5.5 times EBITDA on debt. Graham's limit was 4.5. That gap was huge.

Now the chickens are coming home to roost. Part of the reason why ABInBev halved the market share is that they are not able to pay down debt. Their debt burden is just massive. Even though they have stripped out half of what they bought, they are still battling to cut debt.

It means the ABInBev and 3G Capital boards were far more aggressive to do those kinds of deals than Graham and Malcolm were ever given latitude to do.

When the buyout came, I was quite bleak. I felt it was a sell-out. I felt we could have held out. Almost five years on, we would still have been sweating blood, sweat and tears.

They put a sales manager into corporate affairs to deal with government. They just wiped their hands of it. We would have handled it much better and come out much stronger, I think, because we managed the business in a way that ABInBev never could.

Those layers were not put into SAB because we wanted to be fat cats, they played a role in how the business was run.

If you look at the bum decisions and lost market share that ABInBev has had everywhere, they speak for themselves.

You can't apply a cookie cutter approach to Africa or Latin America.

Ally

I think they thought we were dripping with fat, but they came in and found nothing. And then they had overpaid and wiped out a level of talent that was formidable and put some youngsters in charge, who may have been qualified but just didn't understand the game.

Andrew

They are creating a layer of fairly good generalists. They don't have deep smarts in that business. Which was our big strength. It's like a mechanic becoming the owner of the garage. You can hear what's wrong in the car.

Norman could look at a spreadsheet and know immediately which number was wrong. You can't bullshit guys who've done the hard yards. When you've got generalists who have spent two years in finance and two in HR, you're always scratching the surface. You're never getting into the depths of what's going on.

Ally

I think the whole beer market is consolidated. There's nothing to acquire. Nothing's moving. We were growing in acquisition and organic growth, now there's nothing. The beer industry is in trouble, everywhere.

Andrew

It is, but there will be global growth. We are still going to go to two billion people mainly in Africa in the next 20 years. African GDP must still multiply big time. I think Africa still has lots of legs. Even if ABInBev doesn't keep its market share, it will still grow despite themselves because of its footprint.

Ally

I have heard some people say they should have kept Mark Bowman and a guy like Grant Harries to run Africa and South America the way we were doing, because we were doing so well, and then consolidated around the world and applied their model but left us to run it and learnt from us.

Andrew

It gets back to the point: it's intellectual masturbation. It appealed to the intellect from a theoretical master's point of view. It's theoretically interesting but not necessarily practical in Africa or LatAm. It makes sense if you're a marketing guru, but you're missing the sales and the nuts and bolts at the coal face.

There are two things I think they should have done.

When we went into LatAm, we put Barry and Karl there to run them, and Jonno Salisbury to handle finance, but for the first two years they assimilated how the local market worked. It was only after two years of running it that you could identify where the strengths and weaknesses were, and who would fit in and who wouldn't.

That's the time to start sweeping out the old management. You didn't go in and just cull the whole lot. But ABInBev applied the cookie cutter they used at Anheuser-Busch and stripped the business of its layers of experience.

Ally

They got the executive layer out and just about everyone left. I did think they were fair on the exit packages and rewarding people for tenure, which was quite powerful.

Andrew

That was probably part of the price they were prepared to pay and that was negotiated not by them, but by us. It was good for our HR guys at the time to be able to negotiate that for us. That was an absolute win.

Ally

Not many people complained. They felt that they had been dealt with fairly.

Andrew

So was I happy about the buyout. Financially, we can't complain. Emotionally, I felt we were losing our heart and soul. When I eventually closed my door and left for the last time, I wasn't leaving SAB, SAB had already gone. It was a hollow Easter egg.

I had always targeted retirement at 58, but I would have carried on working at SAB for the fun of it, had it remained.

BARRY SMITH

At the takeover, like many SAB guys I felt very disappointed, not hurt but sore. I believe it would never have happened if Graham and Malcolm had still been in charge. Graham had such credibility among those shareholders; the Santo Domingo family thought he walked on water; the guys from Miller did the same.

What happened was that our share price came off quite a bit at the time. Graham and Malcolm would have been able to tell shareholders: 'Yes, it came off for whatever reason, but you should take the long view, we'll be back up there soon.' They would have believed him and gone along with him.

You hear other rumours, but I don't know if they were true. Malcolm said the same thing: if Graham had been around that would not have happened.

We are lucky to be out of the beer market now. Throughout the world beer markets are maturing. There is very little low-hanging fruit anymore.

I don't study ABInBev's results but when I do see something, they always seem to make out that they are doing so well, the profit margins are increasing, etc., but I think 'guys, you can't be telling the full story because your share price wouldn't be dropping down to the level it is if you're performing so well.'

Ally

At one point their market cap was $96 billion, and they had paid $106 billion to buy SAB. The share price dropped to about R500 at one stage. It's about R900 now from over R1,800 at the time of purchase.

Barry

When they bought SAB the share price was €116, and it dropped right down to €65. That was a helluva drop and if you were a shareholder, you would have been pretty dissatisfied.

Ally

There was a deal where they would take your shares and give you a swap to ABInBev with a 15 percent factor in your favour as an employee of the company. Many of the people took some of that. And there was a five-year lock-in, and that still has about two years to run.

Barry

A merger with Heineken was unlikely ever to happen because of the family control. In Holland they allow a pyramid structure of ownership where the top controls 51 percent of the company, below that it controls 51 percent of a company below it, and so on. So the family at the top can still control the company at the bottom. As far as I know that structure is illegal in many countries, but not in Holland. To buy the company, you would have to get the family out. But it's their name that's on the company standard.

I think Alan and the board tried to do something about Heineken, but at the time I thought that unless they knew something I didn't know, I don't know how they could have wrestled the family out of it.

I often reflect on the SAB times whenever I have a beer. To this day I can't drink a non-SAB beer. I have always liked a draught beer. I want that smooth taste. None of the many craft beers excites me and I really miss Peroni draught. I do like the Castle Tank beer.

Without Peroni around, Castle would probably be my first choice, although it's quite bitter.

In a way I'm glad that now that ABInBev have got it, they can try to make it work. I think: 'You bought us out and you think you can do good, now make good. At the moment your share price is half of what it used to be.'

IAN PENHALE

ABInBev's idea was to buy us at a ridiculous price, but that didn't turn out to be a winning hand. That was their only idea. They're a 'one-idea' company. Over the years, Brito has sounded like a stuck record. It worked with ABInBev because they were fat and badly managed. It didn't work with us because we had cut that out years ago. Heineken have done quite well because they have the only truly global brand, and they manage it very well and stick to their knitting.

It was always going to be difficult when the industry matured into its final form. Graham talked about 'the dance of the elephants'. That's what it was. He spoke about that in around the mid-2000s, so by then the industry was already in its growth death throes. Beer wasn't really innovative; spirits were becoming very innovative. Trends were changing around the world and we weren't geared for it.

I think it was perfect timing for us to leave. Any longer as an organisation, we would have overstayed our welcome. I think we extracted everything we could out of Latin America.

I think Europe lost its lustre in the consolidation days. Making the beer quality better and leveraging the good old on-premise occasion, that all faded away.

Asia was never going to make any money, and even Africa was beset by the fact that the globe faced financial difficulties. Our days of 10 percent growth in dollars and the strategy of 'halving the price of beer, doubling the price, and going farming', was brilliant conceptually, but those days had a timeline.

Australia was always a dog. I don't know why we bought it. You could hear it barking from 100 miles away. You've got to think it was some sort of swinging dick syndrome, or the opportunity to let management make their own mistakes, but it was a big mistake.

I think FEMSA would have been better through regional consolidation. The operational team was stronger than the Asian team. We were never going to win in Australia where key accounts dominate the route to market.

I think Grolsch was a mistake. We paid three billion euros and spent nothing to back it up. It was a funny tasting beer in a funny looking bottle that we couldn't produce anywhere. It was a distant number two to Heineken. It was not a good idea. Nor was Peroni, which was four percent in its own market. It has been successful only in the UK.

Miller was interesting with its flint glass and taste. We tried taking Castle Lager beyond South Africa and though we had a good go, that didn't work. These things don't travel well.

ABInBev also proved that it's hard to force your global brands into a local market successfully. The idea that beer is local was our idea and a good insight.

JOHN COCHRAN

The takeover was a bittersweet pill to swallow, especially for the guys who had worked for the company for more than 30 years. To see it go was emotional and sad, like losing an old friend. It was: 'How can you do this?'

At the time it was bitter, but if you see globally what has happened to the beverage industry generally, and the beer business in particular, it may have been inevitable.

I have made peace with that bitter part. That is gone and I have moved on. I look back with fondness and smiles on the past 30 years.

It was always about the people, the characters, the passion, camaraderie, brothers-in-arms. We were an army rustled up to go into the world without fear. We had brains but, for goodness' sake, we had balls.

KEN HITCHCOCK

I would probably still have been working at SAB today. I left ABInBev because of culture. I couldn't take it anymore.

But I honestly think that the whole Woking thing, and SAP, and the structure of the hub head offices killed the business. Even at the time people were starting to talk about it and say this thing isn't working, it's too big, too expensive, too cumbersome.

They were all hitting their short-term incentives, but the operational guys were battling to reach theirs.

The whole thing just got out of kilter. And I think that broke the back of our business.

When the offer came, we moved from about £34 eventually to £45, it was unbelievable.

The deals they negotiated for people leaving SAB on the back of the takeover... I haven't heard of any other company doing that. They were unbelievably generous.

I haven't heard of one person who took the deal whom was unhappy. It was here's your retrenchment and there are your share options, and off you go into the sunset and enjoy your life.

That was SAB. It was the culture of the company that saw it through. A lot of people could have said: 'Oh well, we've been bought,' and move on. 'Do what you have to do.' But they didn't do that. That was indicative of what SAB was about.

Emotionally it was sad. Financially, it was very rewarding.

MAURICE EGAN

One of the questions that was asked was whether we should have sold. Well f … me, at £45, no question. Look where we are today. We would have been busting a gut for 20 years to recover from the first offer which was £29, I think.

Others will have nostalgic views that we should have teamed up with Heineken but, after reading some of the anecdotal stories about FEMSA, I believe there's always a time to walk away from a deal.

We were doing deals quickly and competently. Business case studies were being written about us as this emerging market brewer. By the time people wiped the shit out of their eyes, we were number two in the world. We had just crept up out of nowhere with a bundle of competent, capable and high-capacity individuals who didn't take no for an answer.

The amount of learning and growth that you got through, you would not have got in any other company in a lifetime.

Remember, we didn't have the deep pockets that the likes of Interbrew had, so we always had to try to keep a step ahead and decide what we wanted to eat for lunch, or whether we wanted to be eaten. So we had to buy Miller. Did we want to? Probably not.

The Miller deal was game changing because it kept us alive for another few years. We had to continue to look for decent deals but now it started to get sticky. As Mackay always said: 'Doing deals with family-owned businesses is sticky.'

Should we have done a deal with Heineken? If you look at it clinically, the numbers made absolute sense (maybe not the price) and it would have made sense technically in terms of the brands and brand portfolios, but culturally it would have been a nightmare.

You'd have all those Heineken guys who believed the sun shone out of their arses, now being taken over by a bunch of hoodlums from the southern tip of Africa. But that would have put us in the spectrum of what Mackay wanted, in a position that we just could not have been passed out on. But it was not to be.

Carlsberg was essentially owned by the Danish people, and it would have required an act of parliament for it to be sold. It's run by, I think, nine trustees and all nine of them would have needed to agree to sell. That would have been good.

Castel was also family owned. The numbers made it look profitable, but they were beefed up by very aggressive transfer pricing techniques, charging back to the Parisian office of Castel for work in the Congo or most of French-speaking West Africa.

In the end we managed to agree that we would have first right of refusal. Whether it would have stuck I don't know.

The FEMSA deal was interesting. It was essentially the second largest brewery in Mexico and would have fitted our portfolio quite neatly, particularly the beer piece. The famous brand was Sol, known internationally, but their bigger brand was Carta Blanca. They were predominantly in Monterrey and northern Mexico, whereas Corona Modella was mainly Mexico City. That would have been interesting.

With Coke, Mackay always said we don't own the brand, so it's not strategic. In the heat of the hunt, Malcolm Wyman was not convinced and as it came down to the wire, FEMSA started to ask for all sorts of ludicrous things way beyond their fighting weight – like a certain number of people on the remuneration committee of SAB, directors here, there and everywhere. It was just a bridge too far. It was one of those deals that we were right to walk away from.

NEIL HOBKIRK

Being at ABInBev was an interesting experience. It's not that SAB was right and ABInBev was wrong, or vice versa. I think there are many commonalities between the two.

While we were predominantly South African, they were predominantly Brazilian. They are going through a transition now. They know they must become truly multinational and that they must be representative of all levels. SAB also started internalising that. Mauricio came as a Latin American to become MD of SAB, so he went through that process as well.

The similarities are being dominant in a place and very proud of it. They are very ambitious, just as SAB was ambitious; with a phenomenal focus, in a slightly different way, on talent, and that people drive the business; a big belief in brands, much stronger on the global brands; a strong desire to give people problems to solve that help them develop their abilities; and giving people an opportunity to achieve things and do big things. I think those are common across both organisations.

The one big difference is – and who knows if it's right or wrong – SAB was a deregulated business that empowered its leaders geographically. ABInBev is centralised.

The capability, quality and intellect of people at the highest levels are very similar, but the massive difference is the deregulated versus the centralised business. It's the main driver of the cultural difference.

In one organisation, you're given strong direction and objectives, people are making it up and pulling it together and if they are achieving those objectives, you don't get invited for that cup of tea. As you know, if things weren't going well in Africa you would come for a cup of tea with John Kirby. You didn't want that cup of tea.

That gave you very capable general managers and good managers who could take decisions, live by them and still achieve the results. There was a lot of personal gratification in that.

One of the downsides of the SAB way was that you always had to force learnings, get things across, get common ways of doing things, and that was very difficult because everyone was doing their own thing. The upside is that ABInBev, because it is a centralised organisation, is a far superior business technocratically, if that's a measure. The direction comes from Brito and it drills straight through the organisation fast – everyone goes at lightning speed. They can turn the world around in a day.

The other thing that ABInBev did faster than SAB, is that they embraced the digital world at speed and aggressively. You can take a guy from China and put him in Latin America, the process will be the same, the templates will be the same, the portfolio map will look the same, it will just have different gaps on it. So that makes it much more efficient, more cost effective.

One of the big downsides of that is that at a personal level you don't get the same degree of gratification, of having to work it all out yourself and doing it. It requires people with a lot less experience and tenure, who therefore cost the company less, which affects your cost base positively. You don't need such experienced managers because the system provides a lot of cover.

The other thing that is more extreme is that it is a much more specialised company; people specialise a lot more within their function, they do a lot more in a narrower area. You can give them an enormous amount to do in a very narrow area. Hence you can flatten the structures quite a lot. That takes out more cost.

The way that they counterbalance that is quite clever. They have created a very deep level of banding. You can take a young person, put them in a function, and they can learn it off by heart in a year to 18 months, and then they're ready to move. Then you put them in another area of specialisation and then another and once they have popped out of that after 10 years, they are now complete.

I'd say those are the main differences: a massive amount of commonality but some fundamental differences that create a completely different corporate culture.

SAB became top heavy in Woking, with less decentralisation. ABInBev is very lean in New York. I don't think there are 100 people there. You can be involved there only if you are operationally engaged. They've got some specialist functions that run some specialised service providers. If you need marketing gurus, they are available. I think it would have been the next logical step for SAB to take.

I would say that if someone like Norman was made the CEO of SABMiller worldwide, that transition would have happened quite quickly, because his nature is to manage and control things from the centre and to create playbooks and 'ways'. I think he would have created a system like that with its own unique SAB character. He would have taken the organisation into that kind of efficient, centrally driven, much faster and nimbler entity.

The advantage that ABInBev has now to be able to do that, is technology. The world is so digitised now, everything is so codified, that you can get away with relying on it. In the old days a lot of people had to pull a lot of information together to make sense of what was going on. That's maybe why Woking got so fat. It wasn't properly technology enabled. Centralisation and digitisation are the two big, structural organisational design differences.

PINE PIENAAR
When ABInBev arrived to take over SAB, I was worried. I benefited in that the share price went up. But it was very difficult, and I

decided to take early retirement. My view was that I worked for brilliant people. I was part of the system. I had come from a low level to a relatively senior management position. I was part of a winning team, a winning culture. I wasn't sure how these guys would manage us, and I didn't want to leave SAB with bad memories.

I felt there were times to come and times to go. I think it was the time to go. It's the best call I made. Because I remain so proud to have been an SAB employee, I still get my benefits, provident fund, O&G (free beer) and medical aid, what more could I want?

My memories of SAB are positive. I can live with that for another 20 years. If I had stayed a little longer and had to take a package then I would be leaving on their terms, and I never wanted to do that. I wanted to leave on my terms with a positive attitude and positive memories of people. I consulted widely with people, and I think I made the right call.

I have no regrets. Maybe a move to Central Office would have helped me, but I enjoyed every single moment in Mpumalanga. My team and I added value. People knew us and trusted us, and if they had issues, they came to us. We were partners.

Of course, we had problems as well. But ultimately, I have not one regret.

WAYNE MCCAULEY

We were in Nigeria when Neil French shouted that we were being bought. Like it or not, from that moment it was never the same, because even there, there was still a lot of water to go under the bridge. We all knew it was the end of something great. As it got closer to the time and reality began to set in, it was a hollow feeling. I was very clear in my own mind, because I had read the book 'Eating the Big Fish' when InBEV took over Anheuser-Busch, and I didn't really want to work for them.

I thought about, and was offered, the role of business unit president, and I said no. I was able to get the package through Johan Nel, who pushed me hard to stay, but I realised it was never going to be for me. I was never going to be that guy that wanted to work for them after what we had done in Africa. It didn't surprise me the way they systematically broke down everything we had done. It was disappointing but it justified my decision.

I felt disappointed that we had let down the layer of people below us, the guys who were coming through, but we had no control over that. I felt very sad for the GMs, the DMs of SAB, for a lot of the people in the countries we left behind. I just felt we had such great people, and they weren't in the fortunate position we were in. I felt we were selling people short.

I do feel the company in London looked after us. The agreements reached with us were very fair. I thought our exit packages were fair. Everybody always wants more but I thought they were very fair.

It was just so sudden. It was like being hit with a blunt instrument. And there was no turning back.

We all went through a bit of a grumpy phase where we all wanted to shoot them down for everything. Some of their decisions bewildered me. Now I've just come to terms with it. It is what it is.

But it was sad to see something we had made so great, just disintegrate. You spent your life on this thing and then just set a match to it. That's just how it felt.

If Graham had been alive and been chairman, and Norman had been there, I don't believe necessarily that they would have come for us. It was obvious that two of the major shareholders that were 48 percent of the business, were already having meetings behind the scenes.

ANDREA QUAYE

I was with Ian when the news came. He had a workshop in Durban and a whole bunch of people were there. Ian stood up and said guys we've just been bought. There had been rumours around it. I didn't know what was happening. It was a very uncertain time. There was about six months of that.

I remember Mauricio preparing us for a meeting with Brito where we all had to present to him. If this conversation took three hours, I would be underselling it. It took three hours, and we weren't even focusing on the content. It was on the perception that they would have of us.

We had to get rid of the secretaries who sat in 'mahogany row' in front of the directors' offices and around the koi pond; the chairs in the boardroom had to be changed, because they looked too plush; we spent an hour discussing what kind of food needed to be served, whether the sandwiches should have crusts. Brito liked bananas so we had to have bananas. It was so stressful, because he wanted us to come across as very frugal. And there was nothing frugal about that building. That art! It was phenomenal.

You'd walk into that mahogany avenue and every director had a secretary out in front of them, and the desks themselves were permanent. The length of time we sat there discussing that, was really funny.

The secretaries were given retrenchment packages. My PA was quite excited about her retrenchment offer. And suddenly my office became a meeting room.

I remember Bonga Moosa: he left and went to the SABC, because he couldn't wear his suits and he didn't have an office. He said: 'I worked my whole career to become a director at SAB and now I don't even have an office. And now I must wear jeans. Haai, no man.'

Ally

I had to dress down from these khaki pants to jeans. I had to get more casual.

Andrea

My office had a toilet. Norman or Mauricio Leyva's office had a shower. I had a waterfall outside my office. Big bucks were something we were never shy about. I was given R100,000 to redecorate my office when I started. I said: 'No I don't think I will.' I just changed the mirror. It was a plush life.

Ricardo Tadeau, vice president of Africa, interviewed me on Skype while I was on holiday in Italy. He was quite formal. He had this formal, distant approach when you didn't know him. I asked him what made him stay at ABInBev. He said: 'I believe that governments have failed society and I believe big corporations are best positioned to change the world.' He was always very philanthropic and had this view of the world. He was brilliant at numbers and running businesses. The reason he did all that was so that he could have a positive impact on the world. I remember after having that conversation thinking this is a company and somebody that I would love to work with.

Then Miguel Patricio, chief marketing officer at ABInBev, also interviewed me. He was a teddy bear. He was kind and accommodating. And so brilliant. He is now group CEO at Heinz.

One of the things I loved about ABInBev was their people process. Miguel always said, when we were sitting discussing people: 'First comes the company and what's best for the company, second comes the individual and what's best for the individual, and only third is you as a manager.' He reminded us about that all the time. That's how he behaved. The people process worked well with that approach.

The difference between SAB and ABInBev was that performance management was about building skills. The people didn't move around as much. It was people development taught in different ways. The SAB version was about creating depth of skills, while ABInBev was about giving people bigger experiences, bigger bones they could chew, moving people across countries.

What I loved about it was that we used to spend three days as a management committee talking about people and how we could help them develop themselves. It was one of the things that I really admired.

I think ABInBev just dreamed bigger than SAB. They had bigger ambitions. They might be unrealistic, but they were just bigger. At SAB we would do a bottom up and say this is how much we can grow by. At ABInBev the approach was: 'Right, 10 percent growth. Here's the gap, fill it'.

It was a totally optimistic outlook, and it was always quite difficult to hit those targets. The targets were always a lot bigger in ABInBev than in SAB.

Ally

It's totally fair to say ABInBev were brilliant at global brands and quite obsessed about them, whereas SAB were more about growing local brands. I think they both had merit and there was positivity on both sides. Local brands were the heroes for SAB. Global brands were everything for ABInBev.

Andrea

If you could marry them that would be something powerful. What ends up happening is that you compromise local brands when you invest in global brands, and that's what we did a bit in South Africa.

Youth and experience – I think there needs to be a balance between the two. In a way, both were extremes. In a way it was because we wanted to push excellence at everything. In SAB, especially the South African business, we had too many layers and too much experience. And we ended up complicating things because everyone was a deep thinker and you ended up arguing and challenging each other, which has its negatives.

Sometimes at ABInBev, things happened too quickly, without enough insight to make that call.

The other things I loved about ABInBev was that they were ambitiously humble. They had huge ambitions in terms of dreaming big and humble enough to steal what's best in class and make it happen. That's a very powerful mindset to have.

The industry was very good to me. ABInBev, SAB ... very, very good to me. I don't think I could have had a better career anywhere else ... on any other continent, in any other category in one industry.

I was there for 16 years. But to keep engaged and to keep growing for 34 years was impressive ... as was to be given the space to prove your value, to be given the support, the belief.

We talk about the giants whose shoulders we stood on. I think about all the people who came before me, who paved the way, who looked after the brands that laid the building blocks so that we could come and do our thing.

The beer industry has a huge dilemma. Over centuries the industry has been built around scale. It's about getting as much of the same thing out there as consistently as possible; but at present consumers want a variety.

GARTH SAUNDERS

Project Crown was a project to centralise everything. If Graham had been there, it would have had some chance of working.

The Project Crown model was never going to work unless we got all the barons on board, and the biggest challenge was that Alan hadn't created his own board. When Graham passed away, he should have got rid of the problem children and that would have given him the chance to have his own men. He had no chance while he had someone else's board there. They were untouchable.

Would Crown have worked? We don't know. Would it have stopped the acquisition? I think the acquisition problem was Graham passing away when he did.

Although I have a view that Graham knew that at some point the value would be in selling. He may well have already had that in mind.

He would probably have done a merger with one of the organisations where he would have ended up as chairman. They tried that with Diageo and that fell over for a number of reasons, one of which was who was going to be top dog. He had set himself up quite nicely to do another merger. A proper big merger. Then we would have been untouchable.

The Miller deal was too big a bite. Australia was probably because we needed bulk. Wyman didn't like FEMSA, I can't remember the reason why. As long as Wyman didn't like something it wasn't going to happen. I think he liked Australia because per capita earnings were high. People had money and the population was growing and the economy was on a growth trajectory. Those were the things that suggested this thing might work. I don't think Australia was ever a player in the way things turned out.

The issue as I understand it is that shareholders Altria and Santa Domingo had a challenge with Alan. I think that people buy into people, not just organisations. Graham had gone, Meyer had gone, and Wyman had gone. I think they just said to hell with this.

GRANT HARRIES

I often wonder, with the industry under the cosh right now, whether we wouldn't have operated in a smarter way than the guys who have taken us over. I am convinced we would have cut our cloth accordingly. Maybe we wouldn't have reached where we hoped we would, but I think we would have gone further than they have. I think we would have adjusted. We were much more agile and very business focused on the beer industry, whereas these guys have come across more as investment bankers. I think we would have done better.

I was very sad when the chapter closed. We had to get over it. It took some of my colleagues a long time to get over it but sometimes you have to accept these things and move on.

For me, it was too early in my career. I always had a view that something big was going to happen one day, but I didn't expect it to happen then. I think they took advantage of the crisis developing countries were having around the world.

During the handover period it was difficult for our people. It was probably my hardest year. I had to look people in the eye. I had one experience before in Russia when we were handing it over to Efes, and there it was worse because the Russians and Turks don't like each other.

I remember a guy called Igor who had been the sales director in Ukraine, and had been sales director in Russia before my time, and we went to meet Alan in Zug in Switzerland. When we got there, it was just him and me. I said: 'What did you do wrong? What did I do wrong?' Igor said: 'You could have sold it to anybody but the Turks.'

It was the same in Colombia. The Brazilians don't have much respect for anyone else in South America. They see themselves as superior. So it wasn't nice at all.

They told me I should come to South Africa and do that country role there, and then told me in the next memo I would need to shed 250 people. I said: 'You haven't even seen the business and you're telling me that, and I must do the dirty work. No.'

Even the people in Santo Domingo asked me: 'Why are they messing with two businesses that are succeeding when their own business in Brazil is failing? They should go and fix their own thing and leave these two that are pumping the money.'

What has been special for me is that I made friends around the world, and I am in communication with most of them, work colleagues and customers. And they're proper mates.

Ally

Positioning beer brands is what really makes the difference between class and second class. I have never had a bad beer, although some beers are better than others.

Before ABInBev acquired SAB, I often looked over the fence at global brands that I admired. Two that came to mind often were Corona and Stella Artois.

So it came to pass that after working on the integration programme prior to the merger, I was asked to stay on in the new 'company'. I agreed to remain for 18 months on one condition: that I could work on the new global brand portfolio coming to Africa.

Corona celebrates the great outdoors, the sun, the sea and the beautiful people who drink the brand. 'This is Living' was a slogan that allowed consumers to escape into another world.

A ritual adds so much value to a brand. Urban legend has it that the lime that's often slipped into the bottle neck was originally done by Mexicans who wanted to clean the residue left in the top of their bottles by rusty crowns. The custom became a global phenomenon, probably the most famous ritual yet, unrivalled by any other beer, in my view.

In October 2016, Corona was selling around 4,000 cases annually at a super-premium price, more than 200 percent above mainstream beer, or double the price of Castle Lager.

We set about entrenching Corona in the South African beer market by customising rich global properties to create equity for the brand in South Africa. The Corona Sunset DJ Festival in Cape Town sold out on our digital platforms in under an hour. The World Surfing League in Jefferies Bay became the number one surfing event in the world circuit with Corona as the title sponsor. The lime ritual captured beer drinkers' attention and limes have been in short supply ever since.

As the tempo gained traction, the brand began to grow exponentially and by the end of 2019, had reached 4.6 million cases in three short years. It's still selling at a premium that has been brought down to around 40 percent.

It's sad that a brand of this stature was part of the naming convention of a global pandemic.

While SAB employed smart people, there was something extra special about the social disposition evident in most, particularly in sales and marketing.

The way in which we tested candidates sought to find a balance of not only 'what' they might deliver but also 'how' they provided the result.

Though there were, of course, exceptions. 'People are our Enduring Advantage' became a pillar of our business model and was the X-Factor that drove the business to achievements beyond expectation and showed that the impossible was possible.

Similarly, 'Accountability is Clear and Personal' became a mantra that encouraged each member of the company to take absolute accountability. The buck stopped with YOU.

It was this empowerment that built trust and pride within the ranks of the business from top to bottom and, with the integrated management systems, was the bedrock for delivery of exceptional performance.

Epilogue

My journey was nothing short of exceptional. I was blessed with a career and life story that is unusual and enviable.

The memories that have been rekindled through writing this book and conducting the interviews with my friends and colleagues (in that order), have made me realise just how special our SAB story was and the value that this has added to countries, communities and colleagues around the world.

I cherish these memories and the stories that will forever unfold when we meet again. I have tried to capture these as far as is possible, though I'm sure there are thousands of examples of these stories among colleagues all around the world that are reflected upon when they meet to rekindle the passion and friendships.

These were the stories as seen through my eyes which I hope will reflect some of the magic that was SAB, the people who were the X-Factor, the brands that were endearing and loved, the systems that were the enablers, the partners that worked as part of our teams, the fun, friendship, and laughter that will endure.

A consequence of the business model and the time spent at work and travelling led to the building of friendships within the business that flourish to this day.

I am part of an annual gathering, at the beautiful Olifants Game Reserve, of 14 previous executives who made meaningful contributions in the SAB journey, to celebrate life and reflect on the stories and achievements that made SAB famous.

Around the world, SAB colleagues gather to reflect, laugh and enjoy the lagers they made famous.

When the curtain came down on SAB in 2016, we hosted a weekend in Cape Town aptly named 'Farewell To Far Flung Friends'.

Two hundred executives from around the world paid their own way to attend and Meyer Kahn addressed the team one final time to pay tribute to and thank the legends gathered, and those in absentia.

Around the world, and particularly in South Africa, you will find SAB executives in top positions in blue chip corporates and in entrepreneurial ventures, mostly transforming them and adding value based on lessons learnt in SAB: a cluster of SAB people who have combined to take a project forward be it in consulting or turning a ship around.

In South Africa, I can think of Distell, Tongaat Hulett, Woolworths, Heineken, The Beverage Company, Blue Label Telecoms, Signal Hill Products, Truman & Orange, Tiger Brands, Coca-Cola and Famous Brands, to name a few.

Other executives ply their skills in fundraising ventures, on club committees, game reserve management, rare game breeding and general leadership roles where their credentials and commercial understanding lead to success.

All are remarkable people who often don't understand how much they really know and what value they can and do add.

Theirs was an era of excellence that will burn brightly for decades to come.

As the sun set on the mighty SAB story, I personally felt a combination of sadness and uncertainty although also a spark of excitement to face up to a new challenge in a different world, but still a golden one in brewing, looking after the immense brands that were Budweiser, Stella Artois and Corona.

I reflect on the varied opinions for how we may have saved the company and what we should have done; if ... but ... and the rest. I do, however, feel like a layer of experience exited the company around this time with many people going into corporates in South Africa and around the world to continue to apply their immense skills and to add value to other companies and organisations and countries. It was a remarkable injection of talent into the wider business world that added an incredible dimension to business in South Africa in particular.

At the same time, the fairness and exit experience of everyone I know who was leaving the company were well received and the dignity and respect shown by SAB and ABInBev to people across the board was remarkable. Beer people, as I have said, are wonderful people!

Our leadership had a hand of cards to play and, at £45 a share, not many could complain, while shareholders were richly rewarded.

What stands out, and remains, in my daily reflections is the wonderful people of SAB and their passion to achieve beyond expectations and to 'Run Through a Brick Wall' to make it happen!

ACKNOWLEDGEMENTS

I am very grateful to my colleagues and friends who gave me their time to provide their passionate input, views and memories of our times at SAB: André Parker, Andrea Quaye, Andrew Wolff, Antonio Rossetti, Barry Smith, Clifford Raphiri, Duane Birkholtz, Garth Saunders, Gavin Hudson, Geraldine Scott, Graham Edmonds, Grant Harries, Ian Penhale, Jacqui Hobkirk, Johan Nel, John Cochran, Ken Hitchcock, Mark Bowman, Maurice Egan, Meyer Kahn, Neil Hobkirk, Norman Adami, Pine Pienaar, Robin Goetzsche, Stuart Scott, Simon Harvey, Steve Bluen, Tony van Kralingen, Vincent Maphai and Wayne McCauley. All these wonderful humans held various positions in their long, distinguished careers at SAB and, as leaders and strategists, were instrumental in creating one of the greatest success stories to emerge out of Africa. Their CVs are remarkable and their contribution is revered in the story of our company. Each of them epitomises the title of this book; 'Through a Brick Wall'.

THANKS

I thank my friend Neville Barber who helped me with the writing, having worked in journalism and as part of the public relations team for SAB over many years; and Reina Luck another SAB stalwart with 37 years of service and now a professional copy editor, for editing the final drafts and making sure it all hangs together.

There are so many other colleagues and friends around the world whose stories would be as fascinating. It took me over two years to pull this together. I felt that I had a story to tell that was worth sharing, so I needed to get this book out of the door. I wish I could have interviewed many more. The meetings and the times together were very special. My thanks again go to all the colleagues and friends for 34 years of fun, friendship, and laughter.

Made in the USA
Las Vegas, NV
28 November 2022

60557232R00193